Excerpts from
GUIDE TO SURVIVAL

"This one is going to set them back on their heels. Nudity alone isn't a drawing card anymore. The public is thirsting for more."   chapter 1

* * *

Some population biology scientists estimate that the population bomb will explode around the year 2000.   chapter 2

* * *

While in another part of the West a "miracle killer" got unwanted publicity recently. There were 6000 dead in Utah.   chapter 3

* * *

God is now an illegal word in the "thank you" verse—*even though only implied.*   chapter 4

* * *

One of these days, millions of people are going to suddenly vanish without any warning! And you are going to wonder why!   chapter 5

* * *

"I remember viewing long cases of arms, legs, hearts, livers and kidneys."   chapter 6

* * *

One of these days some great leader, admired by the world as a man of peace will offer to settle the Arab-Israeli dispute. Watch out when this event happens!   chapter 7

* * *

He will have the power somehow to make this image come to life and to speak and demand that all who will not worship it be put to death.
                                        chapter 8

* * *

If we went on the basis of our present population . . . this would mean that some 750 million people will die through various judgments during this Tribulation Period.   chapter 9

* * *

To those in Israel, the first 3½ years will seem like a heaven on earth . . . But the honeymoon is over and the next 3½ years of the last half of the Tribulation Period ushers in a most horrible period. . . .   chapter 10

* * *

God has a purpose in allowing Russia to come to Israel. God will use Russia as the greatest object lesson this world has ever seen. . . .
                                        chapter 11

* * *

Above are just some of the many startling facts you will read in the first few chapters of **GUIDE TO SURVIVAL.** But you will read much more! For there are 14 fact-filled challenging chapters that will bring you to the **greatest decision in your life!**

GUIDE

TO

SURVIVAL

by Salem Kirban

Each additional printing of GUIDE TO SURVIVAL is completely updated with the most recent statistics and current news events that have prophetic significance.

First Printing .... December, 1968
Second Printing .... February, 1969
Third Printing .... April, 1969
Fourth Printing .... July, 1969
Fifth Printing .... January, 1970
Sixth Printing .... June, 1970
Seventh Printing .... November, 1970
Eighth Printing .... May, 1971
Ninth Printing .... December, 1971
Tenth Printing .... July, 1972
Eleventh Printing .... December, 1972
Twelfth Printing .... May, 1973
Thirteenth Printing .... January, 1974
Fourteenth Printing .... July, 1974
Fifteenth Printing . . . Completely updated .... September, 1978

Library of Congress Catalog Card No. 68-57811
ISBN 0-912582-14-6

ACKNOWLEDGMENTS

To **Jerry Marrello,** Sunday School Teacher, Church of the Open Door . . . who in teaching from the book of Revelation in the Bible, sparked a renewed interest in my life in writing a book on God's prophecy in a clear, easy-to-read style.

To **Eileen Kirban,** who painstakingly typed the original manuscript from reels of dictated tape.

To **Bill Goggins** and **Bob Krauss,** artists, who were able to capture the central message of God's prophecy for these Last Days and graphically portray them in easy-to-read charts.

To **Dr. Gary G. Cohen,** President of Graham Bible College, Bristol, Tennessee, who carefully checked the final manuscript to assure its accuracy to the Scriptures.

To **Dr. Paul R. Ehrlich,** whose book THE POPULATION BOMB brought to sharp focus one of the critical problems the world now faces.

To **Edward Edelson** and **Fred Warshofsky,** whose book POISONS IN THE AIR, made me aware of the growing danger air pollution is bringing to our country.

As in a war, everyone remembers the General but few recall the privates . . . so it is often in Acknowledgments. I want to especially acknowledge those who indirectly had a major part in this book . . . those who served me coffee breaks while I scanned daily newspapers for news events vitally related to prophecy:

    Eleanor Grove, Sophi Kasper, Lillian Lamon, and
    Doris Taylor of The Hot Shoppes . . .
                and
    Max and Bea Stroll and Ginny Burns of TALLY HO.

DEDICATION

To my wife
MARY
Who provided encouragement and a foundation of prayer while I researched through the maze of theologically heavy books to write **GUIDE TO SURVIVAL**, simply, graphically . . . so everyone could understand.

To our children
DENNIS, DOREEN, DIANE, DUANE and DAWN
Who know that God is indeed still alive . . . for they, with their parents, have accepted Jesus Christ as personal Saviour and Lord.

To
YOU
That this book will bring you face to face with the greatest decision of your LIFE. My sincere prayer is that when you read the last chapter . . you might choose **LIFE.**

Why I Wrote This Book...

Today, it is not the most popular thing to believe that the Bible is the verbally inspired Word of God.

But I do!

And the more research I do on the prophetic books of the Bible . . . Daniel and Revelation . . . comparing them with current events happening today . . . the more convinced I am that (1) there is a God, (2) there is a Heaven and a Hell, (3) the WORLD IS RAPIDLY COMING TO AN END and (4) the period of 7 years of Tribulation will soon begin.

Whether you agree or disagree with me...you should know the premise on which I wrote **GUIDE TO SURVIVAL.**

My only request is that you read this book with an open mind and with a Bible next to you...to look up substantiating verses. It matters not whether that Bible is the King James Version (which I prefer), or the Catholic Duoay Version. To my Jewish friends...if presently you prefer not to read the New Testament...you will find that the prophecies in the book of Revelation in the New Testament will be backed up by similar predictions made in the Old Testament book of Daniel.

If you have not made a study of the Bible it will interest you to know that one-fourth of the Word of God was prophetic at the time it was written.

Just as there is a Heavenly Trinity (Father, Son and Holy Spirit), the Bible reveals there is also a Satanic trinity (Satan, the Antichrist, and the False Prophet). The Bible sometimes refers to Antichrist as The Beast because he will become the leader of the end-time Beast empire which will be animal-like in its wickedness (Revelation 13; Daniel 7). He will be a human being inspired by Satan.

> **Satan** imitates the work of **God the Father.**
> **The Beast (Antichrist)** imitates the work of the **Son** in subjecting the world to himself.
> **The False Prophet** imitates the work of the **Holy**

Spirit in praising the false king (Antichrist) who will reign on this world's throne.

Who will this Antichrist be? Will he be known to us as a President or a King? This book will explain his role in detail.

Just briefly, however, if one could amicably settle the Arab-Israeli dispute and bring peace to the world...this man's wisdom would be compared to the wisdom of Solomon. He would be considered a diplomat with no equal in the history of the world. Because of his accomplishments he could "write his own ticket." People would bestow on him unusual powers because of his amazing accomplishments.

For the past 25 years Presidents or their spokesmen have cautiously supported Israel.

President Truman in 1948 said Israel "must be large enough, free enough and strong enough to make its people self-supporting and secure."

John Foster Dulles, Secretary of State during the Eisenhower administration, said "the preservation of Israel is one of the essential goals of U.S. foreign policy."

President Kennedy in 1963 said U.S. policy in the Mideast was to halt all aggression because "we support the security of both Israel and her neighbors."

President Johnson repeated his pledge. And Presidents Nixon, Ford and Jimmy Carter have said the U.S. is committed to the integrity of Israel as a free and independent state.

The U.S. Congress, by joint resolution of both houses in 1957, declared "the preservation of the independence and integrity" of all Mideast nations, Arab and Israeli alike, to be "vital to the national interest" of the U.S.

President Ford hinted that he would use force in the Middle East if the Arab-Israeli situation affected U.S. economy.

Thus, according to prophetic Scripture, we are seeing the stage being set for the eventual clash between Russia and her allies on the side of the Arabs and the United States on the side of Israel.

Despite Vietnam the U.S. may still enter into conflict to "preserve the independence and integrity" of Israel because such preservation is "vital to the national interest" of the U.S. In any case a Man of Peace will someday appear on the scene to resolve this conflict by means of a peace pact in favor of the preservation of Israel.

When this occurs...and it will...BEWARE...for this man may be the Antichrist! (Daniel 9:27)

Events right now in the United States are helping set the course for these prophetic Scriptures to become a reality.

Arthur Krock, well-known newsman for 60 years, recently reflected his fears regarding the United States and its decline.

In his book, *Memoirs: Sixty Years on the Firing Line,* he says: "I have contracted a visceral (inner) fear. It is that the tenure of the United States as the first power in the world may be one of the briefest in history."

Mr. Krock contends that, between 1933 and 1968, "the United States merits the dubious distinction of having discarded its past and its meaning...."

Among the changes for the worst he notes:

> "A federal union almost replaced by a mass federal democracy controlled by an alliance of politicians and special-interest groups...
>
> Fiscal solvency and confidence in a stable dollar driven from the national and foreign marketplace by continuous deficit spending, easy credit...
>
> The free-enterprise system shackled by organized labor and a Government-managed economy...
>
> The Republic transmuted into a welfare state subsidized from Washington...
>
> A Supreme Court assuming overlordship of the Government and all the people to fit the political philosophy of the current majority."

Herbert V. Prochnow, former U.S. Deputy Under Secretary of State in a recent article in U.S. NEWS & WORLD REPORT said,

> "We know what we are, a nation professing to believe that respect for the law is the foundation of a free society and essential to the survival of freedom, and yet:
>
> A nation in which the number of crimes is increasing four times as fast as the population.
>
> A nation in which 15 and 16-year-old children

have the highest arrest rate.

A nation in which one third of its citizens feel compelled to keep firearms in the house for protection.

A nation in which there is violence in city after city, with widespread disrespect for law and property."

How true the Scriptures are and how prophetic when we read:

But realize this, that in the last days difficult times will come. (II Timothy 3:1).

And you will be hearing of wars and rumors of wars; see that you are not frightened, for those things must take place, but that is not yet the end.

For nation will rise against nation, and kingdom against kingdom, and in various places there will be famines and earthquakes. (Matthew 24:6,7).

Of Christ's second coming, the Scriptures tell us prophetically:

Behold, He is coming with the clouds, and every* eye will see Him, even those who pierced Him; and all the tribes of the earth will mourn over Him. Even so. Amen. (Revelation 1:7).

*Up until a few years ago people would have not believed the verse "every eye shall see Him." Now with TV satellites it will soon be possible for an entire world to watch one event together at one time!

There are more than 300 Old and New Testament Scriptures which promise that Jesus Christ will return to earth!

And these promises will be fulfilled just as literally as the 200 Old Testament prophecies of His virgin birth, death, burial and resurrection were fulfilled in His first coming when He suffered and died for man's sin.

The events occurring right now in the United States and in the world have an alarming parallel with the prophetic Scriptures in Daniel and Revelation regarding THE LAST DAYS.

And how true II Peter 3:3-4 and 10 are today...

Know this first of all, that in the last days mockers will come with their mocking, following after their *own lusts,*

and saying, "Where is the promise of His coming? For ever since the fathers fell asleep, all continues just as it was from the beginning of creation."

But the day of the Lord will come like a thief, in which the heavens will pass away with a roar and the elements will be destroyed with intense heat, and the earth and its works will be burned up.

GUIDE TO SURVIVAL is not meant to be a deep theological discourse. I have purposely tried to present God's blueprint for tomorrow in as simple, understandable language as possible. I hope I have succeeded.

Sometime in the near future...several MILLION people will suddenly disappear from this earth..."in the twinkling of an eye" (I Corinthians 15:52).

I sincerely hope you will be among them!

But, when this happens—and if you still remain on earth—then READ THIS BOOK for it will be your **GUIDE TO SURVIVAL.**   (October, 1968)

Revised Edition

Although **GUIDE TO SURVIVAL** was written in 1968 its message is as current as today. In fact, world conditions are even more acute.

The increasing problems of ecology, air pollution, famine, and wars in the last few years have made the message of **GUIDE TO SURVIVAL** even more clear. We are seeing Bible prophecy being fulfilled at a pace quicker than any of us anticipated!

I hesitate to guess what type of world we will be living in when 1985 arrives. Events are moving so rapidly that the next few years could see dramatic changes . . . changes, I believe, that will not be for the better.

Now, more than ever before, it is important to study God's Word, the Bible. For it will be your **GUIDE TO SURVIVAL.**

Salem Kirban

Huntingdon Valley, Pennsylvania
August, 1978

CONTENTS

How IT ALL BEGAN

It was just a little missionary church in Clarks Summit, Pennsylvania. Services were held in a rented room on the second floor of a quaint building in the center of town. Rev. Pryce was the pastor. Here my brother Lafayette, my sister Elsie and I were brought to church each Sunday.

The photograph above was taken at the annual church picnic at Covey's Farm in Clarks Summit. I am indebted to Mrs. Lulu D. Thomas for sending me this picture. It was taken about 1938. I am that little boy in the circle on the front row. I can remember vividly at this picnic the various church members discussing the book of Revelation and prophecy.

And this discussion was the first spark that kindled a flaming desire for me to understand God's prophetic promises better. This was really how GUIDE TO SURVIVAL began.

                                             Salem Kirban

Facts You Should Know About The Bible

Since the source of reference we use in our book, **GUIDE TO SURVIVAL,** is the Bible, you should know why the Bible is the Word of God.

The Bible (Old and New Testament) is comprised of 66 books of about 40 authors and was written over a span of about 1600 years.

These authors were fishermen, kings, philosophers, physicians, scholars and poets. Since (a) their lives were lived in various countries, and (b) their writings were distributed over 60 generations of human history...this one volume exhibits the most perfect continuity of thought the world has ever seen.

It sweeps the universe from the heights of Heaven to the depths of Hell and traces the works of God from beginning to end.

It reveals the minutest details of the plan and purpose of God and the perfection of His creation.

And this is important...though written in the earlier days of human knowledge, when the present world discoveries could not reasonably have been disclosed, it is in complete harmony with every discovery made by man.

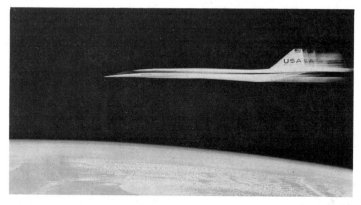

Man's scientific accomplishments sometimes causes him to boast of his own abilities, drawing him away from God. But all knowledge is God-given and the universe is evidence of His creation.

THE THRILL OF PROPHECY

Everyone who has discovered the marvel and miracle of definitely fulfilled prophecy knows that the Bible is not an ordinary book but is God's message to man and undeniably divine. Only God knows the future and can foretell it with accuracy.

In this connection Peter writes in II Peter 1:16

For we did not follow cleverly devised tales when we made known to you the power and coming of our Lord Jesus Christ, but we were eyewitnesses of His majesty.

Not only were many of these writers eye-witnesses of Christ's ministry but God used them to write down His prophetic message.

The fact that *one-fourth* of the Word of God was prophetic at the time it was written is astounding enough.

But to this we know that hundreds of years before Christ was born the Old Testament told us the time of His birth in Daniel 9. Isaiah 7 tells us the fact of the virgin birth. Micah 5 tells us the place of His birth. In Psalm 22 and Isaiah 53 we have recorded prophetically the intimate details of His life and death. In Psalm 16 we find the fact of His resurrection.

Prophecy is two-fold in nature. It is both didactic and predictive. It is important to realize that the prophetic utterances of the writers were not deductions of human reason, but were imparted to them by the Holy Spirit.

For no prophecy was ever made by an act of human will, but men moved by the Holy Spirit spoke from God. (II Peter 1:21).

Remember this also: The prophecy that has been fulfilled, HAS BEEN FULFILLED LITERALLY.

More than half of the predictive prophecies concerning Christ, are as yet unfulfilled.

As the fulfilled prophecies were fulfilled LITERALLY...so the unfulfilled prophecies WILL BE FULFILLED LITERALLY!

There is no fact in history more clearly established than the fact of Christ's First Coming. But, as His First Coming to suffer did not fulfill all the prophecies associated with

His Coming...it is evident that there must be another Coming to completely fulfill the prophecies which speak of His reigning over the earth in power and glory.

We find that one of the greatest doctrines in the Bible, next to salvation (accepting Christ as your personal Saviour and Lord), is the doctrine of the Second Coming of Christ.

One verse in every 30 in the New Testament refers to Christ's Second Coming. There are 20 times as many references in the Old Testament to Christ's Second Coming as to His First Coming at Bethlehem!

WATCH, THEREFORE

In writing this book **GUIDE TO SURVIVAL**, I wrote it (a) believing the Bible of the Old and New Testaments to be the Word of God, (b) verbally inspired, (c) infallible and inerrant in the original writings, (d) that God's final and complete revelation of Himself is in His Son, our Lord Jesus Christ, (e) Who by His substitutionary death on Calvary, purchased our redemption, (f) that He is coming again for His saints and we as believers will meet Him in the air (I Thessalonians 4:13-18).

If you, too, believe the Bible as the whole Word of God and have accepted Christ as your personal Saviour and Lord... you will find this book a thrilling account of your spiritual inheritance.

However, if you deny that the *entire* Bible is the Word of God...if you have not personally accepted Christ as your Saviour and Lord...this book will be a startling revelation of the terror and tragedy that awaits you.

2 Timothy 3:16 tells us that "...all Scripture is given by inspiration of God..." Christ also tells us in Matthew 24: 42,44

> *Therefore be on the alert, for you do not know which day your Lord is coming.*
>
> *For this reason you be ready too; for the Son of Man is coming at an hour when you do not think He will.*

Will you be ready when this event of His Second Coming occurs? I pray that you will!

Explanation Of Terms
Used In This Book

Abomination of Desolation

A desecration of the temple of Israel by Antichrist. His final attempt to force the Jews to worship him (Matthew 24:15; 2 Thessalonians 2:3,4; Daniel 9:27).

Persecution under Antiochus IV, a forerunner of Antichrist. A Temple priest, compelled to eat pork, prefers to die rather than desecrate the altar.

Antichrist

A name taken from I and 2 John. In Daniel he is referred to as the little horn and the vile person; In 2 Thessalonians as the Son of Perdition; and in Revelation as the Beast out of the sea.

Satan so completely possesses the man as to amount almost to an incarnation. Scriptures appear to indicate that he, like Judas Iscariot, will become indwelt by Satan.

Antichrist will oppose Christ, the saints, and the Jews. He will be first hailed as a Man of Peace and given unlimited power by the European countries, the United States and Israel. At his rise, Antichrist will be only a man, but with satanic power. His sudden, sensational rise as the saviour of a world threatened by destruction will be one of the marks of the beginning of the Time of the End.

His later attempt to annihilate the Jews will bring about his defeat at Jerusalem by the return of Christ. All prophecy up to the return of Christ at Armageddon will be fulfilled by the close of his day.

A future world leader, Antichrist, will come first as a messenger of peace but after 3½ years of command, will attempt to annihilate the Jews!

Born Again

When Nicodemus, a ruler of the Jews, asked how he could enter Heaven, Jesus answered, "...Except a man be born again, he cannot see the kingdom of God" (John 3:3).

The condition of this new birth is faith in Christ crucified (See John 3:14, 15 and Galatians 3:24).

Through the new birth (being born again) the believer becomes a partaker of the divine nature and of the life of Christ Himself (Galatians 2:20).

The term "born again" and "saved" are used synonymously.

For further light on this, read the definition for SAVED and also THE SAINTS.

The False Prophet

Antichrist will be the political ruler who will work the works of Satan. **The False Prophet** will be the religious ruler who will undergird the work of the **Antichrist.** Both get their power from Satan. (Revelation 13:11-18; 16:13; 19:20)

The False Prophet never will attempt to promote himself. He will never become an object of worship. He will do the work of a prophet in that he directs attention away from himself to one who he says has the right to be worshipped (the Antichrist).

The False Prophet will imitate many miracles of God. He will cause fire to come down from heaven copying the miracles of Elijah in order to convince the nation Israel that he (The False Prophet) is the Elijah whom Malachi promised was yet to come (Malachi 4:5-6)! Having achieved this deception the False Prophet will declare that since this miracle (bringing fire from heaven) shows that he is Elijah...then, therefore, the Antichrist is truly Christ and should be worshipped.

He will also build a statue, and through some satanic miracle cause this statue (image) to talk and somehow come to life. When the people see this miracle they will fall down and worship the Antichrist believing him to be a Christ.

Last Days

Our reference to the Last Days means the *days immediately* prior to the "Rapture" of the saints and the ushering in of the Tribulation Period of 7 years.

Mark of the Beast

During the second half of the seven year Tribulation Period, the Antichrist (who previously was setting himself up as a Man of Peace) will suddenly move against the Jews and all those who have accepted Christ as Saviour during the first 3 1/2 years of this Period. In Revelation 13:16, 17 we read that "...he (False Prophet) causeth all, both small and great, rich and poor, free and bond, to receive some mark in their right hand, or in their foreheads: And that no man might buy or sell, save he that had the mark..."

Therefore those who refuse to submit to the authority of this system by having this mark (the Mark of the Beast), either starve to death slowly, or else are slain by the representatives of the government, who will treat as traitors all who refuse to accept this identifying mark.

Rapture

This refers to the time, prior to the start of the 7 year Tribulation Period, when believing Christians (both dead and alive) will "in the twinkling of an eye" rise up to meet Christ in the air.

For if we believe that Jesus died and rose again, even so God will bring with Him those who have fallen asleep in Jesus.

For this we say to you by the word of the Lord, that we who are alive, and remain until the coming of the Lord, shall not precede those who have fallen asleep.

For the Lord Himself will descend from heaven with a shout, with the voice of the archangel, and with the trumpet of God; and the dead in Christ shall rise first.

Then we who are alive and remain shall be caught up together with them in the clouds to meet the Lord in the air, and thus we shall always be with the Lord. (I Thessalonians 4:14-17).

A mark of identification will be placed on the right hand or on the forehead. No one will be able to buy or sell without this mark during the Tribulation Period.

The Saints

Those who accept Christ (in their heart) as both personal Saviour and Lord.

> Truly, truly, I say to you, he who hears My word, and believes Him who sent Me, has eternal life, and does not come into judgment, but has passed out of death into life (John 5:24).

> For the wages of sin is death, but the free gift of God is eternal life in Christ Jesus our Lord. (Romans 6:23).

*For by grace you have been saved through faith;
and that not of yourselves, it is the gift of God;
not as a result of works, that no one should boast.
(Ephesians 2:8, 9).*

*Blessed be the God and Father of our Lord Jesus
Christ, who according to His great mercy has
caused us to be born again to a living hope
through the resurrection of Jesus Christ from the
dead, to obtain an inheritance which is imperishable and undefiled and will not fade away, reserved in heaven for you. (I Peter 1:3,4).*

Through the quoting of the above Scripture verses
God's Word defines (a) how you can be a saint, (b)
the rich promises that will be yours when you accept Christ as your personal Saviour, and (c) your
eternal rewards in heaven.

Saved

The term "saved" and "born-again" are used interchangeably. In our terminology, one who is "saved"
is one who has accepted Christ as His personal Saviour
and is thereby saved from the wrath of God against
the sinner and from an eternity in Hell and is assured
of an eternity with Christ in Heaven.

In Acts 16:30, 31 we read:

*And after he brought them out, he said, "Sirs,
what must I do to be saved? And they said, Believe in the Lord Jesus, and you shall be saved,
you and your household.*

And the well known verses in John 3:16, 17 tell us:

*For God so loved the world, that He gave His
only begotten Son, that whoever believes in Him
should not perish, but have eternal life.*

*For God did not send the Son into the world to
judge the world; but that the world should be
saved through Him.*

For further light on this, read the definition which
begins on the previous page on THE SAINTS.

Second Coming of Christ

This is one of the most prominent doctrines in the Bible. In the New Testament alone it is referred to over 300 times. His First Coming was over 1900 years ago when He came on earth to save man from sin. The Second Coming is an event starting at the Rapture and comprehending four phases: **First,** at the Rapture Christ takes the believers out of this world to be with Him (I Thessalonians 4). **Second,** Christ pours out His judgments on the world during the 7 year Tribulation Period. **Third,** Christ at the end of the 7 year Tribulation destroys the Antichrist and his wicked followers at Armageddon (Revelation 19). **Fourth,** Christ sets up His millennial Kingdom prophesied so often in the Old Testament (Revelation 20).

Tribulation

In our reference to the Tribulation Period we mean that period of phenomenal world trial and suffering that occurs during the seven-year reign of Antichrist. Daniel 12:1 tells us, "...there shall be a time of trouble, such as never was since there was a nation."

It is at this time that the Jews (and those who accept Christ as Saviour during this seven-year period) will be severely persecuted through imprisonment, torture and death.[1]

1Some scholars reserve the title **"Great Tribulation"** (Matthew 24:21), for only the latter half of this seven year period. During this latter half...the troubles of the period will reach their zenith.

1

Guide to Survival

A Slumbering World • Current News Reveals Shocking Fulfillment of God's Prophecies • Self-confidence • President Requires Fortress Protection • Alcohol • The Crime Wave Keeps Growing • Shocking Films • A Civilized Nation Thrives on Uncivilized Music • Strikes Becoming More Crippling • The United Church and its Courtship with Destruction • Growth of Super Church • The Clock Nears Midnight • The Sterile Church Offers the World False Hope • Your Guide to Survival

A SLUMBERING WORLD

As a small girl walked past the cathedral that she always passed on her way to and from school each day, the clock in the steeple chimed the hour but, apparently broken, it didn't stop after striking 12—it kept on: 13, 14, 15, 16, and on it went. The little girl, becoming somewhat alarmed, ran home quickly. As she entered her home, she shouted to her mother, "Mommy, it's later than it's ever been before!"

If this book can accomplish any one thing, echoing the cry of the little girl, it is to show **that the hour is later than it has ever been before.**

The world is rapidly coming to an end. It is on an irreversible course.

When this end will come no one can accurately predict. All we can do is judge today by the signs given to us in the Scriptures.

> *Be on the alert then, for you do not know the day nor the hour. (Matthew 25:13)*

And by those signs it is safe to assume that we are indeed living in the Last Days.

It was Billy Sunday who said: "It is better to be 100 feet from Hell headed away from it than 1000 miles away headed toward it."

The sad fact is that while politicians are espousing that the world and America is getting better and better—they are, in reality, casting a veil of illusion over the populace and lulling them into a slumber from which they will awake too late.

Never before in history have so many events so rapidly in succession pointed to the Last Days. The amazing thing is that because they appear to be everyday occurrences most people are taking them for granted and overlook them as having any important significance in relation to God's Word.

CURRENT NEWS REVEALS SHOCKING FULFILLMENT OF GOD'S PROPHECIES

However, if one takes the time to study all of the news reports and read all of the magazines that are available in America and sift those things which are not related to prophecy—one will come up with an array of news data that will shock you because they coincide with the amazing prophetic revelations as found in the Bible.

Of course, if you believe that God is dead and if you believe that there is no such thing as the Rapture (which will occur when the believers rise up to meet Christ in the air)—then this book will appear to be a fairy tale to you. However, may I suggest you hold on to this book and keep it in a prominent place in your home because someday if you are still living, this book will be worth its weight in gold. Every page will be a reality to you and a road map as to what lies ahead in your future life on earth.

Let's look at Matthew 24:3-14:

> ...the disciples came to Him [Christ]...saying, "Tell us, when will these things be, and what will be the sign of Your coming, and of the end of the age?"
>
> And Jesus answered and said to them, "See to it that no one misleads you.
>
> "For many will come in My name, saying, 'I am the Christ,' and will mislead many.
>
> "And you will be hearing of wars and rumors of wars; see that you are not frightened, for those things must take place, but that is not yet the end.
>
> "For nation will rise against nation, and kingdom against kingdom, and in various places there will be famines and earthquakes.
>
> "But all these things are merely the beginning of birth pangs.
>
> "Then they will deliver you up to tribulation, and will kill you, and you will be hated by all nations on account of My name.
>
> "And at that time many will fall away and will betray one another and hate one another.
>
> "And many false prophets will arise, and will mislead many.
>
> "And because lawlessness is increased, most people's love will grow cold.
>
> "But the one who endures to the end, it is he who shall be saved.
>
> "And this gospel of the kingdom shall be preached in the whole world for a witness to all nations, and then the end shall come."

Many things mentioned in these Scriptures are already occurring in the world in greater intensity than they have ever occurred before.

There are wars which are not the conventional wars that America has been used to fighting. There are wars that are dividing nations from within and from without. There are famines. Living in America, one cannot always fathom their intensity. The recent famines in Africa and the continuing famines in India are just a few of the many that are appearing throughout the world.

There are earthquakes which appear to be becoming more and more frequent and more and more devastating.

But as horrible as these are the Word of God tells us that this will only be the **beginning** of the horrors to come.

Let us look at some of the events that are occurring in today's world which have set the course of the world on an irreversible trend to destruction and are opening the gates to the Last Days.

SELF-CONFIDENCE

Prior to each election, we hear many speeches. The candidates tell us that America is getting better and better and that soon America will be able to take care of the needs of everyone. We are still told that the United States is heading despite the current inflation, towards better times and certain figures are being used to prove this. As an example, it has been estimated that about 14 million Americans have left poverty behind them during the last 7 years. A proportion of families earning $7,000 or more annually has risen from 22% in 1950 to about 55% in 1969. And in 1976, for the first time, the average family earned $11,000 a year.

25 million more American families have savings accounts than in 1963. Other millions despite inflation have had sufficient funds to buy and sell shares of stock in a declining market, hoping for an upswing to come soon.

Home ownership has gone up from 33 million families to 40 million since 1960. Multi-car ownership has gone up from 9.5 million to 23 million.

Now 99% of all American families have at least 1 television set—often 2 in the house.

In economic terms—America, with 7% of the world's land area and about 10% of its population, accounts for 1/3 of the world's production of goods and services.

Its farmlands produce 13% of the world's wheat, 46% of its corn and 21% of its meat—enough to feed 215 million Americans and much of the world besides.

Its factories produce a flow of goods almost equal in size to the combined output of the Soviet Union and western Europe.

The U.S. automobile factories produced over 12 million passenger cars last year or 41% of the world output. Half of all the cars in the world are registered in the U.S. California, with 10 million autos, has more cars than any single foreign country except West Germany, France and Britain! Right now in the United States there are over 105 million autos, trucks and buses on the highways!

Today Americans are the best educated people the world has ever known.

More Americans—50%— have finished secondary school than any other people.

The Gallup Polls reported that 45% of all Americans attended church during a typical week and 70% thought religion "very important."

It is very apparent that never before in history has America been so affluent. And yet never before has America been weighed in the balances and been found so wanting.

PRESIDENT REQUIRES FORTRESS PROTECTION

For in spite of its affluence, in spite of its education, in spite of its economic prosperity, it is a sad reflection on America when the President of the United States must ride in a $500,000 automobile designed to withstand small scale military attacks.

This new Lincoln limousine which was built for President Johnson and his successors is unlike any car on the road.

It has a fighter plane canopy and more than 2 tons of armor. This shielding is designed to stop a 30 caliber rifle bullet, a barrage of molotov cocktails, or both.

The window glass and the plastic bubble top canopy, all bullet-proof, are thicker than the glass and plastic used in air force fighter planes.

The limousine runs on 4 specially designed truck tires. Within each tire is a hard steel disc with a hard rubber tread which would allow the limousine to be driven up to 50 miles at top speed with all four tires flat.

If the government were to pay for this vehicle at $1,000 down and $100 a month, it would have the principal paid off in 416 years—or just in time for the Democratic Convention in the year 2384. All this protection is necessary because of this lawless age.

Eleven persons were killed when a pick-up truck traveling on the wrong side of a four-lane highway collided head-on with this station wagon. Four of the victims were children. There were no survivors. Some 30,000 deaths annually are caused by drunken driving.

Secret Service agents mount President's car while motorcycle police accompany motorcade. Presidential limousine is $500,000 fortress on wheels. The Bible tells us ". . . in the last days perilous times shall come" (2 Timothy 3:1).

In the chapter POWER THAT DESTROYS we will cover the Democratic Convention that was held in Chicago in August, 1968 and relate how disastrous this convention was and yet how prophetic it was in showing the people first hand what happens when a Democratic country is forced to impose actions similar to those of a police state upon a nation.

ALCOHOL

The profit motive is so intense in the United States that unscrupulous manufacturers will go to any length to put their product into the hands of the public for monetary gain.

One of the worst enemies of the American people is alcohol.

Alcohol is the No. 3 cause of hospitalization in the United States.

Just recently the World Health Organization reported that the United States has achieved the dubious distinction of replacing France as the nation with the highest incidence of alcoholism in the world.

It is estimated that more than 5 million Americans are alcoholics. That's one in 40 persons.

The social and emotional costs of the disease are difficult to measure but some statisticians have made some dollar and cents estimates. It costs industry $2 billion a year in work loss.

Dr. David J. Pittman, Chairman of the 28th International Congress on Alcohol and Alcoholism called alcoholism "mankind's most neglected, most serious and most tragic health problem."

Recent reports show that the drunken driver is the biggest killer on the highway, causing 25,000 deaths and 800,000 crashes annually.

Especially tragic is the fact that much loss of life, limb and property damage involves completely innocent parties.

During the past 35 years, surveys made in every area of the country have found alcohol to be the largest single factor leading to fatal crashes.

This corruption of the body, while not new, is something

which is increasingly on the rise and indirectly causes first an individual, then a family, and eventually a nation to turn away from God and toward material ambitions.

THE CRIME WAVE KEEPS GROWING

Recently the Federal Bureau of Investigation announced that in 1976 the crime wave rose by 15% over the same period of just a year ago. In 1976 all major crimes were up sharply in number—robbery 13%, murder 20% and larceny up 30%.

In 1959 we had 1,592,189 crimes. By 1969 this has risen to an annual crime rate of 4,989,700 or a 21% **increase in crimes in a 10 year period!**

In murders there was a 66% increase within the same 10 year period and in forcible rapes a 115% increase.

In what was supposed to be a "great society" the crime picture has changed it into what may be known as a "violent society."

One of the hottest issues in Congress has been the issue of how to restrain crime. The only thing that senators seem to agree upon is that lawlessness is a big and growing problem and that something has to be done about it.

Since 1960 there has been an increase in serious crime of 176% while the population of the nation has increased by only 13%.

One of the sad revelations is that more than 20 million citizens own more than 100 million firearms and that every year there are 17,000 gunshot deaths or 2 every hour.

Senator John L. McClellan, a Democrat from Arkansas said recently in the Senate: "Crime and the threat of crime stalk America. Our streets are unsafe. Our citizens are fearful, terrorized and outraged. They demand and deserve relief from this scourge of lawlessness, which today imperils our internal security."

Perhaps inadvertently the Supreme Court itself has, through its recent rulings, encouraged crime. One of the problems of Congress is to attempt to overcome the effects of recent adverse Supreme Court decisions.

The shortsightedness of some people is found in a recent ad put in a metropolitan city newspaper by the Retail

Liquor Dealers Association which had as its headline:
"Is Law Enforcement Also Dead?"
In the ad, they deplored the fact that the proprietor of a liquor store was shot while defending his own property. It apparently had not occurred to them that liquor has been one of the major sparks that ignites crime in the hearts of men.

In the U.S., FBI Reports Show—

Every 30 minutes . . . . **A murder**
Every 12 minutes . . . . **A forcible rape**
Every 1 1/2 minutes . **A robbery**
Every 1 1/2 minutes . **An aggravated assault**
Every minute . . . . **12 serious crimes, including a violent crime**
Every 32 seconds . . . **An auto theft**
Every 17 seconds . . . **A larceny**
Every 14 seconds . . . **A burglary**

Police solved about 17% of all crimes in 1977. In 1960 they solved over 31%.

In a recent poll, where 45,000 persons were interviewed, 78% said they feel unsafe even in their own homes!

Source: Federal Bureau of Investigation
Copyright © 1978 Salem Kirban, Inc.

SHOCKING FILMS

In a recent issue of the Wall Street Journal, one of the feature articles carried this headline:

TOP "NUDIE" FILM MAKER SCRAMBLES TO
OUTSHOCK BIG STUDIOS

Public "Bursting For More" So
Producer Turns To Rawer Sex & Violence

This particular producer said in a recent interview: "This one is going to set them back on their heels. Nudity alone isn't a drawing card anymore. The public is thirsting for more."

The increasing exploitation of sex and violence by U.S. movie makers is incontestable. It is a well chronicled fact. The trend suggests a good deal about changing U.S. traditional customs.

A sociologist stated, "The blatant sex saturated movies today is just part of an exuberant, initial over reaction of a society breaking loose from old restraints and rules."

The producer of sex films stated that every one of the 20 movies he has made in the past 9 years has grossed at least 4 times its cost. His first film, which took only 4 days and $24,000 to produce, has grossed $1.2 million so far or a 40 to 1 return on investment — which has been matched only by Gone With The Wind.

COURT STRIKES FCC BAN ON OBSCENE WORDS

On Thursday, March 17, 1977 a U.S. Court of Appeals ruled that the Federal Communications Commission may not ban indecent language on radio and television, and may not even limit it to certain times of the day to prevent children from hearing it.

The U.S. Court of Appeals ruled that the FCC order banning obscene words "...ignored both the statute which forbids it to censor radio communications and its own previous decisions and orders which leave the question of programming content to the discretion of the licensee."

The Court added: "We should continue to trust the licensee to exercise judgment, responsibility and sensitivity to the community's needs, interests and tastes. To whatever extent we err, or the commission errs in balancing its duties, it must be in favor of preserving the values of free expression and freedom from government interference in matters of taste."

Freedom without responsibility is not freedom! And it is easy to see how in the last 10 years freedom **with** responsibility has drastically eroded.

Once satanic forces get their foot into the door ... there is no holding back. All is done under the guise of freedom of speech. What begins as one or two minor incursions into good taste suddenly blossoms into total obscenity without any shame. We see it in the rash of motion pictures on the screen. We hear it on radio. We see it on the so-called television comedy and serious drama. And we read it in our newspapers and magazines.

For the Christian it will soon become time to limit his viewing to the 6 o'clock news. In one way, this may prove a blessing. It may drive the Christian to spend more time reading and studying God's Word.

Today in some cities in our Western Hemisphere, sex films are shown on TV late at night—after a suitable warning. Pay the fee and in many U.S. motels R (Restricted) movies will be cabled privately to the TV set in your room!

With America being fed this type of entertainment and then going home and reading pornographic books while drinking a cocktail ... it is no wonder that the seed which America is sowing is now reaping its harvest of wickedness and lawlessness!

And in the wake of this unrest we find that the important family unit is disintegrating at a much more rapid rate. The number of divorces is rising. In 1974, over 1 million divorces and annulments were granted in the United States compared with 490,000 in 1966. A government survey has estimated that more than one-third of all first-born children in the U.S. are conceived out of wedlock.

A CIVILIZED NATION THRIVES ON UNCIVILIZED MUSIC

Not only is our music getting more and more suggestive but the decibel rate is getting higher and higher (Decibel—unit for measuring the loudness of sound). Recently a researcher at the University of Tennessee conducted a study with guinea pigs.

On some days the animals listened to as much as 4 hours of popular teenage music. On other days they heard none.

Both ears were exposed for the first 45 hours of listening and after that the left ear was plugged.

After 88 hours and 30 minutes of exposure to this hard sounding music, the cochlear cells were photographed. Cells in the left ear were normal. But many of those in the exposed right ear had collapsed and "shriveled up like peas." This study was prompted last fall when screening of freshmen at the University of Knoxville revealed a high proportion of students with a measureable hearing loss.

Dr. David M. Lipscomb, director of the University's audio-clinical services said: "We were shocked to find that the hearing of many of these students had already deteriorated to a level of the average 65-year-old person."

Daily Mirror, London

In the interest of decency we do not believe this portion of photo should be printed by us.

Daily Mirror, London

Pop Goes the Bible: "The Old Testament depicts human life, warts and all," gamely explained the Archbishop of Canterbury. His bemused reaction to a London exhibition of illustrations for a new edition of the Bible was understandable. The Oxford University Press edition features some 700 contemporary drawings ranging from a couple making love (The Song of Solomon) to a startling illustration (above) of Job 14:1-2: "Man that is born of a woman is ... full of trouble. He cometh forth like a flower."

STRIKES BECOMING MORE CRIPPLING

More than ever before we are seeing strikes becoming the way of life among professional people as well as blue collar workers.

With each new school term we see a wave of teachers' strikes.

In recent years there have been no less than 50 strikes set for the opening of public schools each September. It is not unusual for classes for thousands of youngsters to be suspended one month, two months or an entire semester because of strikes.

More than half of the nation's 1.8 million elementary and high school teachers are now organized in either the National Education Association or the American Federation of Teachers.

While most strikes called by these organizations are "illegal," since nearly all states have laws prohibiting walkouts by public employees including teachers — angry teachers, in this age of unrest, choose to defy the law and strike. In 1960 there were only three strikes by teachers. In 1961, only one. In 1965 there were only seven strikes by teachers, 1966 saw 33 strikes.

Then suddenly in 1967 there were 81 strikes and by 1976 there were over 100 strikes by teachers.

In New York City, garbage workers are better paid than teachers, and in Washington, D.C. the pay for teachers is $1,000 a year less than it is for policemen and firemen.

This chapter is not to point out the deficiencies in pay for teachers but simply to show that there is a continuing unrest throughout the nation, not only among those in the ghetto or those in blue collar jobs, but also those in professional areas of skill.

These problems will not be resolved — regardless of what politicians may tell us. They will become increasingly more complex and increasingly more severe in intensity. Every 3 days somewhere in the United States, municipal workers —policemen, firemen, schoolteachers, sanitation workers —go on strike.

This unrest is particularly evident in slum areas. Slums were supposed to be rebuilt during this "great society."

Seen in rear-view mirror of police motor scooter, helmeted policemen guard front door of Public School 20 in New York. Crippling
strikes are causing greater havoc and creating an era of unrest.

Yet, "ghettos" grow instead of shrinking—and become centers of riots.

Poverty was to be eliminated by a national "war on poverty" and yet we find welfare costs continuing to climb.

Neither America nor the world will be able to resolve this perplexing situation.

And while this unrest continues, confession magazines will rake in an estimated $40 million in newsstand and subscription sales this year. This is up from $30 million 5 years ago.

And surprisingly enough, book sales from across the nation doubled in dollar volume in the last few years. A "paperback explosion" has brought popularity in America and overseas to novelists whose main stress is on sex.

One prominent publisher of books who deals heavily on sex and who has thrived financially in book sales throughout America recently wrote me the following:

> "...I'm a total atheist. I feel sorry for people who are superstitious, obsessive, compulsive, fearful or for any other motivations believe in a personal god or gods. As long as they keep (what I consider) their silliness to themselves and don't intrude on my life with such nonsense, I don't object...I don't know an intelligent person among my hundreds of friends or acquaintances who feels committed to any formal or ritualistic religion..."

I sent him a New Testament and asked him to at least read it before he made any further commitments to atheism. He promptly wrote me back that as soon as he received the New Testament he threw it in the wastebasket.

THE UNITED CHURCH AND ITS COURTSHIP WITH DESTRUCTION

While America should be looking to the church for an answer—the church is woefully lacking in providing the answer that will meet the needs of the human soul.

For the Bible speaks of a time when the church will depart from the faith and will offer only social answers to spiritual problems.

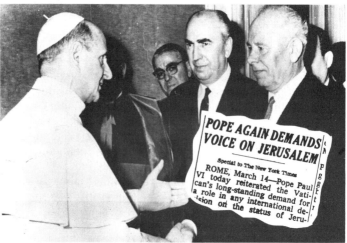

Top: An Orthodox prelate looks on as a volunteer bus driver displays the World Council of Churches' *Oikoumene* (ecumenical) symbol. Symbol represents the universal world church.

Below: In a January, 1967 meeting at the Vatican, Pope Paul VI and former Soviet President Nikolai Podgorny met privately to discuss world peace.

More and more we are seeing the dissolving of individual church groups and the unifying of church denominations with the goal of a One World church.

At a 1968 World Council of Churches meeting in Uppsala, Sweden, where over 2,000 persons attended (including 880 delegates from the 232 member churches of the WCC of the Protestant, Orthodox, Anglican, and old Catholic communions), more steps were taken toward religious unification.

LOOK Magazine in its report at that time on the Uppsala World Council of Churches Assembly wrote:

> With 15 Roman Catholic observers on hand this time to do everything but vote, the Assembly at Uppsala became the most complete Christian gathering in 900 years. Pope Paul VI gave it the Vatican's first blessing. Fr. Roberto Tucci, a key Jesuit, surprised the delegates by suggesting that they "seriously consider the possibility that the Roman Catholic Church might one day become a member...of the World Council." Nine Catholics have already been elected to the Council's Faith and Order Commission. Protestant theologian Robert McAfee Brown predicts of the Catholics: "They won't hold the Council back. The really good Catholics are way ahead of traditional Protestants."

It further reported in one of the Council Assembly's working sessions that there was much discussion on World Economic and Social Development.

> But the World Council's agony of conscience is real. It is too aware that Christians are, as economist Barbara Ward said, "in the main, members of the exclusive white man's club with incomes rising into the stratosphere." To narrow the gap, the Assembly proposed that rich nations start "growing richer slower" by giving one percent of their gross national product to the development of poor nations.

This World Council now represents some 2 billion people.

GENERAL CHURCH MEMBERSHIP URGED

The director of Ecumenical Affairs for the National Council of Churches, in a recent magazine article, projected his views on hastening the unification of all churches into a one-church body.

What could be done immediately, he says, is for the Roman Catholic Church and the major Protestant communions to recognize the existence of a "general church membership."

In his words, "This means that, if you become a Christian, other Christians acknowledge that you are fully a Christian...anyone who belongs to one church belongs to all. Thus, if you should become a member of the Methodist Church, you would become simultaneously a full member of the African Methodist Episcopal Zion Church, the Roman Catholic Church, the United Church of Christ and the Episcopal Church."

> Further in the article he states, "In practice, of course, some people will maintain life-long fidelity to a single tradition. Others will expose themselves to many traditions at once—participating perhaps in a Lutheran Bible study class, a Methodist prayer group, a Roman Catholic Mass, a United Church of Christ service project and Episcopal enterprise in education."

This is but another step towards a One World Church idea that Scriptures tell us usher in the Last Days. In Revelation this is referred to as the Laodicean church, one that has a form of godliness but denies the power thereof. Christ's message for them is found in Revelation 3:15,16...

> *I know your deeds, that you are neither cold nor hot; I would that you were cold or hot.*
>
> *So because you are lukewarm, and neither hot nor cold, I will spit you out of My mouth.*

Even in the Catholic church we see a growing unrest and a lessening of power by the Pope.

For the first time, Catholics were shocked to learn that about 200 Catholic priests had joined a union to gain a voice in the affairs of the Catholic church in America.

For the first time in the open, many priests are questioning tradition, and Catholic laymen are protesting and ignoring the Pope's decision regarding the use of birth control devices.

Louis Cassels, Religion columnist for UPI, wrote in his October 5, 1968 syndicated column the following:

> Washington—When Pope Paul VI issued his encyclical on birth control last July, many people thought it would be a severe setback to the Christian Unity Movement.
>
> They felt that the Pope had dashed ecumenical hopes by reiterating rather than modifying a Catholic teaching which is almost universally rejected by Protestants.
>
> But that judgment is now up for reappraisal. Astute observers are beginning to think that the birth control controversy may be more of an asset than a liability to the cause of Christian reunion.
>
> Their reasoning goes like this:
>
> The greatest obstacle to unity is Protestant fear of papal power.
>
> Despite the example of Pope John XXIII, and despite the pronouncements of the Vatican Council, most Protestants have remained dubious about the existence of real freedom of conscience in the Catholic Church.
>
> In the words of Dr. Robert McAfee Brown, a Presbyterian observer at the Vatican Council, Protestants have "feared that if organic reunion with the Roman Catholic Church ever came to pass, we would be required to submit our individual judgments of conscience to the voice of authority emanating from Vatican City and subordinate our personal convictions to whatever was definitely spoken by that voice."

PROTESTANT VIEW IS REAPPRAISED

This Protestant view of the arbitrary force of papal authority is now undergoing a considerable modification, in light of the Catholic response to the Pope's birth control encyclical.

Some members of the Catholic hierarchy, such as Cardinal Patrick O'Boyle, of Washington, D.C., have taken the position that Protestants expected: Namely, the Pope has spoken so the discussion is over.

But other cardinals and bishops in several Western European Countries, and many leading Catholic theologians in the United States, have taken a different view of the encyclical. As papal teaching, they have said, it deserves respectful consideration from every Catholic. But is not infallible, and a Catholic who disagrees with the Pope's conclusion, after sober and prayerful study, has the right and indeed the duty to follow his own conscience.

AN ECUMENICAL BREAKTHROUGH?

"What more could a Protestant ask?" says Dr. Brown. "What Protestant could not fully subscribe to this way of making decisions?"

Writing in the Catholic magazine *Commonweal*, the Presbyterian theologian concludes that the birth control encyclical "is inadvertently the greatest gift to the ecumenical scene since the election of Pope John back in 1959.

"Its reception shows that the traditional views of papal authority simply cannot be taken seriously any more, and that Catholics feel no greater sense of being bound to unquestionable doctrine than do Protestants."

GROWTH OF SUPER CHURCH

While the need for missions and missionary endeavors becomes even greater, the number of workers becomes even fewer. This appears to be in direct proportion to the desire of the churches to become even bigger and bigger.

We are seeing the growth of the super church in suburban America.

The church seems to be employed in the same numbers game that is overtaking other areas in America.

While they may not admit it, many a church is more interested in a numbers game than they are in the individual souls of men. For the individual souls of men require individual personalized attention and counseling and this is something that cannot be done when a local church grows to such proportion that its members hardly know each other.

One of the largest congregations in California is a Baptist church with 3500 members and an auditorium that overflows twice on Sunday morning. Another church in Texas has a 15,000 membership and a $7 1/2 million physical plant.

And while the church becomes preoccupied with buildings and programs, not only a nation—but a world is fast slipping into eternity.

The trend is irreversible.

THE CLOCK NEARS MIDNIGHT

We have approached a point of no return and the only hope for the world is that the individual might turn to Christ and might accept Him as his personal Saviour. It is interesting to note that the Bulletin of the Atomic Scientists has on the cover of their magazine what they term their doomsday clock.

The clock is now set at 11:57.

The Bulletin editor, Dr. Eugene Rabinowitz said: "In sad recognition that the past six years have brought mankind farther down the road to nuclear disaster, the Bulletin clock has moved closer to midnight."

The late Dr. Ralph J. Bunche, U.N. Undersecretary, said in a meeting at the World Affairs Council at the Stratford Hilton Hotel in Los Angeles that: "It is equally inevitable that sooner or later the world finds itself in a nuclear war... Fear of a nuclear war motivates Secretary General U Thant in his efforts not only to save the U.N. but to save the world."

War games studies at a British defense research establishment have led to the conclusion that a concerted Russian advance into western Europe possibly could not be held up for more than two or three days even if all the west's 7,000 battlefield nuclear weapons were used.

Russia is fast advancing towards closing the missile gap between herself and the United States. While this is going on many churches continue merrily in their luxury of erecting mammoth buildings.

THE STERILE CHURCH OFFERS THE WORLD FALSE HOPE

Churches in the United States have over $80 billion invested in real estate, mostly in church and Sunday School buildings, and this property is fully utilized less than 1% of the time. Yet it represents 80% of the total resources of religious bodies in the United States.

If half of this wealth were invested in income producing securities, the return would amount to more than $2 billion a year which could be used for missionary endeavors.

Churches now spend more on construction and upkeep of buildings than they spend on any other activity in which they engage.

Even the mission-minded Southern Baptist in 1968 spent more money on construction than on missions. Their total outlay for construction was $161,691,000, the outlay for missions was $120,455,000.

The book of Revelation speaks about 7 churches which I believe have a prophetic significance in world history.

The church in **Ephesus** existed approximately 95 A.D. and is described in Revelation 2:1-7. This was the backslidden church of which Christ says: "...I have somewhat against thee because thou has **left thy first love**" (Revelation 2:4).

The church in **Smyrna** began around the same time. It continued until 313 A.D. This church is described in Revelation 2:8-11. This was the **persecuted church.** Christ told them "...be thou faithful unto death and I will give thee a crown of life" (Revelation 2:10).

The church in **Pergamos** began about 313 A.D. with the Emperor Constantine's proclamation of toleration toward Christianity. It extended to about 590 A.D. This is recorded in Revelation 2:12-17. It is known as the **state church** wherein the world and the church blended into one confusing whole. Christ admonished them saying "I know thy works..." (Revelation 2:13).

The church in **Thyatira** was in existence in the Dark (Middle) Ages from about 590 to 1500 A.D. and a description is found in Revelation 2:18-29. It is known as the **lax church.** Christ told them "...you are permitting that woman Jezebel, who calls herself a prophet, to teach my servants that sex sin is not a serious matter..." (Revelation 2:20).

The church in **Sardis** existed from 1500 to about 1800 A.D. and is recorded in Revelation 3:16. This is known as the world church of the reformation era or the **dead church.** Christ told them "I know your position as a live and active church, but you are dead" (Revelation 3:1).

The church in **Philadelphia,** which is the 19th century church, continues on up through the 20th century. It is found in Revelation 3:7-13 and means *brotherly love*. It is the church with an **open door** of opportunity. This is the only church of the seven which has the promise of being kept from the Great Tribulation. Christ says to this church: "I know thy works: behold I have set before thee an open door, and no man can shut it...I will also keep thee from the hour of temptation..." (Revelation 3:8,10).

The **Laodicea** church, which is the last church, begins in the 20th century and continues until the Last Days. It is the **lukewarm** church.

At that time, it, being the one-world church, will be cast out of the Lord's mouth (Revelation 3:14-22). Christ's message for them is "I know you well—you are neither hot nor cold; I wish you were one or the other! But since you are merely lukewarm, I will spew you out of My mouth" (Revelation 3:15,16).

As we look at this day and age we find ourselves in what is termed the Laodicean Age.

More and more, people are believing less and less about the Saviour and the necessity for accepting Him as Christ and Lord in their life.

More and more they are relying on personal gain and material wealth to give them a "heaven on earth."

And while many would have us believe that the world is getting better and better...when one looks at the facts they show a tragic picture. One sees the evidences of wickedness and moral decay from seeds that have been sown in corruption. In light of this, one can only accept the fact that we are on an irreversible course to self-destruction. This course is headed by church leaders who have in their power the opportunity to offer the world every hope of salvation, and, instead they return to the world these same seeds of corruption through its priests and prophets who have fallen away from the faith which was once delivered to the saints.

In this day and age it is becoming increasingly difficult for the non-church and churched individual to believe in God.

Worshiper dances in the aisle with Chaplain at a communion service in the Perkins Chapel at Southern Methodist University in Dallas, Texas.

YOUR GUIDE TO SURVIVAL

If we are to survive as individuals we must first believe that God **is** and believe that He rewards those that diligently seek Him by His gift of eternal life. "...without faith it is impossible to please Him (God), for he that cometh to God must believe that He is (exists), and that He is a rewarder of them that diligently seek Him" (Hebrews 11:6).

Noah has returned to the United States and to the world!

That Noah represents the millions of Christians (those believing in Christ) throughout the world who have accepted Christ as their personal Saviour and are looking forward to His coming. They are building their ark plank by plank and, with the small voice that they have, calling in those who would enter into the ark of safety.

But they find few takers, for the world is relaxing in its wealth, in its supposed self-sufficiency. The world is listening to its leaders tell them that heaven is here on earth and that we are getting better and better.

And so the small still voice of the believers is falling on deaf ears...and while there is still plenty of room in the ark, a rather empty ark will someday soon leave this world because there are many millions who will not believe.

In the cellar in Cologne in Germany after World War II, these words were found written on the wall:

I BELIEVE...

I believe in the sun,
>   even when it is not shining;

I believe in love,
>   even when I feel it not;

I believe in God,
>   even when He is silent.

While the words of God may be silent to many in the world, His message is ever present; his warnings are found on every page of the Bible.

In the hurry of today's living, why not take a few minutes to read about them?

Those few minutes may save your life.

2

Destiny Death

In the past chapter we discussed some of the factors that indicate we are living in the Last Days.

These include a growing self-confidence that the world is getting better and better, increasing use of alcohol, a crime wave that keeps growing, more and more discontent through strikes, the rise of pornography (and its acceptability in the eyes of the Supreme Court), the continuing desire of major church denominations to unite into a one World Church, coupled with the rise of super churches where emphasis is put on building and structure at the expense of missionary evangelism. These, combined with a continued cold and hot war atmosphere and increased arsenals of destruction, are rapidly bringing the world to the brink of disaster.

The above are some of the important signs of the Last

Days, but there are a few others that are even of greater importance and are creating areas of self-destruction which place us on an irreversible trend towards the End Times.

A few years ago you did not read too much about these particular events in the newspapers. But scientists are continually warning us about the tragic consequences that the world will reap because it has failed to correct these measures that will lead to self-destruction.

Two of these major catastrophes are (1) air pollution and (2) the continuing rise of world population.

AIR POLLUTION

More and more, some of the country's top weather experts are of the belief that dirty air may be triggering the unusual weather conditions that we have been experiencing in the last few years.

Each year, Americans spew more smoke, dust, heat, steam and chemicals into the atmosphere. At the same time, the weather seems to be getting worse.

This has been evident by the extremes of weather which become greater and more frequent. Droughts appear longer, thunderstorms more violent, cloudbursts heavier, and snowfalls deeper. Fog has become a common thing and most important, airline pilots complain of murky haze over the once-clear airports.

This problem of fog and haze will become more critical as the country turns to nuclear power for electricity, for nuclear plants release great quantities of moisture into the air creating just-right conditions for man-made fog.

Recent weather bureau statistics show that in La Porte, Indiana, over the last 30 years, there has been a 31% increase in rain now falling each year on this area. They also have received more destructive storms with lightning and hail in the last few years.

La Porte is 35 miles east—and downwind—of the giant steel mills at Gary, Indiana.

The thousands of jet planes that fly over the U.S. each day are also modifying weather conditions.

Through the large water vapor trails that they leave, a series of chain reactions take place, which some weather

New York City as seen on a rare clear day.

The same scene covered by a blanket of polluted air.

experts believe, have caused the Northeast droughts. It is also believed that this is partly responsible for the world-wide cooling trend.

COOLING TREND

This cooling trend started about 10 to 20 years ago and reversed a warming trend that had been taking place for about 50 years.

Some scientists say that a few degrees of cooling will bring on a new ice age with rapid and drastic effects on the agricultural productivity of the temperate regions. On the other hand, if we have a few degrees of heating, the polar ice caps would melt and perhaps raise the ocean levels 250 feet.

By polluting the earth on which we live, we tamper with the energy balance of the earth. This results in an "environmental roulette."

The National Center for Air Pollution Control recently estimated that in 1965 there were 129 million tons of air pollutants rising into the air and that by the year 2000 this will increase to 404 million tons of air pollutants annually rising into the air.

The yearly pollution by the year 2000 will be made up by the following: 76 million tons of sulphur dioxide, 217 million tons of carbon monoxide, 53 million tons of hydrocarbons, 30 million tons of nitrogen oxides and 28 million tons of particles such as dust, coal smoke and soot.

While problems of air pollution have been with us a long time, recent years have shown a great acceleration in the volume of air pollutants to the point where we are reaching the critical stage.

THE TOLL OF AIR POLLUTION

As early as 61 A.D., Seneca complained of the heavy air of Rome and pestilent vapors from the smoky chimneys.

It is odd that we once thought of smoke as an indication of economic prosperity. But today, scientists recognize it as harmful to human lives.

You will recall that at Donora, Pennsylvania, a town of 12,500 not too far from Pittsburgh, 20 people lost their lives and close to 6,000 people sought medical help during a five-day "smog" in 1948. London and New York have also had these killer fogs and in 1952, 12,000 deaths in London were attributed directly or indirectly to this killer fog.

What are pollutants and what is air pollution?

Pollutants—and this includes smoke—are the residues of things we use and then throw away. The unfortunate thing is that as the earth becomes crowded, there is no longer any place to throw anything away and therefore, the trash basket of the world becomes the air above them.

To an ordinary citizen, air pollution may not be recognizable as an immediate threat. However, scientists consider the air pollution threat as already "overwhelming."

It is estimated that the annual loss in the United States from air pollution is $15 billion. The average family of 4 in New York City spends $800 a year to undo the damage of air pollution and to clean up the dirt that settles.

In a few years, one may find it difficult to sing the song "America the Beautiful" with any real meaning.

While quite a bit of America is still visible as a beautiful country, it is becoming increasingly dirty with polluted air, filthy streets and clogged and polluted rivers.

It seems odd that in a day of tremendous progress (someone recently said that 50% of the world's inventions have been created in the last decade) that the by-product of this progress can be a slow, agonizing death through the pollutants emitted into the air.

One thing that we may not realize is that nature has an efficient way of getting rid of its wastes through the process of decay and then reclamation.

The wastes of man's products, however, produce huge quantities of synthetic materials which almost totally resist natural decay. And more and more, such wastes are poisonous to man's fellow creatures, to say nothing of himself.

Air Pollution Can Be Fatal
Medical Researchers Show

TRIGGERING DISASTER

Time magazine in a recent essay on pollutants said the following:

"Man has tended to ignore the fact that he is utterly dependent on the biosphere: a vast web of interacting processes and organisms that form the rhythmic cycles and food chains in which one part of the living environment feeds on another. The biosphere is no immutable feature of the earth... years ago, terrestrial life consisted of some primitive organisms that consumed oxygen as fast as green plants manufactured it. Only by some primeval accident were the greedy organisms buried in sedimentary rock (as the source of crude oil, for example), thus permitting the atmosphere to become enriched to a life-sustaining mix of 20% oxygen, plus nitrogen, argon, carbon dioxide and water vapor. With miraculous precision, the mix was then maintained by plants, animals and bacteria, which used and returned the gases at equal rates. About 70% of the earth's oxygen is thus produced by ocean phytoplankton: passively floating plants. All this modulated temperatures, curbed floods and nurtured man thousands of years ago.

To primitive man, nature was so harsh and powerful that he deeply respected and even worshiped it. He did the environment very little damage. But technological man, master of the atom and soon the moon, is so aware of his strength that he is unaware of his weakness—the fact that his pressure on nature may provoke revenge. Although sensational cries of impending doom have overstated the case, modern man has reached the stage where he must recognize that real dangers exist. Indeed, many scholars of the biosphere are now seriously concerned that human pollution may trigger some ecological disaster."

Coincidentally, as man has devised pesticides which have sharply improved farm crops—these same pesticides have also caused spectacular kills of fish and wildlife—thus upsetting the balance of nature which was created by God.

Let's look at a typical example. In the Canadian province of New Brunswick the application of only one-half pound of DDT (Dichloro-Diphenol-Trichlorethane!) per acre of forest was used to control the spruce budworm. This control procedure, however, has twice wiped out an entire year's production of young salmon in that locality. And this triggers further destruction as follows: In this process the rain washes the DDT off the ground and into the plankton of lakes and streams. The fish eat this DDT-tainted plankton.

This pesticide becomes concentrated in their bodies. The original dose ultimately reaches multifold strength in fish-eating birds, which then often die or stop reproducing.

DDT is almost certainly to blame for the alarming decrease in New England's falcons, hawks and herons.

While these on the surface may not seem too important, every step along the way is another irreversible step in upsetting the balance of nature created by God.

THERE IS A LIMIT

Some falsely believe that the sky is unlimited. They believe because of the vast amount of space up there that pollution will never have an irreversible trend or represent a danger to the world.

This is far from the truth, however.

The earth is basically a closed system. The waste-disposal process that we have produced clearly has limits. It is important to realize that the winds that ventilate the earth are only 6 miles high. Above this level the air rapidly thins out to almost nothingness by the 15 mile level.

More and more we are rapidly filling every inch of air space in the limited six mile umbrella that covers the world.

Deaths caused by air pollutants have already demonstrated their capacity to disaster, but even greater disasters will be forthcoming in the future.

It has been said that in the sense of pollution—Man is the dirtiest animal and he cannot continue to casually clog the rivers with sewage and the sky with air pollutants.

But man is on an irreversible course and in the expediency of progress—there has yet been no real answer to solving the ever increasing problem of air pollution.

This problem is coupled with the disasters that come with over population which we will discuss in another part of this chapter.

IMMORTAL DUMPING GROUND

In the days before scientific technology, we used to use tin cans which would rust away. Now we have become scientifically advanced and use the immortal aluminum which some scientists say may outlast the Pyramids.

Each year, the United States produces 48 billion cans, plus 28 billion long-lived bottles and jars. The average American would be surprised to know that his average output of solid waste in these items approximates about 1,800 lbs. and is rising by more than 4% a year.

Each day New York City dumps 200 million gallons of raw sewage into the Hudson River. Each square mile of Manhattan produces 375,000 lbs. of wastes a day. And over 70% of Americans live on only 10% of the country's total land area.

The air we breathe circles the earth 40 times a year, and America contributed 140 million tons of pollutants: 90 million tons from cars—we burn more gasoline than the rest of the world **combined!**

Tetraethyl lead in auto exhausts can have a drastic effect on human reactions. Scientists tell us that this lead is found in auto exhausts and affects human nerves, increases irritability and decreases normal brain function. Like any metal poison, lead is fatal if enough is ingested.

In this age of progress—during the rise of the automobile— the average American's lead content has risen an estimated 125-fold, to near maximum tolerance levels. It is surprising to learn that Arctic glaciers now contain this wind-wafted lead.

It is estimated that by the year 2000 about 90% of Americans will live in urban areas and drive perhaps twice as many cars as they do now. You can imagine what this will do to produce a higher concentrate of the deadly Tetraethyl lead.

There are some indications to show that overexposure of lead was even a factor in the decline and fall of the Roman Empire. We are now faced with the same type of exposure.

Oxygen which is vitally needed for the human to exist, is rapidly being depleted because of the pollutants and mounting sewage.

It has been estimated that by 1980, these pollutants may well dangerously deplete the oxygen in all 22 U.S. river basins.

This has already happened in Lake Erie where a once magnificently produced inland sea was turned into a sink of pollutants. It has been estimated that two-thirds of the U.S. sewage systems are now below health standards.

In 1940, there were a little over 1 million cars in the United States. Today there are over 100 million cars—not only

Tokyo's special pollution patrol uses a measuring device to check exhaust gas from car during periodic testing. Tokyo's pollution problem is reaching crisis proportions.

more powerful—but more deadly in their emission of Tetraethyl lead.

On a January day in 1957, Richmond, Virginia, was hit by an unusual plague. Girls walking down the street suddenly discovered that the nylons on their legs literally dissolved and disappeared.

No one knew what caused the mystery of the missing nylons until it was referred to a city chemist, who analyzed the stocking remnants. Some detective work turned up the fact that the girls had been on the same street corner at about 8:30 that morning. There was a high humidity and virtually no wind. But a large amount of sulphur was in the air from air pollutants.

This unhappy combination made the nylons pop into nothingness.

In further checking, they discovered that this was not a startling discovery, for 300 women in Jacksonville, Florida had an identical experience.

MAJOR CAUSE OF ILLNESS

Some feel that the pollutants are the major cause of respiratory diseases. And the number of people dying from respiratory diseases is doubling every five years.

The chance of a man between the ages of 50 and 70 dying of respiratory disease are doubled if he lives in a polluted area.

Emphysema—a disease of the lungs—has achieved a grim position of eminence as a killer with almost no recognition. In 1935 there were only 135 emphysema deaths reported in the United States. By 1962 that number had grown to 12,350. Since then it has grown distressingly upward.

There are more emphysema patients in the country today than the combined total of lung cancer and tuberculosis victims—more than one million!

Only heart disease disables more men than emphysema.

And the cause of emphysema has as its major contributant —air pollution.

Perhaps the chemistry of air pollution may be difficult for you to understand. However, the arithmetic is very simple. And it is a numbers game that America and the world is losing.

Thousands of fish cover a beach near downtown Chicago . . . victims of polluted waterways.

New York's Calvary cemetery losing ground in a race for inner space. As the population explosion threatens the future of the living, so does it also pose a dire and growing problem for the dead.

THE POPULATION EXPLOSION
AND
OUR RACE TO OBLIVION

While you are reading these words, four people have died of starvation. And the sad fact is that most of them will be children. Every day over 10,000 people throughout the world die from starvation.

It is no wonder that former Secretary of Agriculture, Orville Freeman predicted that: "The world will literally run out of food by the mid-1980's."

Why not take a moment right now to open your Bible and read Matthew, chapter 24. You will recall that the disciples came to Christ asking Him what would be the signs of His Coming.

He replied that we would hear of wars and rumors of wars, but this would not signal the End "...for all these things must come to pass, but the end is not yet." (verse 6).

Then in verse 7, He notes "...there shall be famines."

And verse 8 states "...these are the beginning of sorrows."

The time bomb of population explosion is coupled with air pollution. When one studies the statistics, it is with a bit of irony to note that man, placed on this earth, and then rebelling against God, sought a more modern technological age...and in so doing—is causing his own destruction.

HUGE SURPLUS A MYTH

Many Americans are under the false assumption that we have a huge surplus. But, however, as bread prices started to climb in 1974 partially because of a shortage of wheat (Remember our sale of surplus U.S. wheat to Russia?) the buyers were beginning to wake up.

It's been at least 10 years that the world has not seen food surpluses because since that time the population increase has exceeded the per capita food supply. And stockpiled food surpluses are gone.

Recently an advisor in India's government said: "The world is on the threshold of the biggest famine in history...affecting hundreds of millions, or possibly billions, of persons."

What is this population bomb and what will be the consequences?

Population biology experts state that every year underdeveloped countries fall a bit further behind their population growth in providing proper food production.

The results: mass starvation.

Right now about 3 1/2 million people starve to death each year—mostly children. But this number will be a mere handful compared to the numbers that will starve to death in 10 to 20 years from now.

Tragically, no action we take now is going to reverse this trend.

FRIGHTENING ARITHMETIC

Dr. Paul R. Ehrlich, in his book THE POPULATION BOMB has revealed some startling figures on the population explosion.

Previous to 1650 A.D. it is further estimated that about once every thousand years the population doubled.

Estimates have placed the human population of 1650 A.D. at 500 million.

In 1850 the population was 1 billion people. This doubling took 200 years.

But it only took 80 years for the next doubling as the population reached 2 billion around 1930.

Now look at this: We have not completed the next doubling to 4 billion yet, but we now have well over 3 billion people. It appears that the doubling time at the present rate seems to be about every 35 years. This is quite a reduction in doubling times: 1,000 years, 200 years, 80 years, and now the doubling rate is every 35 years!

To more graphically present this to you, let's examine what might happen on the assumption that the population continues to double every 35 years into indefinite future.

If this growth continues at that rate for about 900 years, there will be some 60,000,000,000,000,000 people on the face of the earth. This is sixty million billion people.

And this represents about 100 persons for *each square yard* of the earth's surface *including* the land and the sea.

J.H. Fremlin, a British physicist, guessed that such a large number of people might be housed in a continuous 2,000-story building covering our entire planet.

Here is how he envisions it.

The upper 1,000 stories would contain simply the apparatus for running this gigantic unit. And half of the bottom 1,000 stories would be occupied by pipes, wires, and elevator shafts. This would leave 3 or 4 yards of floor space for each person.

Can you imagine this unusual apartment living. An individual perhaps, could take elevators through all 1,000 resident stories but could travel only within a circle of a few hundred yards' radius on any floor. This would permit him, however, to choose his friends from among 10 million people.

But this would create another problem which is called "heat limit." As you realize, people themselves, as well as their activities, convert other forms of energy into heat which must be dissipated. This would create tremendous problems.

In fact it would take only 50 years to populate Venus, Mercury and Mars and the Moon to the same population density as the Earth.

Scientists tell us that the next 10 years will reveal some drastic problems in population. While the average doubling time of population in the United States is about 35 years one must keep in mind that doubling rates in other countries are far shorter.

As an example in Kenya the doubling rate is every 24 years. In Brazil it is every 22 years, in Costa Rica it is 20 years and in the Philippines it is every 20 years.

Just to keep living standards at the present *inadequate* level the food available for the people must be *doubled right now.* Every road must be duplicated. The amount of power must be doubled. The number of trained doctors and administrators must be doubled. And this is impossible—particularly when many of these countries have none of these facilities now to any great extent.

Some of the side effects of the rapid doubling rate of our population is not just the garbage that we throw into our

Hunger at its worst! A young Biafran woman seems very happy as she prepares a dead rat for cooking — and eventual eating. In the grim fight against starvation Biafrans were instructed on how to catch rats and snakes as well as insects for eating.

environment, but overcrowded highways, growing slums, deteriorating school systems, rising crime rates, and general unrest including riots.

We have already witnessed this in the United States and it is growing in intensity.

D-DAY

Some population biology scientists estimate that the population bomb will explode around the year 2000 (How coincidental this is to our remarks on page 137).

Their reasoning is that 40% of the population of the underdeveloped world right now is made up of people under 15 years of age. And as these young people move into their reproductive years, you will see the greatest baby boom of all time which will generate the gunpowder for the greatest population explosion of all times.

Developments of medical science have been the straw that broke the camel's back. For through the marvelous techniques of prolonging life and also reducing death at birth we are contributing to the complex factor of an exploding population.

The battle to feed humanity is already lost and in the next decade we will see large-scale famines.

But deaths from starvation generally go unnoticed even when they occur in our own country...simply because starvation is undramatic.

In 1966 as an example, the population of the world increased by some 70 million people but there was no compensatory increase in food production. Actually in 1966, each person on earth had 2% less to eat.

In 13 years India is going to add 200 million more people to its population and yet they can't adequately feed the population that now exists.

WATER, WATER, EVERYWHERE?

India is already investing about 50 million a year to try and control the rapid rise in population.

It is not meeting with great success. India's current population is estimated at 600 million and statistics on its growth are shocking.

An Indian is born every one and a half seconds. Twenty-one million will be born this year but less than nine million will die. At the present rate of growth, the population will be one billion by 1994.

What about our own farmland?

In Iowa, which is commonly considered as good a land as we have, the farmland is declining by 1% per year. Even in irrigated lands of the west coast we face a constant danger of salination from the rising water tables.

In some areas we find that salt water is seeping into the aquifers (water bearing rock strata).

In 1987, it is estimated that the United States will need 600 billion gallons of water a day or *two-thirds more* than it is presently using today. No one knows where this water can possibly come from.

With the misuse of our watersheds and the current population growth, it is quite possible that by 1987 the United States will quite literally be dying of thirst.

This is the picture of affluent America. At the moment, the United States uses well over half of the raw materials consumed each year.

Look at this. The United States, which is less than 1/12th of the population of the world requires more than all the rest of the world to maintain its prime position.

It has been stated that if present trends continue that in 20 years we will be much less than 1/12th of the world's population and yet we may use some 80% of the resources consumed.

Each American baby will consume in a 70-year life span directly or indirectly:

> 26 million gallons of water
> 21 thousand gallons of gasoline
> 10 thousand pounds of meat
> 28 thousand pounds of milk and cream
> $5,000 to $8,000 in school building materials
> $6,300 worth of clothing
> $7,000 worth of furniture

Feeble attempts are being made to correct the problem, but the problem has reached such magnitude that these attempts are like trying to move an ocean across a desert taking one thimbleful at a time.

The recent affirmation of the Pope, against mechanical means of birth control is one of the evidences of what is an insurmountable problem—that of over population.

Even attempts at controlling the population in India have proved insignificant.

Let's look at California. California's population is over 20 million people. This is larger than all Canada and 1.5 million ahead of New York.

And almost half of the state's 20 million people live in five counties surrounding Los Angeles.

Anyone going to Los Angeles can almost daily see the curtain of death which hangs over the city each day causing smarting eyes and leaving in its wake, a population suffering from myriad types of respiratory illnesses. But in spite of all of these inconveniences and in spite of the multiple complex of interconnecting highways built in this area, the population in the Los Angeles area continues to grow very rapidly instead of declining.

This is one indication that people will not recognize the disasters that come from air pollution and from the population explosion. These disasters have reached an irreversible trend that can only contribute to a final world disaster.

A GOOD EXAMPLE OF BAD PLANNING
Los Angeles International Airport (pictured above) handles an average of 36,000 passenger cars daily, which produces 26 tons of carbon monoxide and over 2 tons of nitrogen oxide just from traveling the traffic loop shown. Within 4 miles is located the Hollywood Park racetrack, which during a 75-day season, attracts almost 900,000 passenger cars for a daily average of 12,000.

CEMETERIES, WATCH OUT!

Philadelphia, finding itself running out of land, has already made plans to look at urban cemeteries—long considered too sacred to touch—as prime sites for new construction projects.

City planners in Philadelphia say using cemeteries would help ease the squeeze that is coming from rapid population growth.

For 2 acres of cemetery land, the city of Philadelphia paid $50,000 which they consider a cheap price for the end result.

Before they used this 2 acres, they had to move over 11,500 graves to a suburban site.

Look at America today. It is the most technologically advanced country in the world, from the standpoint of industrial, social and medical technology.

It has the highest rate of employment, the highest per capita income, the greatest sources of material wealth. But in the last 10 years, while its scientific technology has rapidly increased, its spiritual values have rapidly declined.

From its leadership in public places—to its clergy in United World type churches, it is relying more and more on the social gospel and fast becoming a nation that is forgetting God.

Can it be that America is reaping a harvest of destruction brought about by sowing seeds of corruption?

It would appear to this author that the dual problem of air pollution and population explosion have reached an irreversible point.

And the heritage that they will rapidly leave to the world is fast bringing us to Destiny Death.

3
Civilized Cruelty

Starvation • Rampant Disease • Walls • Weapons of Destruction • Napalm • The Arms Race and Power • Growing Gun Menace • America...Land of Broken Homes

Recently one of the candidates for President of the United States said that in the past years the country has been deluged by government programs for the unemployed, programs for the city, programs for the poor, and that these programs reaped an ugly harvest of frustration, violence and failure across the land.

He promised his listeners that "The long night is about to end."

Realistically, when one examines the areas of disaster affecting not only the United States but the entire world—one can only say "The long night is not about to end—It is just beginning."

It seems difficult to believe that in an era when we have greater and greater involvement in social programming and social concern for our fellow human beings—that we have also developed more refined means to inflict civilized cruelty on our fellow man.

Civilized cruelty raises its ugly head several ways.

STARVATION

Tragic events in the little country of Biafra, in its 32-month war with Nigeria...showed that in spite of all the efforts of well-meaning people, they were unable to stop the tragic deaths of thousands of people.

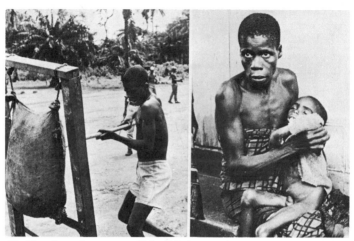

Civilized cruelty a way of life. While a Biafran recruit goes through bayonet practice using a stick in place of a weapon until supplies of weapons come through . . . a woman at an Owerri Refugee Camp holds her starved child awaiting food that never arrived.

West Berlin children play "ring-around-the-rosey" in the shadow of the hated wall that cuts Berlin in two. The wall of sin separates man from God. Christ said, ". . . except ye be converted (born again) and become as little children, ye shall not enter the kingdom of heaven" (Matthew 18:3). How hard it is for adults to have the same trusting faith as little children. How easy we allow walls of distrust and doubt to creep in under the guise of "intelligent thinking."

The civil war in Nigeria was killing an estimated 120,000 people a month—by starvation.

Henry Labouisse, Executive Director of the United Nations Children's Fund, reported after making a visit to Southeast Nigeria:

> "I witnessed the frightful suffering of the many thousands of refugees who have poured into that area. Many are dying from starvation, particularly children, on both sides of the fighting. A great many others are on the verge of starvation."

The International Red Cross had stocked 3,500 tons of food nearby, but in mid-August of 1968 they still had not been able to get it through to the estimated 7 million encircled Biafrans.

Other relief organizations also had little success in breaking this effective blockade.

While this is a dramatic episode of death by starvation, the fact is that 10,000 people starve to death every day under less dramatic situations and very few people are concerned.

For the inequities of life, right or wrong as they may be, are ever present.

While 10,000 people are starving to death every day in other parts of the world, Americans are treating the 4-legged household pets as part of the family. Fifty-five million dogs and cats eat 3 million **tons** of food every year in the United States!

Table scraps are not good enough. This means that the nations' 3,000 dog—and cat—food makers and marketers realized 1976 sales of over 2½ billion, up more than $500 million since 1975.

This far exceeds the expenditures people spent last year on baby food ($500 million) and breakfast cereals ($914 million)!

And pet-food makers spent over $110 million last year to advertise this fact. Pet food, which is reported to be the fastest-growing product on grocery shelves today, is **four times as big** as the baby-food business!

It is estimated that the U.S. has 35 million dogs, 25 million cats and 33 million pet-owning families.

It has been stated that with all the concern over care and feeding, today's cats, and dogs have a better balanced diet than most humans. Yet America still must pay farmers not to farm, while humans today starve.

How reminiscent today is of 2 Timothy 3:2 & 4 which reads:

For men will be lovers of self, lovers of money, boastful, arrogant, revilers, disobedient to parents, ungrateful, unholy, (verse 2)

Treacherous, reckless, conceited, lovers of pleasure rather than lovers of God. (verse 4)

RAMPANT DISEASE

While modern medical technology has controlled much of America's diseases, one must realize that other countries are still enslaved by disease and harassed by malnutrition and starvation.

Oftentimes, in reading of the triumphs of modern medicine such as heart transplants, brain surgery and cancer chemotherapy, it is hard for one to realize that these are almost irrelevant to the health needs of more than 200 million Africans as an example.

The health problems of Africa constitutes a grim picture indeed.

Half the population of Africa is under 15 years of age. And half of all children die before the age of five.

Life expectancy varies enormously by geographic location and, in some places, according to sex.

Malaria is the continent's overwhelming problem. One-third to one-quarter of the adult population suffers from active malarial attacks.

The death rate from malaria in Ghana approaches 12%.

And while these type of health problems do not concern America—doctors in America are as equally concerned about the run-away epidemic rate of syphilis and gonorrhea. While these are not greatly publicized, the more virulent streams of these diseases are becoming increasingly more difficult to arrest. And because of this, their effect on tomorrow's children will directly affect the health and course of this nation.

WALLS

Civilized cruelty not only finds itself prevalent in the areas of starvation and disease but also in barriers people place between themselves.

The Berlin Wall, erected in 1961, is now a bigger barrier than ever. It keeps getting higher and tougher to cross and harder to overlook.

In the last few years, the East German authorities have pushed work along 100 miles of frontier with West Berlin, replacing the old wall with a new and higher version.

The flow of refugees has been cut to a trickle.

Most of the 2.2 million West Berliners try to stay away from the wall believing that "out of sight, out of mind."

Every day 16,000 guards atop 629 observation towers keep this Berlin Wall secure. The Berlin Wall is just a stone barricade, highly sophisticated with a series of obstacles, mine fields and flood-lit no-man's zones.

It was made possible, however, partially because of the wall of indifference of people throughout the world.

It has always been the policy of communists to use this indifference to their advantage. And it paid off handsomely for them.

There are no pat solutions to the problems of individual, national and world-wide indifference that produce a civilized type of cruelty on fellow man.

Perhaps because there is no pat answer, this is more indicative of the Last Days and of the type of impossible world in which we now live.

We find ourselves in a world that on one hand decries cruelty, yet on the other hand creates elements of force with capabilities of destruction that defy description. And while we expend billions of dollars to create these elements of destruction, it is difficult to secure a few million dollars to alleviate human suffering.

WEAPONS OF DESTRUCTION

A few years ago, the Atomic Energy Commission carried out its biggest underground test yet of a nuclear device. The device was exploded 3,800 feet beneath the desert

Two sheepherders start the mammoth task of disposing of some 6000 dead sheep accidentally killed by a whiff of nerve gas developed by the U.S. Army.

surface and was equal to 1 million tons of TNT or 50 to 60 times the force of the bomb dropped on Hiroshima. This device was developed principally because of the missiles believed being readied by Communist China.

Though the device was exploded 3,800 feet beneath the desert surface, its shock wave was felt for hundreds of miles. The explosion generated temperatures in the millions of degrees and liquefied the volcanic rock—creating a vast cavern underneath the floor of the desert.

NERVE GAS TRAGEDY

While in another part of the West a "miracle killer" got unwanted publicity in the late 1960's.

There were 6,000 dead in Utah. It could have been people. Fortunately, however, it was SHEEP. It was like any other day in Skull Valley, Utah. Over 6,000 sheep were grazing... when suddenly strange things happened. Alvin W. Hatch, General Manager of the vast Anschutes sheep ranch, noticed the sheep stagger in the snow, then flail their legs in agony and then die.

First a few...then a few hundred...and within three days the sheep were "dropping like flies." The final count listed over 6,400 sheep dead! For a while, no one knew what caused these massive sudden deaths.

Intensive investigation by agricultural agents and Army experts brought forth these facts:

On March 13 a jet plane flown by an Air Force pilot released 320 gallons of "nerve gas" it had developed.

This gas was released over the Dugway Proving Ground.

The wind, up at the altitude of 2,290 feet, varied from 5 to 25 m.p.h. and was generally to the north. The sheep were grazing on the other side of a mountain range, 20 to 30 miles to the east.

Marker cards showed that at least 95% of the sprays had fallen within the target area, which was a mile wide and four miles long.

However, portions of the remaining 5% must have been somehow spiraled upward to an altitude where the winds may have been different and they remained in the atmosphere until 2 hours later when there was a shift in the surface winds, apparently toward the east.

These winds settled down over the 6,400 sheep and brought with them the 5% balance of the nerve gas which attacked the central nervous system of the sheep and killed them.

What we read in science-fiction is now becoming a reality. Man has developed ingenious ways of mass destruction which in the hands of irresponsible people can lead to world chaos.

> But realize this, that in the last days difficult times will come (2 Timothy 3:1).

This untimely accident also brought to light the fact that America has developed a deadly nerve gas that can cause massive human disaster using extremely minute quantities of a chemical.

Death can occur within a few minutes if the agent is inhaled, or within an hour if only a drop or two gets on the skin.

This deadly nerve gas causes the pupils of the eyes to close, extremely labored breathing—because the nerves controlling the muscles of the heart and lungs have gone wild—and fatal spasms and convulsions.

This particularly catastrophic weapon of destruction—created by U.S. scientists—came to life only because of an accident. No one knows how many more deadly elements of destruction have been created not only in the United States but in other parts of the world that can bring instant death to multiplied millions within a short span of time.

Recent revelations of a secret death-dealing Laser ray, developed by both Russia and the United States are frightening!

In a CBS news broadcast the commentator stated that the United States was the only major country that refused to sign the Geneva Protocol of 1925 which outlaws development of chemical and biological weapons. While one would have to study the circumstances surrounding the United States decision before reaching a judgment, the decision itself reflects the world situation. In fact, recently, the U.S. has ordered more than 1½ million nerve gas protective suits for its Armed Forces.

They didn't have refrigerators and television sets in Robin Hood's day when the primary weapon of destruction was a bow and arrow. But then they could do without those luxuries, if having these luxuries, also brings with them such deadly elements as nerve gas, germ warfare, hydrogen bombs and napalm.

It is not the purpose of this chapter to discuss the right or wrong of war but simply to point out to the reader that in this modern day and age we have come up with highly civilized forms of mass cruelty that must make one wonder in what direction this world is headed.

NAPALM

Napalm is an incendiary substance made by the gelation of gasoline. It was invented by L. F. Fieser in 1942. Oddly enough, the preparation of napalm is a simple procedure, utilizing inexpensive and abundantly available materials. No special techniques are needed for the mixing or the creation of this tragic invention.

It is an extremely tough and stable substance, capable of withstanding the blast of an explosive charge without shattering. It will not thin out at 150° F (such as in the tropics) nor will it become brittle at —40° F (the temperature reached in a bomb bay). It can be stored indefinitely and will not deteriorate during transport. The temperature of a napalm flame can approach 2060° C.

It is hard for anyone to fathom how hot this is. It can also be projected with speed and accuracy to a small target over 150 yards away.

Just 165 gallons of napalm dropped from a low flying airplane can spread this deadly fluid over approximately 2,500 square yards.

Napalm burns are likely to be deep and extensive. The adhesiveness, prolonged burning time and high burning temperature of napalm favor third-degree burns in all affected areas. This brings coagulation of muscle, fat and other deep tissues. Burns of this depth usually result in severe scar contractures and deformities and make skin grafting very difficult.

Many people fail to realize that saturation of Japanese cities with napalm during the last months of World War II caused many more deaths than the atomic attacks themselves.

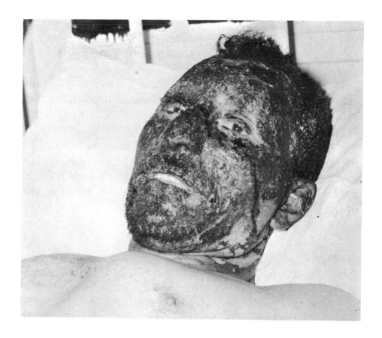

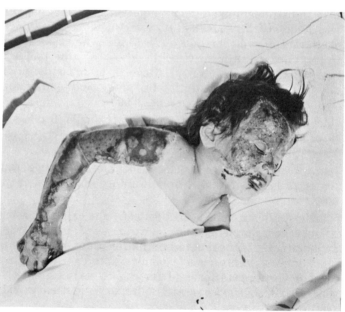

Here are two recipients of the "benefits" of man's scientific achievements. Permanently scarred by napalm, these are Arab victims of Arab-Israeli war. "... peace, peace; when there is no peace" (Jeremiah 6:14).

Rescue workers entering an area after a napalm raid often suffer from heat stroke because of rise of temperatures to intolerable levels. Victims also succumb to heart collapse and the attending carbon monoxide poisoning becomes a major cause of death in large incendiary raids.

Napalm has the capabilities to cause such mass destruction on the human being that, even if he survives, it will scar him for the balance of his life both mentally and physically.

War knows no moral code, for every major country engaged in war right now uses napalm extensively. This includes the United States. If civilians could witness the horrible burns that napalm inflicts on men, women and children... if they could visit these victims in the hospitals and witness the tragic deaths on the field...perhaps there would be enough righteous indignation rising from the populace to stamp out this, which is just one of many, forms of civilized cruelty.

THE ARMS RACE

Doesn't it seem that the logical step would be to cut down on our weapons of destruction?

This, of course, is impossible, for world conditions demand that the United States be militarily prepared. And since the Soviet Union also feels the same way we are helplessly blocked in an arms race that grows in intensity.

In May, 1972 former President Nixon met with Russian leaders in Moscow...signing several treaties...in his "journey for peace." He met with them again in 1974, just before his resignation. History, however, shows that in 25 summit agreements, Russia broke all but 1 treaty!

Russian arms aid to North Vietnam has daily taken a toll of American dead. The latest Communist squeeze on West Berlin and its march into Czechoslovakia show that there are no signs of this being relaxed. And both the Soviets and allied powers are continuing to meddle in the affairs of the Middle East. In future chapters we will see that this is following God's plan for the world.

While Russia has gone ahead in antimissile defenses and fractional orbital bombardment systems and has bigger and more powerful nuclear warheads—the United States still maintains the lead in submarine-borne missiles and long

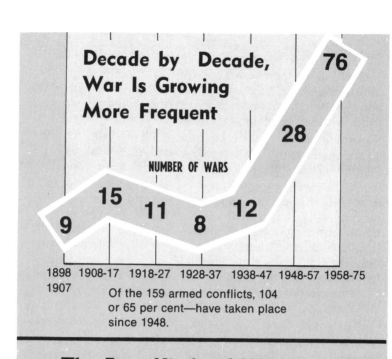

Decade by Decade, War Is Growing More Frequent

NUMBER OF WARS

76

28

15

11

9

8

12

| 1898 1907 | 1908-17 | 1918-27 | 1928-37 | 1938-47 | 1948-57 | 1958-75 |

Of the 159 armed conflicts, 104 or 65 per cent—have taken place since 1948.

The Four Kinds of Wars

Of 159 conflicts since 1898 —

60 have been be-
tween nations

63 have been
insurgencies

31 have been
civil wars

14 have been
coups d'etat
or mutinies

range intercontinental bombers. However, Russia is on the verge of gaining clear superiority over the United States in the field of nuclear arms. The Soviet Union is lengthening its lead in intercontinental ballistic missiles!

And so the arms race goes on. The Soviets have developed a space weapon called FOBS—for Fractional Orbital Bombardment System—which can attack the U.S. with a very short warning.

ARSENAL OF DESTRUCTION

THE ATOM FOR WAR

Five nations of the world together have amassed more than 50,000 atomic devices—the U.S., Soviet Russia, Britain, France and Communist China.

Two of the five are superpowers:
U.S. has stockpiled more than 30,000 atomic devices with a total power of 25,000 megatons. It takes 50 Hiroshima-type atomic bombs to equal 1 megaton, the equivalent of 1 million tons of TNT.

Russia has more than 15,000 atomic devices, with a total power of 12,000 megatons.

And these figures get higher every day.

Among today's nuclear arms—

A-bombs and H-bombs for long and short-range bombers.

Nuclear warheads for missiles based on land and at sea.

Warheads for antiaircraft defenses, for antimissile missiles.

And on the battlefield—atomic shells for artillery, for demolition charges, for mobile launchers, for tactical missiles and free-flight rockets.

IN THE YEARS AHEAD—

Danger of more and more nuclear weapons. Seven countries could—if they so desired—produce A-bombs within 8 months to 2 years—India, Japan, Canada, Switzerland, West Germany, Sweden and Israel.

On top of that: Use of atomic energy is expanding so rapidly that by 1980, civilian reactors in 40 countries will turn out as a by-product plutonium enough to make 5,000 A bombs a year. If only 1 per cent of that plutonium were diverted, it could be used to make several dozen atom bombs a year.

The big goal now is to convince the world's smaller nations to renounce use of the atom for war—instead, to concentrate on harnessing it for peace.

Russia has surrounded Moscow with an anti-ballistic-missile system.

Just in the last five years, the Soviets have caught up with the U.S. in the missiles race. Some say the Soviets have surpassed the U.S. in the space race.

In 1962 Soviet Russia had 50 Intercontinental Ballistic Missiles ready to fire. At that time the United States had 233. Now Soviet Russia has over 1,400 Intercontinental Ballistic Missiles ready to fire and the United States has 1,054. By the time this is printed, even these figures will be changed upward!

In this race for international death there has been a growing concern over the United States being able to survive a nuclear offensive.

While the United States and Russia are concerned with each other's progress, they are more concerned about what might happen if an atomic bomb got into the hands of criminals or terrorists.

Scientists state that it is far too easy for a crazed man, a revolutionary or criminal to make a bomb.

It takes only 13 pounds of plutonium to make an atomic bomb as powerful as that that devastated Nagasaki. And with the secrets of nuclear warheads now fully developed by both France and China, the increasing struggle for power dominance becomes even more complex in a world that is more and more becoming accustomed to this civilized cruelty.

It would seem anti-climactic to tell you that New York's school system, plagued for years by rock-throwing vandals, has turned to plastic instead of glass windows. The School Board has estimated that the city had to pay out OVER THREE MILLION DOLLARS a year just to replace broken school windows, etc.

It may also be anti-climactic to tell you that in the first 6 months of one school year Philadelphia schools had 425 break-ins in which tens of thousands of dollars worth of typewriters, tape recorders and projectors were stolen. So serious has the problem become that the school district plans to operate its own mobile, radio-equipped patrol force.

This might seem very insignificant but it, too, is an indication of the type of civilized cruelty that compounds itself first in little things and then grows to epidemic proportions.

THE GROWING GUN MENACE

Recently Americans witnessed how difficult it was to propose a registration of guns in the United States.

Americans have turned this country into an arsenal. Today they own somewhere between 90 million and 100 million pistols and revolvers, shotguns and rifles, as well as uncounted machine guns, hand grenades, bazookas, mortars, and even antitank guns. At least 2.5 million more are bought each year.

Consider the words of a magazine ad that recently advertised replicas of the derringer pistol as the dandy little model that killed "two of our country's Presidents, Abraham Lincoln and William McKinley."

Another suggested: SUBMACHINE GUN FOR FATHER'S DAY?

Yet another offered, for $99.50 a 20-mm. antitank gun, "ideal for long-range shots at deer and bear or at cars and trucks and even a tank if you happen to see one."

One individual estimated that there are more guns in Los Angeles than there are in Saigon—perhaps 3 million.

In Massachusetts, 1,100 gun dealers last year sold enough arms to equip an army of 56,000.

A mayor of a Michigan city recently exhorted his town's folk "to take up arms, learn to shoot and be a dead shot."

And as a result almost 500 women are regularly taking pistol practice.

What has been the harvest?

Since the turn of the century, nearly 800,000 U.S. citizens have been killed by privately owned guns, vs. 630,768 Americans killed in all of the nation's wars. Hijackings of commercial airplanes is a common occurrence.

Last year the United States suffered more than 21,000 gun

fatalities including 7,000 murders and homicides. Another 100,000 were wounded by gunfire.

Governor George C. Wallace was the 10th man seeking or holding the office of President to be an assassin's target, and the fifth to survive the attack. In nine out of ten cases, including that of Wallace, the weapon used was a handgun.

In 1975, two assassination attempts were made on the life of former President Ford. Both occurred in California.

Only 10 other nations surpass the United States in overall homicide rates—and all of these are in Latin lands where violence is a way of life.

JAMAICA

In 1973, the little Caribbean nation of Jamaica found itself locked in at night in fear of hoodlums with guns. Then they did something almost unheard of...despite the screams of the do-gooders...they made Jamaica safe overnight! It became an offense to own a gun of any kind without a hard-to-get license; police were allowed to search and raid on suspicion; and long sentences were handed out even for possessing a bullet...and foreign visitors were not excepted. Then too, violators were placed in RED PAINTED publicly exposed prison compounds in the center of cities.

All of a sudden violent crime in Jamaica fell down, down, down. Natives and visitors now are able to walk the streets at night for the first time in years. Jamaica was saved by a no-nonsense elimination of the gun.

AMERICA...LAND OF BROKEN HOMES

There is a saying "Charity begins at home." And civilized cruelty is rearing its ugly head across the nation with the growing toll of America's broken homes.

The rates of divorce, desertion and illegitimacy are rising. Also increasing is an army of fatherless children—many of whom are heading for trouble in years to come.

The divorce rate per 1,000 married women aged 15 years or older has been climbing steadily, with only two interruptions since 1958.

Last year, 820,000 U.S. marriages were dissolved in the courts, more than in any other year in the nation's history!

It is estimated that by 1985 there will be over 8 million divorced women in the United States.

Estimates also place over 10% of all births as illegitimate. This situation is compounded by poverty.

Government records reveal that 3 out of 5 children being brought up in homes where the father is absent are "poor" families.

A juvenile court judge recently said "This is a symptom of our times. The rapid flow of American society brings a high divorce rate, so that young couples live several lifetimes in a few years."

If past experience is a guide, the nation may be paying further costs in the years ahead in emotional and mental illness—an element coming to the surface in the form of violence and lawlessness.

Whether it is starvation, the refined elements of war or the rapidly moving society that leaves in its wake broken homes —all of these elements and many more contribute to a civilized cruelty which is inflicted on our fellow man.

We have become so immune to the many reports of cruelty throughout the world that life holds little significance and we measure progress in war by the weekly reports of the "kill rate."

This refined form of civilized cruelty is just one more step that points without question to the heralding of the Last Days.

4
Power That Destroys

A Growing Power • The Arms Race • The Power Over Money and the Dwindling Power of the Dollar • Rising Taxes and Rising Needs • Police Power State • Sorry, No Praying Allowed • The Age of Lawlessness • Trying Decisions

A speech is to be made in Scranton, Pennsylvania.

The Vice President of the United States summons a helicopter which whisks him away to the Washington airport.

Waiting for him there is his personal $3 million Air Force One jet. In a few minutes, he is in the air and on his way to his speaking engagement in Scranton.

Upon arrival it is discovered that he forgot his tuxedo.

The $3 million Air Force One jet takes off again to return to Washington where it lands—picks up the waiting tuxedo—and makes a return trip to Scranton.

Total cost to the United States taxpayers to pick up this forgotten tuxedo; $704.00.

While this is the power of the Vice-Presidency there is no doubt that the power of the President of the United States is even far greater. His office represents the most powerful position in the world.

No one doubts the sincerity of our nation's presidents throughout the years. Undoubtedly, they have devoted their time to what they believed to be the best interest of the United States. Being human, they are, of course, subject to making mistakes. Watergate is a prime example. However, the one difference is that their life is constantly under the limelight day and night and their mistakes (unlike ours) are broadcast within seconds to a waiting world.

Perhaps no other man in the world is under as much pressure and tension and has to make so many important decisions affecting the lives of millions of people as the President of the United States.

Inadvertently, sometimes these decisions are ones that go down in history as decisions which cause great travail and many problems. But any man in similar circumstances could make equally as tragic decisions.

Perhaps, this all points out to the fallibility of man and the infallibility of God.

What is it that makes a man expend all of his energies and all of his mental and financial resources in striving for years to become President of the United States?

There are so many other avenues of occupations that would offer him far greater rewards and leave him far richer with far greater time for his own personal life to spend with his wife and family.

In fact, almost every President when he comes near the end of his term, is thankful to get rid of the job and return to normalcy.

Then, if this is true, there is most likely only one basic reason why any human being strives so diligently to seek an office that can only cause him years of anguish and perhaps leave him disheartened, disillusioned and broken in health.

If one would study each situation closely, perhaps the real basic reason for so many people striving for this high office is because **no other office in the world offers an individual so great an opportunity for recognition and power.**

While it is true that Communist Russian leaders exercise great power, their power structure is of such a nature that one mistake by its leader can result in his execution or overnight removal from office.

This is not true of the President of the United States. The President of the United States once elected into power has at least four years of what amounts to an almost supreme

The Philadelphia Inquirer

Oldest Daily Newspaper in the United States— Founded 1771

Vol. 291, No. 40   O O   Friday, August 9, 1974   15 CENTS

Nixon Resigns;
Ford to Step Up

Successor Hails 'Great Sacrifice'

Kissinger To Stay, He Says

By JULIUS WITOVER

WASHINGTON — Gerald R. Ford Jr., a 61-year-old Grand Rapids, Mich., lawyer never exposed to national office but had it thrust upon him as a result of two of the greatest political scandals in American history, will become the 38th President of the United States today.

Appearing outside his Alexandria, Va., home 31 minutes after President Nixon's resignation speech had ended, Ford praised Nixon's act as "one of the greatest personal sacrifices for the country."

He also announced that he would keep Henry A. Kissinger as his Secretary of State and follow the foreign policy developed by Nixon. He said Kissinger had accepted his invitation to stay and called him "a very great man."

Wearing a gray, pin-striped suit and standing in a light drizzle, the President-designate spoke for about 30 minutes without notes.

He read a crowd of newsmen and about 200 onlookers that he considered this "one of the most difficult and very saddest periods, and one of the very saddest occasions I have ever witnessed."

Ford said he expects "a spirit of cooperation between the President and the Congress."

"I've been very fortunate in my lifetime to public office to have a great many adversaries — in the Congress," he said. But I don't think I have any enemies in the Congress."

Ford said he and Kissinger will be working to the pursuit of peace as we have achieved in the past."

Betty Ford lived a quiet life in Grand Rapids in First Lady.

(See FORD on 2A)

President-Designate Ford after the speech

Ford to Fight Inflation First

By PAUL FRIEDMAN

WASHINGTON — As President, Gerald R. Ford can be expected to follow the domestic and domestic policies of his predecessor. But with a tougher, less expedient brand of conservatism.

Aides who have been meeting Ford's attack on his priority target — the rock American economy — warn that the new President will use the firm's between dear to sell are to take "brutal measures" to wring the rate of inflation and re-expose 12 5 A a become the

Ford is expected to invoke the cycle of inflation and recession 3 4 5 a a

Index

National and international news are related in Pages 9 to people accused of being far behind the B section and on Pages 9-D and 24-A

Amusements 18-E
Business News . . . 16-H to 14-H
Classified Ads . . . 3-R to 14-E
Comics 16-E
Crossword 16-E
Editorials 13-A
Entertainment . . . 14, to 4-d
Finance 3-A
Horoscope 12-F
Living 14, 15,
Obituaries 4-29
Sports . . . . . . 1-D to 4-D

President Nixon embraces Julie after telling family he'd resign

President Forced Out By Scandal

By ROBERT S. BOYD

Inquirer Washington Bureau

WASHINGTON—Richard Milhous Nixon, the 37th President of the United States, resigned in sorrow Thursday night, the first chief executive torn from office by scandal in the 198-year history of the Republic.

The resignation is effective at noon today, when Gerald Rudolph Ford will be formally sworn in by Chief Justice Warren Burger in the Oval Office.

Nixon will not attend the ceremony.

In a subdued but emotional nationwide television address, the President said:

"I would have preferred to carry through to the finish, whatever the personal agony it would have involved. My family unanimously urged me to do so, but the interest of the nation must always come before personal considerations . . . Therefore, I shall resign as President at noon tomorrow."

Describing himself as one who has "never been a quitter," the President said, softly, "To leave office is abhorrent to every instinct in my body."

"There was no admission of guilt or shouldering of responsibility for Watergate-related crimes in the 17-minute speech. The closest to that was the statement: "If some of my judgments were wrong — and some were wrong — they were made in what I believed at the time to be the best interests of the nation."

The momentous but peaceful transfer of authority from the scandal-plagued Nixon to his chosen successor will occur as the outgoing President and his family fly to their estate in San Clemente, Calif.

Mr. and Mrs. Nixon plan to bid farewell to the White House staff at 9:30 A.M. today and then board a helicopter on the south lawn for Andrews Air Force base and their final flight in Air Force One.

Nixon called on the nation Thursday night to give its "help and support" to the new President and to put "the bitterness of the recent past behind us."

"I feel great sadness that I will not be in this office marking up your behalf," he said, "but I sense the leadership of America will be in good hands."

To continue the fight for his personal vindication, he said, would have diverted the attention of the President and Congress when they should be concentrating on peace abroad and prosperity at home.

Ford watched the 18-minute address on his home television set. Afterward, looking solemn, he came out on the front-lit lawn of his modest home in suburban Alexandria, Va., to make a short, informal talk.

He praised Nixon for his "personal sacrifice" in stepping down and promised to carry on his policies, at home and abroad.

He announced that he had named Secretary of State Henry

(See NIXON on 2A)

Nixon Could Face Criminal Charges

By WILLIAM VANCE

WASHINGTON — Richard Nixon is leaving office with no doubt to protect him from prosecution as a private citizen.

He could, however, take another from one thing by Speaker Carl Albert (D-Ill.) announced Thursday night that impeachment proceedings would "come to a halt" in the House.

Albert's statement indicated that he had rejected a proposal by Senate Democratic lead-

or Mike Mansfield (Mont.) that impeachment and a historic trial continue regardless of whether Nixon quit.

But, stripped of his Presidential immunity, he now would be exposed to the threat of criminal and civil prosecution.

The President did not, perhaps, and may not, demand Congressional immunity from prosecution as a price for stepping down. And his failure Thursday night to acknowledge any wrong-doing, even thus did

"some of my judgments were wrong," made the prospect for immunity seem more remote.

So far, there is the evidence that Nixon has attempted to bargain with Federal prosecutors, as did former Vice President Spiro Agnew, for a plea that would keep him out of jail.

Watergate Special Prosecutor Leon Jaworski and Charles Ruth, his deputy, have been in agreement or understanding of any sort between

(See HIGH CITY on 2A)

Shrieks of Joy, Polite Applause Greet the News

"We're going to have a party," attendant Richard Pryor told his audience at the Bijou Cafe. "It's going to be part of history."

And at 9:04 P.M., when Richard Nixon told America, Therefore, I shall resign the Presidency effective at noon tomorrow," cheers bursting with the pop of champagne corks throughout the world cabaret on Broad and 16th hand it.

Down at the Spectrum, the 16,000-plus fans attending the lacrosse game between the Kings and the Buckeye

raid in particular cheers once the start of the game.

And when the basketball suddenly Stood, "Spread the homeroom." Effective 12 noon tomorrow, Richard M. Nixon, President of the United States, has resigned, the crowd drinking inside and empty it out and applauded.

But soon, as was a a a little quieter and less joyful. As the a a a a feel the loss of a and thin a a I heard there a a a a a a a a a a a a a and the announcer a a a a

news's knocked off a rather somber and was joyfully, tolerance ends in their tables.

For a minute Greg-Psychiatric Clinic and willing to treat tomorrow, Richard Nixon, President of the United States have resigned. I a a a a a a a

Well and boxes Mr. fro the being a probably full town a a few, but no trades a a a long a and a a a a and Heart a a a now was the atmosphere a a a a a a a a

night, but not when — you a a hourself. "he I a a said, He found with me, a a and say what he had to say. And we have a great theater on the exit.

When people already were cascancing in a stream at Broad and the Temple Jazz Festival in Ambler.

a a Deli and the Temple a a

a a a a a a a gathering a a a a a a a a a and the a a a a a Gus a a a a a a a a a a a a a a a a a a a a a a a a and the boring a a a in a a

On August 8, 1974, President Nixon became the first President forced to resign from office because of scandal. John Mitchell became the first Attorney General to serve a prison sentence. Are we witnessing dramatic changes in U.S. Government that will eventually lead to the emergence of Antichrist?

power in directing the affairs of state. Should he choose to run for a second term, he more than likely can achieve this goal without any great problem.

A GROWING POWER

In the last few years, more and more power has been placed in the hands of the President of the United States and less and less power has remained in the hands of elected state representatives to Congress.

It is not the purpose of this chapter to comment on present or past administrations in the United States, but simply to show how easy it would be for a president so inclined to use this ever increasing power to the detriment of its citizens and yet create a police state approved by the majority of its citizens.

Let's take a recent example in history which shows how a country run by elected representatives divests its power and transfers it to the President of the United States.

In 1964 it was alleged by the State Department that the ship Maddox was attacked by North Vietnam in the Gulf of Tonkin. Acting swiftly, the Congress of the United States extended to the President of the United States the power to "exercise any means" to protect the military arm of the United States.

This gave almost unqualified power to one man to make the decisions of entering into war and sending over a half million people into a foreign country to continue a war. This initiative began a disastrous war that was to see as many as 541,500 American servicemen involved of which over 55,000 died. And while the U.S. watched, North Vietnam flouted the Paris peace agreements and captured Vietnam Wednesday, April 30, 1975!

Recent investigations have questioned whether this step by Congress was a wise one and whether the Gulf of Tonkin situation was as critical as it appeared at the time.

Whether one agrees with the Gulf of Tonkin resolution or disagrees is not the subject or point of discussion in this chapter...that's for history to decide.

One must agree however, that regardless of personal opinion, this type of action (rightly or wrongly) places in the hands of one man the greatest exercise of power in the world.

In tomorrow's world, whether it be one year, two years or ten years from now—this type of power in the hands of the wrong leader can be the power that destroys.

As an example, in the Nixon and Ford administrations, a non-elected official, Secretary of State Henry Kissinger, played a major role in shaping not only U.S. but Asia and Mid-East policies! Speaking of decisions the President makes that could lead to nuclear war one paper commented: "He was in that moment as true an emperor as ever existed and scarcely more accountable; a people who want peace could still be given war at his dictate; and what good would it do to vote him out of office six months from now if the world were an ash..."

Let us look at some of the areas of power in the United States today and see how such evidences can be a reflection on the Last Days and be a mirror of what we read in the Book of Revelation.

THE ARMS RACE AND POWER

We are living in a day and age that demands that our President have power and also demands that our country be equipped with the elite in nuclear arms. Both of these desires on the part of the nation and its leader are desires which basically are created because of a need for protection and guidance.

Current politics is guided by the thought that the way to disarm is to arm. It is an acknowledged fact that a country has to have more arms than its potential enemy in order to negotiate disarmament from a position of strength. It is assumed that once we have arms superiority the Russians will presumably be forced to disarm. However, history has taught us that this theory does not work. For when we did have arms superiority—when we had the A-bomb and the Russians didn't—neither they nor we disarmed. And they unfortunately closed the gap.

Even as early as the days of Krushchev, scientists were talking about the "doomsday bomb." This weapon, when hitched up to an electronic brain, will be able to destroy the remainder of mankind even if no survivors are left in the attacked country to set it off.

The problems that a President of the United States must face today seem monumental compared to the problems that Washington or Lincoln faced in their days. For never before in history have we been engaged in an all out race for survival where one mistake could literally obliterate the entire world.

And in spite of all this—every four years—some of the leading men of our country drop everything in order to engage in a frantic race to become President of the United States.

It was Seneca who said: "He who has great power should use it lightly."

And it was Noah Webster who quite prophetically stated: "Power is always right, weakness is always wrong."

But perhaps, Lord Acton summed it all up in this statement: "Power corrupts, and absolute power corrupts absolutely."

James F. Byrnes, the former Secretary of State remarked: "Power intoxicates men. When a man is intoxicated by alcohol he can recover, but when intoxicated by power, he seldom recovers."

THE POWER OVER MONEY AND THE DWINDLING POWER OF THE DOLLAR

Any of the decisions regarding the budget of the United States and the disbursement of funds into certain channels rests primarily with the President of the United States.

Every President naturally would welcome the opportunity to be the President who eliminates poverty in the United States and makes America a Utopia.

It was back on November 27, 1934, President Franklin D. Roosevelt wrote a friend of his the following:

"There will, of course, be a certain number of relief cases where work will not furnish that answer, but it is my thought that in these cases all of the relief expenditures should once more be borne by the states and localities as they used to be.

"The lessons of history, confirmed by the evidence immediately before me, show conclusively that continued dependence upon relief induces a spiritually and moral disintegration fundamentally destructive to the national fibre."

This was written by President Franklin D. Roosevelt before the old-age benefits system or Social Security or the unemployment compensation system were inaugurated. These were problems originally designed to relieve states and localities of their burden.

In the growing complex societies, instead of these new social benefits relieving the problems on hand, poverty is still very much with us and many millions more are being expended in an attempt to relieve the condition.

This is being done through taxation.

In no other time in history have taxes been higher than at the present time. Individuals paid over one-third more in income tax in 1976 than they did in 1966. In the two years prior to 1976, as the total income went up 17%—correspondingly—the federal income tax went up 32%.

If the recent 6% inflation rate continues for the next 30 years, the American breadwinner earning $10,000 in 1976 will have to earn $57,435 to maintain a comparable standard of living! A $20 bag of groceries of 1976 will cost $114.87 in the supermarket of the year 2000!

In this case, former Presidents Nixon and Johnson found themselves fighting a war of "containment" in Vietnam, and a war on poverty at home with mounting increased costs. As a result, in the last four Nixon years the federal budget increased by 146%—from $100 billion in 1964 to 246 billion in 1972.

To compensate for this—between 1961 and 1966, the money supplied in the U.S. was increased 4% by "creeping inflation."

PRESIDENT CARTER URGED TO TAKE STRONG STEPS

Even in this day of inflation, it is perhaps still difficult for the reader to envision the possibility that this country could within a short time drift to a dictator type leadership reflected in the prophetic Scriptures of the Bible. People, however, are calling upon President Carter to take "strong" measures. They want results and are not worried now about any possibility of growing executive power (as long as he, the President, files his own private Income Tax form honestly)!

Let's for a minute look at what happened to Germany after World War I.

Her treasury was low in gold. Her budget was unbalanced. Inflation moved to a run-away stage. In 1919 the German mark was worth 25¢. Within four years it declined in value until 4 trillion were needed to equal $1 in buying power.

Here's what the Reader's Digest reported:

> "The German middle class had lost all their savings. The value of every pension was wiped out. All security was gone. Then the people were ready to listen to any demagogue who would voice their bitterness: His name was Adolf Hitler."

Quite prophetically it was Lenin who said: "The surest way to overthrow an existing social order is to debauch the currency."

It was only a couple of years ago that foreign banks and business interests, concerned about the stability of the U.S. dollar, increased their demand for payment of American obligations in gold instead of dollars. In one month, about one-twelfth of the total American gold supply disappeared. And more economists discussed the idea of a unified world monetary system.

RISING TAXES AND RISING NEEDS

The trend for increased taxation is irreversible. There is a steady pressure for more spending, followed by requests for higher taxes, followed by widespread grumbling from taxpayers. And yet the trend continues upward, for people want better housing, relief from poverty and now, a guaranteed minimum income.

In fact, in a few years, one may see in the United States a negative taxation which guarantees every family a minimum of perhaps $3500 in guaranteed income—whether the individual works for this income or not.

This guaranteed negative income has already received wide acclaim from businessmen, financiers and people in high levels in government. But perhaps the greatest threat to democracy is the threat of "gradualism."

For not in one big swoop, but gradually step by step—and with acceptance by the majority of the population either

THE UNITED STATES GOVERNMENT
Is it getting too BIG?
The BIGGEST Organization on Earth:

EMPLOYS

6.4 million people and pays them 39 BILLION dollars a year!

1 out of every 13 Americans works for the U.S. Government!

OWNS

760 million acres of land or 1/3rd of the Nation

PLUS
422,000 BUILDINGS valued at 103 BILLION dollars!

PLUS
about 250 BILLION dollars in EQUIPMENT including 409,000 vehicles, 54,000 airplanes and over 1000 ships.

SPENDS

$8 MILLION a MINUTE and this is increasing! That makes 5 BILLION DOLLARS A WEEK!

and all this contributes to a
DEBT

of $694 BILLION DOLLARS with 55 million Americans sharing 1/4 TRILLION dollars of federal income support annually!

through apathy or desire—we see the original tenets of our democracy slowly fading away as evidences of a socialistic state creep in.

Much of the power to direct the affairs of this nation lie with the President of the United States. However, it would be extremely unpopular for the President of the United States to protest a guaranteed negative income or to protest wide expenditures that make it possible for employment of millions of people in government held offices.

It is no wonder that a President ends his term with a sincere desire to get out of the "quicksand of office" and back to normalcy.

For as the country raises its income taxes, it also forces states to boost their taxes. Thirty-five states now collect personal income taxes. Forty states now collect corporate income taxes. Forty-four states now collect general sales taxes and all fifty states tax gasoline.

In addition to state taxes, about 6,000 cities and counties have already imposed local, income or sales taxes. And special local levies on cigarettes, gasoline and utility bills and similar goods or services are also increasing.

In a recent news article, the headline stated that "American Debts Total 2 Trillion; $10,000 a Person." The private and public gross debt rose by over $100 billion just during the year 1969. It may be surprising to the reader to realize that in all, government this year will collect $250 billion in taxes of all kinds—or about double the tax burden of just 10 years ago!

To show you the complexities of government growth...it took 60 years, from 1789 to 1848, and the first 11 Presidents, combined, before the U.S. Government spent its first 1 billion dollars. Today, it takes *less than two days* for the Government to spend 1 billion dollars.

Yet in spite of the soaring taxes and record spending, this country is found to have been skimping on public improvements needed by the growing population—roads, bridges, parks, schools, recreation areas, adequate police and fire protection, water and sewer facilities.

On July 30, 1972, the U.S. Treasury announced that the previous fiscal year showed the biggest deficit since World War II or $38.8 billion "in the red." In the past 5 years, spending has exceeded income by over $50 billion. The 1976 debt was $70 billion!

Not so long ago the United States stood at the pinnacle of world power. Gold was piled high. The dollar was King. However, in December, 1971 the European Common Market nations forced the United States to devalue their dollar. Half the gold is gone. Once the U.S. had plenty of gold, but in two decades gold stock of the U.S. has been cut to less than half its former size.

Over the years since 1945, overall cost of Foreign Aid by the U.S. to the outside world has soared to more than 190 billion dollars.

We have sent to the foreign nations of the world over $36 billion more than they have returned to us. While our national debt has soared to over $400 billion, the debt of all the other nations of the world is only around $305 billion!

One authority talks of the U.S. as a "reverse Horatio Alger —a nation that has gone from riches to rags...."

A continued trend in this direction may yet bring about the inclusion of the United States in a Federated States of Europe-type combine...perhaps first on a cooperative common market basis.

Nations economically forced into federations, such as a Federated Europe, would be the fulfillment of prophecy as found in Revelation and another indication of the Last Days.

From a practical standpoint, while we were taking the freedom of a coffee break, our nation was spending over $500,000 on the war in Vietnam! That's right! Over one-half million dollars was spent every ten minutes on the war.

It took 100,000 bullets, statistically speaking, to kill or maim one Viet Cong...or about $7000. It took only 20,000 bullets to produce an enemy casualty in World War II. More than 4,100 U.S. helicopters were destroyed in Vietnam. Value of helicopters—over $1 billion.

Some would optimistically believe that when the war ended there would be a huge drop in military spending...and billions of dollars will be released to alleviate the nation's suffering.

This is far from true, however. Billions of dollars were needed for a catch-up on military programs that were allowed to lag during the war.

Joseph W. Barr, former Under Secretary of the Treasury, stated, "I would seriously doubt that any sizeable reduction can be made in the defense budget in the foreseeable future."

Mr. Barr pointed out that a cessation of hostilities would result in great pressures to rebuild stocks in military supplies...more tanks...more ships...more planes to replace obsolete equipment and keep ahead of the Russians.

Although the Vietnam War has ended, this did not usher in a holiday on military spending but simply gave us a breather to prepare for the next crisis.

✓ ASTRONOMICAL IS THE WORD FOR IT

The President of the United States has the dubious honor of presiding over a payroll which is best described as: Astronomical.

In 1955 the number of civilian Government employees averaged 2,367,290. Federal expenditures for this civilian payroll were $9,621,000,000.

In the fiscal year 1968 the average civilian employment was 2,947,720 (580,430 more!).

BUT LOOK AT THIS! The payroll expenditures for fiscal 1968 were $22,425,000,000. Therefore the increase over 1955 was $12,804,000,000!

The largest employer in the United States is the United States Government. And the President, through his office, governs this work force.

All the above is said to say this: At no time in history has the position of President required so many decisions of monumental importance as it does today.

The complex continued growth of our country demands more and more money and greater and greater taxation.

While some may question the advisability of spending money in some directions or maintaining as large an army of government employees as is currently being employed—this is not the point of this article.

The point is this, that it is the responsibility of any Presi-

A Czechoslovak student waves National flag while standing on Soviet tank in Prague, Czechoslovakia. While this tiny country was invaded by some 500,000 Russian army and satellite troops . . . the

dent who comes into office to wield an even greater power with even greater consequences—whether he desires to do so or not. It is these responsibilities of office which he automatically inherits.

And because he does inherit these powers, he does also become the most powerful person in the world.

It is no wonder that more control and more desire for world unity become the objectives of our nation whether directly or indirectly.

In a desire for world unity—from 1945 to present, American taxpayers have authorized our government to give or "loan" to other nations over 190 billion dollars.

This ranges from $300,000 to Tonga Island to $1,133,300,000 to United Arab Republic and $1,104,500,000 to Israel and over $5,000,000,000 to Vietnam.

As a nation we actively support the World Bank which is also supported by 108 other nations throughout the world.

Currently the World Bank has approved 44 loans, totaling $847 million, to borrowers in 31 nations in the past year. Prophetically, the creation of the World Bank is just one step further towards the coming Last Days.

POLICE STATE POWER

In the previous paragraphs we have discussed how the responsibilities of fiscal control rest initially under the powerful leadership of the President of the United States. By his direction, he can increase spending and create more government positions which result in increasing budgets, which in turn require more taxation.

By his direction, he can also encourage an abandonment of the financial system of gold backing of U.S. currency and can encourage world unification through a World Bank. This in itself gives a President large avenues of power.

However, there is another avenue of power which directly and indirectly is generated by the President...

Directly—through appointments of individuals who he feels are qualified to handle certain offices and whose policies may create adverse conditions in the United States.

And indirectly by allowing certain events to occur without speaking out against them and taking corrective measures.

Demonstrations are now a way of life. A demonstrator confronted
National Guard troops in early morning clash in front of Chicago
Hilton Hotel during 1968 Democratic National Convention.

In 1968 the nation watched in horror as they saw over one-half million Russian and Russian satellite armies march into tiny Czechoslovakia and "save" the country overnight. They watched huge Russian tanks lumbering into the streets of Prague as aroused people shouted epithets and threw rocks at their self-appointed "saviors."

Americans—as was the world—were understandably upset. Here was tyranny and dictatorship in its most blatant form.

But the same eyes that witnessed this would have great difficulty in recognizing the seeds of a police state gradualism that occurred just a few days later in the city of Chicago.

Let's look back just for a moment. It was Lenin who stated that his blueprint for taking over America would include the creation of a climate that would "make America's people so rotten and decadent morally that they will not resist an eventual communist takeover."

Recent rulings by the Supreme Court favorable to the smut industry made it possible for this industry to create over $2 billion in volume last year, making this country the pornographic capital of the world.

It has been alleged that one of the publishers to benefit by the Supreme Court ruling was formerly a client of a Supreme Court Justice. This allegedly is the same former Supreme Court Justice who accepted a $15,000 fee paid for nine two-hour lectures to 17 law students—about $800 an hour.

It is rather prophetic to read in the "Rules for Bringing About Revolution" published by the Communists in 1919 the following: "Corrupt the young; get them away from religion. Get them interested in sex. Make them superficial. Destroy their ruggedness."

While America pays lip service to God—this same Supreme Court which opened the flood gates to pornography—has banned prayer and Bible reading from American schools.

And this seed that was sown soon came to harvest in the city of Chicago in the 1968 Democratic Convention and in Miami in the 1972 Democratic and Republican Conventions. The results were disastrous.

It is not the purpose of this article to explore the merits of the protestors or the merits of the action taken by the Chicago police, but simply to make some observations for you to consider.

When the Russians took over Czechoslovakia, one of the first things they did was to jam the radio broadcasts of Voice of America. Once their troops were firmly entrenched in Czechoslovakia, they became annoyed by the "distorted" news reports which were coming out of Czechoslovakia by U.S. newsmen which were unfavorable to them. It was then they imposed censorship.

One of the first actions of any police state is to control the news media or to ban the freedom of news and issue carefully worked out documents to be doled out to the public.

In entering the Democratic National Convention of 1968 the newsmen were faced with a week of grievances against the restrictions of the convention, the alleged highhandedness of the police and the general air of news repression. In fact, the convention city of Chicago looked more like an armed camp than a city where Democratic processes were soon to be initiated.

Whether this armed camp was justified or not is for you the reader to decide. The important fact is that the day in which we live and the general conditions of our country have brought about a situation which necessitated such an armed defense of a city.

It was David Brinkley of NBC that told his network audience that: "We gather that the Democratic leadership does not want reported what is happening." It appeared to the newsmen that the police were singling them out as special targets and blaming them for attracting the undesirable elements. On the first night of the convention, some 20 newsmen were beaten up and three were hospitalized.

When a Chicago Daily News reporter protested to the police the clubbing of three girls in a convertible, his reward was a beating and a scalp wound.

A CBS cameraman, while filming a clash between police and populace, was clubbed from behind. While an NBC cameraman was filming this very event, he, too, was hit in the face and toppled.

And while an entire nation was watching on television,

CBS Floor Reporter Dan Rather was flattened by two security men; one hit him in the stomach, the other in the back. His colleague, Mike Wallace, was belted in the jaw by a guard and hustled out of the hall.

So vigorous were the attacks on newspaper and television reporters that eight top executives of news-gathering organizations strongly protested the treatment in a telegram to the Mayor of Chicago.

In this age of social order and progress, Chicago found itself a bristling camp.

It was faced with a 14 week old strike of telephone installers and further impeded by a strike by major cab companies.

Expecting trouble, Mayor Daley put his 11,900-man police force on twelve-hour shifts, called up more than 5,000 Illinois National Guard troops. In addition, some 6,500 federal troops were flown in. Over 23,000 men were armed and ready for whatever was to come.

As a further precaution the convention hall was protected by barbed wire and packed with policemen and security agents.

The scene was so ominous that one demonstrator held up a sign "WELCOME TO PRAGUE."

Against this army of 23,000 police force it is estimated that about 10,000 demonstrators showed up. So tight was the security at the Chicago Democratic Convention that delegates had to have two forms of identification—one of them being a plastic identification tag which hung around their neck. This special tag had to be inserted into a "computer" machine which would verify the authenticity of the tag by flashing a green light. If the tag were a forgery, a red light would flash and an alarm would be sounded.

While the machine appeared to be a hoax when one delegate got a green OK by inserting his Dartmouth's identification card—this very stringent marking system bears a very strong similarity to what we read in Revelation 13: 16,17

> And he causes all, the small and the great, and
> the rich and the poor, and the free men and the
> slaves, to be given a mark on their right hand, or
> on their forehead,

> *and he provides that no one should be able to buy*
> *or to sell, except the one who has the mark, either*
> *the name of the beast or the number of his name.*

The shocking thing is that even though the over 30 reporters, photographers and TV newsmen had visible credentials and attempted to identify themselves to police, they still were attacked and in several instances had their cameras, film and tape recorders destroyed.

While one delegate could not even bring the New York Times into the convention hall to be used in a speech—bus loads of Chicago patronage workers were hustled into the Amphitheatre by a side door to take up seats in the gallery—from which the general public had been officially excluded.

Therefore, while authorized press representatives were beaten and excluded from these same galleries, the powers that be made it possible for unauthorized individuals to flood the galleries and create a wall of vocal approval for their candidate.

There is no question that America should be a land of law and order.

On the other hand, this law and order should be achieved through lawful and equitable means.

There are many eyewitness reports of newsmen who stated that clubs were used indiscriminately to subdue already subdued or cooperating individuals.

The purpose of any police force is to maintain peace and order and to effect an arrest when a law has been broken.

It is not the purpose of a police force in the United States to be both judge and jury.

Yet, this is what they do become in non-emergencies when they use clubs instead of their arresting powers.

There is no excuse for policemen—if they have to use clubs—to use them on an individual's head.

For medical doctors will attest to the fact that this is the most sensitive part of the body and can lead to irreparable damage in the life of an individual for years to come.

And yet we found not only the guilty being clubbed but also the innocent.

The Democratic National Convention brought to the American public very visually two important facts:

1. It revealed the powers of a desperate city with the police force acting as both judge and jury.
2. Never before in recent United States history has there been so great a desire for the suppression of news.

What is surprising is that over 72% of those interviewed in one poll unwittingly condoned this action and by so doing, through gradualism, will one day find themselves condoning what will be a police state...if it is allowed to continue.

Violence met with violence begets violence.

And regardless of what issues were at stake at the Chicago Democratic Convention or what laws were broken—the fact still remains that this convention will go down in history as a period of lawlessness and erosion of democracy.

It is extremely important to the preservation of Democracy in the United States that law and order prevail. It is also important that the insidious communist elements in our society, that have misled some of our errant youth, be checked before our country becomes a lawless anarchy.

It is also extremely important, however, that in our desire to accomplish the above we do not swing the pendulum too far in the opposite direction where we condone a police state where justice no longer prevails.

Shortly after the Chicago Democratic Convention the Attorney General of the United States commented: "Of all violence, police violence in excess of authority is the most dangerous. *For who will protect the public when the police violate the law?*"

On one hand we have an intense desire for law and order at the expense of individual freedom. On the other hand we have an element of irresponsible youth who, in many cases without morals or a belief in God, blindly seek a "better way" but offer no real solutions on how such a way can be accomplished.

The end result will be continued chaos!

SORRY NO PRAYING ALLOWED

Can we blame only those 10,000 dissenters who became disenchanted with their country or does some of the blame originate with the parents who raised them and with the Supreme Court of the United States? It was the Supreme Court which decreed that the kindergarten children can no longer recite a "thank you" verse in unison as they partake of a morning snack.

The forbidden expression of gratitude is this:

> "We thank you for the flowers so sweet;
> We thank you for the food we eat;
> We thank you for the birds that sing;
> We thank you for everything."

This illegal utterance was originally even more "nefarious" (VERY WICKED)—for it once contained the word "God" in the last line and read "We thank you God for everything."

The objectionable word was removed from the verse when parents of a child in DeKalb County, Illinois, won a regional court decree that such language violated previous U.S. Supreme Court decisions.

"God is now an illegal word in the "thank you" verse—*even though only implied.*

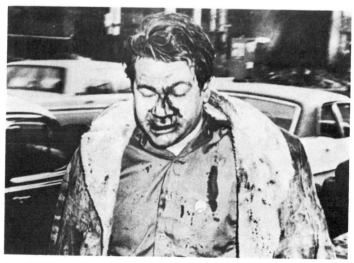

Attacks on teachers by students are commonplace now. Pictured is a New Jersey teacher who was beaten by youths in Newark.

It is no wonder that this writer recently issued a calling card which read:

IN CASE OF
ATOMIC ATTACK
THE FEDERAL RULING AGAINST
PRAYING IN THE SCHOOLS WILL BE
TEMPORARILY SUSPENDED!

Perhaps, some of America's leaders are not acquainted with the verse in Galatians 6:7 which reads:

Do not be deceived, God is not mocked; for whatever a man sows, this he will also reap.

It has been estimated that the average American child who reaches the age of 18 has passively watched a television screen for some 22,000 hours. And on this screen he has been fed the elements of sin and violence which in many instances reaps a bitter harvest as he reaches adulthood.

While on one hand we have youth seething with unrest, dissatisfied with a world they have inherited from their adults...on the other hand, we have an ever increasing desire by a majority of the populace towards maintaining law and order apparently regardless of the means by which this is attained. Thus we reach an impasse which can only lead to further destruction.

And which eventually—whether he desires it or not— places greater power in the hands of the President of the United States.

THE AGE OF LAWLESSNESS

Never before in our history have we seen such mass outbreaks of lawlessness as has occurred in the last few years. College students sealing off entire campuses, holding officials in hostage, rioting, wanton destruction, stealing in the face of the law which helplessly stands by lest their actions ignite an even greater powder keg.

One has only to look at II Thessalonians 2:7-12 to see this prophetic picture.

For the mystery of lawlessness is already at work; only he who now restrains will do so until he is taken out of the way. (7)

And then that lawless one will be revealed whom

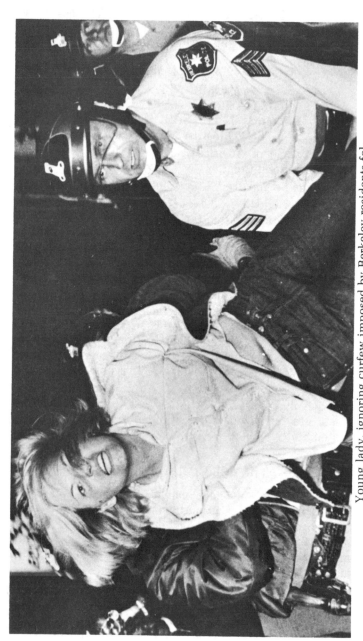

Young lady, ignoring curfew imposed by Berkeley residents following outbreak of violence near campus, is forcibly ejected from

> the Lord will slay with the breath of His mouth
> and bring to an end by the appearance of His
> coming. (8)
>
> That is, the one whose coming is in accord with
> the activity of Satan, with all power and signs and
> false wonders. (9)
>
> And with all the deception of wickedness for
> those who perish, because they did not receive
> the love of the truth so as to be saved. (10)
>
> And for this reason God will send upon them a
> deluding influence so that they might believe
> what is false. (11)
>
> In order that they all may be judged who did not
> believe the truth, but took pleasure in wicked-
> ness. (12)

So rabidly anxious are many people for law and order
that one crowd listening to a presidential candidate
stood on its feet in unison shouting yells of approval
when the candidate stated: "...and if any demonstrator
ever lays down in front of my car, it will be the last car
he'll ever lay down in front of...."

For while they yell their approval for this type of power,
they fail to realize that this same power may divest them
of their own individual freedom at some future date.

As an example, a controversial atheist, Mrs. Madalyn
Murray O'Hair, began a weekly series of talks on religion
on an Austin, Texas radio station. It was Mrs. O'Hair's
lawsuit which resulted in the U.S. Supreme Court ruling
banning prayers in public schools.

While Mrs. O'Hair has every right to the airwaves to
broadcast her views on atheism, the sad fact is that
many religious broadcasters cannot secure time on many
radio stations throughout the country even though they are
willing to pay for it.

At a time when this country should be turning to God...
His message is falling on deaf ears as we enter even
greater eras of prosperity.

II Peter 2 is very revealing in this situation.

An ex-convict who was "Minister of Information" for the
Black Panthers addressed a group of some 15 attorneys—

all under the age of 36—in a San Francisco dinner meeting.

"America is up against the wall," he declared. "This whole apparatus. This capitalistic system and its institutions and police...all need to be assigned to the garbage can of history and I don't give a—who doesn't like it."

"If we can't have it, nobody's gonna have it..."

This is the moral climate a president must face.

TRYING DECISIONS

In conclusion, the President of the United States is faced with the greatest power ever confronted by a man in history. He knows that man now has the equipment and the knowledge to inflict havoc on the earth through the power of the atom.

He knows that Red China now has this same capability. He knows that soon she will acquire the capacity to deliver the nuclear bombs to any far location.

He knows that Russia has the know-how to plant a hydrogen bomb 200 miles off the West Coast of the United States —and they could detonate it. He knows that this explosion could cause a giant tidal wave over 800 feet high that would travel at least 1000 miles inland.

He knows that there has also been developed multi-missile units than can circle the earth 100 or 200 miles out and that can be set off by ground instructions and hurtle their atomic destruction over many target areas covering thousands of miles—*all at one time.*

He knows that an entire nation could be wiped out in a matter of seconds by one push of a button.

He knows that if elected the complex problems of race, poverty, law and order cannot be solved regardless of how good his intentions.

He knows that he will have to expend more and more money, put this nation's economy deeper and deeper in the red, and work towards a guaranteed income for everyone.

He knows he must be all things to all people.

He knows that his future administration will bring him even greater day by day crises that will make the armed camp episode in Chicago seem like a Boy Scouts' picnic.

THIS MAY "NEVER COME ABOUT !!

About 285 A.D. the Roman Empire was under the reign of Diocletian.

He had gone quickly up the ranks from governor of Maesia, to the honors of the consulship, and to the important command of the guards of the palace.

While Emperor, in order to organize the government better and to lower the risk of his own assassination, he divided the Empire with a second-in-line successor in the West. He also created a third and fourth who were also sure of eventual promotion to the Imperial office in a definite term of years.

But after 20 years of serving his country, he became tired of the pressures of the day and it was in the 21st year of his reign that Diocletian decided to abdicate the empire.

The population was getting restless and dissatisfied with some of his edicts. But Maximian, whose passion was the love of power, begged Diocletian to remain in office.

Diocletian's remarks while made in 300 A.D. reflect even more truth in light of today's more complex problems.

He rejected the temptation with a smile of pity, calmly observing that, if he could show Maximian the cabbages which he had planted with his own hands at Salona, he should no longer be urged to relinquish this enjoyment of happiness for the pursuit of power.

As a result of his over 20 years of reigning, he admitted that the most difficult art was the art of ruling and told Maximian that he would rather continue in his farming and raising of cabbages than to become embroiled again as the reigning Monarch of the Roman Empire.

He had progressed up to the office which bestowed upon him the greatest power in the world at that time—Emperor of Rome. For years he had sought to achieve this power—but after tasting the power—he longed to return to a quiet and unfettered life.

And yet in spite of all of this, presidential candidates during the Presidential Election of 1976, expended over $500 million in order to secure the coveted post of President of the United States.

What is it that would make an individual leave his own personal prosperity and sacrifice everything he has in order to reach this command?

In two words—"power" and "recognition."

In 1973 came the revelation that President Richard Nixon's re-election committee had received millions in campaign gifts from Defense contractors. Then came the news that President Nixon had secretly taped all conversations in several of his White House offices. This plus the Watergate episode and charges made against Vice-President Sprio Agnew resulted in the general public losing confidence in those in high office.

U.S. LEADERS RESIGN

And on October 10, 1973 came the dramatic announcement that Vice-President Spiro Agnew had resigned! Then at noon on Friday August 9th, 1974 President Nixon himself became the first man in history to resign the Presidency— as impeachment proceedings stared him in the face. Yet these were the leaders who were committed to bring a "heaven on earth" with a lasting peace for the world!

A well-known philosopher wrote "Every man would like to be God if it were possible; some few find it difficult to admit the impossibility."

It was Tacitus who said: "Lust for power is the most flagrant of all passions."

Archimedes—who had no knowledge of the hydrogen bomb or the power of the President of the United States— prophetically stated many hundreds of years ago: "Give me a lever long enough, and a fulcrum strong enough, and single handed I can move the earth."

It was back in 1770 that Pitt stated: "Unlimited power corrupts the possessor."

Though this nation was originally founded so that its individuals could have a truly representative power, it is slowly drifting, because of the complexities of growth, to where more and more power is invested in the President of the United States.

It is no wonder that men with sincere desire strive valiantly to reach this post.

And yet one must accept the fact that sooner or later this vast concentration of power will be invested into leadership that may exercise a POWER THAT DESTROYS!

5
The Vanishing Christians

As in the Days of Noah • An Increasing Materialism • Explanation of Terms Used in This Book • False Christ • Wars, Earthquakes, Famines • The Second Coming...How It Will Occur • The Seven Days and The End of the World

One of these days, millions of people suddenly are going to vanish without any warning! And you are going to wonder why!

Up to this point of the book we have discussed current events and their relationship to events that will occur in God's plan for man.

It most likely was very easy for you to understand the current events discussed in the first four chapters...because these are events you have witnessed first-hand.

It may be far more difficult for you to understand the next few chapters because, to the non-believer, they may seem utterly fantastic and because they relate to things that will happen in the future.

No one knows exactly at what point in the future these will occur. But it is my belief that the events related in the first four chapters of this book point up to the fact that God's timetable is right on time and that these events which we will discuss in the next few chapters will start to occur very soon.

> You will recall the first four chapters outlined events that are bringing us to the threshold of the Last Days. They include (a) an increasing crime wave, (b) lawlessness, (c) avalanche of pornography and nude films, (d) trend towards a World Church, (e) air pollution, (f) population explosion, (g) increasing famine, (h) earthquakes, (i) onrush of more virulent germ strains, (j) fantastic new weapons of mass destruction, (k) a breakdown of the family unit through increased divorce rate, and (l) the building up of East and West powers into two strong opposing factions with the Mid-East as the tinder box.

Now in order to understand the prophetic teachings of God's word—one must first believe that the Bible is the literal (true to fact) word of God.

One must also realize that it is necessary for one to accept Christ as his personal Saviour first if he expects to gain entrance into God's Heaven.

It is a false assumption to believe that there are many religions which all lead to the same place.

This is in direct contradiction to Christ's words found in John 14:6 in which He states:

> Jesus said to him, "I am the way, and the truth, and the life; no one comes to the Father, but through Me.

Even the majority of church going people and the majority of clergymen in the world either do not understand God's teachings or simply want to create their own little religion.

In so doing they mislead their congregations.

You will find many churches and clergymen who, for example, do not believe that the blood of Jesus Christ has any power to wash away sins. They do not believe in Heaven. They do not believe in the Second Coming of Christ.

They believe that heaven is here on earth and that the world will get better as people become more educated and more mature.

The Apostle Paul understood these conditions which would appear and wrote in I Corinthians 2:12:

> Now we have received, not the spirit of the world,
> but the Spirit who is from God, that we might
> know the things freely given to us by God.

Naturally, someone who has not accepted Christ as his personal Saviour cannot be expected to understand those things in God's Word which deal with the Second Coming of Christ.

Just because a man is well educated in this world does not mean that he is able to understand spiritual things.

In fact, quite often the opposite occurs. The Bible tells us that in these Last Days there will be people who will be "Ever learning, and never able to come to the knowledge of the truth" (2 Timothy 3:7).

The Bible also tells us in 1 Corinthians 2:14:

> But a natural man does not accept the things of
> the Spirit of God; for they are foolishness to him,
> and he cannot understand them, because they are
> spiritually appraised.

Let's assume you are a man of the world. You may be a friendly skeptic. Or you may simply feel that the only life that is going to exist for you is the life here on earth.

Blaise Pascal, one of the acknowledged masters of calculus in the 17th century, was asked why he believed in eternal salvation or eternal life.

In essence his remarks were as follows: "Let's assume that I am wrong and there is no life hereafter—then I have lost nothing. On the other hand, let's assume that I am right and there is life hereafter, then I have gained everything."

God's plan for man is not a hit and miss plan based simply on ideas or theories.

God's plan for man is a very definite blueprint which can be substantiated through previous scriptural events which have been fulfilled and can be followed with scriptural prophecies which have yet to be fulfilled.

However, God's plan requires faith on your part. And this is something that many people, although they practice it in their daily life—find it difficult to practice in their spiritual life.

Every year millions of people go on vacation and by faith follow the markings on the road maps when they are traveling in areas they have not previously traveled.

They believe in the road map because this map has been charted for them and shows them things to come such as detours, connecting roads, etc.

However, man in his finite mind, finds it difficult to read the Bible and discover that God has, in the Old Testament, charted things that have occurred—which have been historically confirmed. God has also charted events that have occurred in the New Testament, and both in the Old and New Testament he charts things which *will* occur with the Second Coming of Christ, the Great Tribulation, and the Millennial Reign of God's people. As we mentioned before, there are more than 300 Old and New Testament Scriptures which promise that Jesus will return to earth. *And these promises will be fulfilled just as literally as the 200 Old Testament prophecies of His virgin birth, death, burial and resurrection were fulfilled.*

It is not our desire to become theologically deep in our explanation of God's prophecies. The purpose of this book is to very simply outline to you what will occur beginning with the vanishing of millions of people suddenly from this earth. This vanishing is termed the Rapture. Briefly this means the calling up (or translation) of born-again believers to meet Christ in the air at the Second Coming.

> *For the Lord Himself will descend from heaven with a shout, with the voice of the archangel, and with the trumpet of God; and the dead in Christ shall rise first.*
>
> *Then we who are alive and remain shall be caught up together with them in the clouds to meet the Lord in the air, and thus we shall always be with the Lord. (1 Thessalonians 4:16,17).*

Let's look for a minute at God's blueprint on the next few pages and after the blueprint is explained to you, we will go into detail on each facet of God's blueprint.

AS IN THE DAYS OF NOAH...

Concerning the Last Days, look what Christ said.

> *For the coming of the Son of Man will be just like the days of Noah.*
>
> *For as in those days which were before the flood they were eating and drinking, they were marrying and giving in marriage, until the day that NOAH ENTERED THE ARK.*

> And they did not understand until the flood came
> and took them all away, so shall the coming of
> the Son of Man be. (Matthew 24:37-39).

Just for a moment, let's look back to the days of Noah as found in Genesis, chapter 6.

In Genesis: we read:

> And God saw that the wickedness of man was
> great in the earth, and that every imagination of
> the thoughts of his heart was only evil continually.

God was so disturbed by the situation of the day that He told Noah:

> Then God said to Noah, The end of all flesh has
> come before Me; for the earth is filled with
> violence because of them; and behold, I am about
> to destroy them with the earth. (Genesis 6:13).

One can imagine the ridicule that Noah received when he was building an ark in the middle of dry land. You can

Are we again living "... in the days of Noah"?

imagine what the townspeople thought when they came up and questioned Noah and asked him what he was doing. Noah, of course, replied that the Lord had promised to destroy the earth by a flood and that he was building an ark so that he and his family could be saved.

This apparently was an age of great prosperity and also great wickedness and it was inconceivable among these people of affluence that such a thing as a world flood could occur.

And yet the flood did occur and Noah and his family were saved, and this is the first and last time that God's wrath was poured out upon the world through the means of a flood.

In fact, God promised to Noah in Genesis 9:12-15 that he would make a covenant with him and with every living creature that this would be the last time the world would be destroyed by flood. And the sign of this covenant would be that He would set a rainbow in the cloud and this would remind His people of this promise.

However, God goes on further to relate in other portions of Scripture that there will be destruction on the earth, but it will be destruction caused by other elements and not by another great flood.

In fact, let us look at the comparison between Noah's days and our days.

There are more and more evidences that we are living in a materialistic world where people are more concerned about worldly pleasures and their own financial gains — than about the spiritual welfare of others or for that matter, the spiritual welfare of themselves and their own families.

AN INCREASING MATERIALISM

General Foods spends $35,000 to film a 30-second commercial for its dog food called Gravy Train. This comes to about $1,200 per second of finished commercial.

Industry sources indicated that General Foods will spend over $1 million in the next year buying TV—network and local—station time to show this commercial.

And what is the message of this great investment?

It is this: "Gravy Train makes your dog feel like Rin-Tin-Tin".

General Foods is not to blame for this age in which we live. This is the type of thing that people want and are looking forward to—simply because we are living in an age of materialism, bathed in an aura of luxury.

Yet in spite of our sophistication in being selective in the purchase of dog food (influenced by over $1 million expended to get us to buy one dog food over another) it was virtually impossible for the world to get in any type of food into the tiny nation of Biafra where thousands of people were dying daily of starvation and where cruel and inhumane killings became commonplace.

To anyone studying world events, it is not difficult to see that as highly modernized and industrialized as we are, such progress seems to put us back even further in our concern for the spiritual destiny of the human race.

It all serves to reinforce those who believe in God's Word that we are truly living in the Last Days.

Before we get further into the signs that point to the coming of the Lord, it is important that we understand the definition of the terms that we are going to discuss.

Very briefly, let's look again at the definitions so that you can understand the terms that we are discussing in succeeding chapters.

EXPLANATION OF TERMS USED IN THIS BOOK

Abomination of Desolation

A desecration of the temple of Israel by Antichrist. His final attempt to force the Jews to worship him (Matthew 24:15; II Thessalonians 2:3,4; Daniel 9:27).

Antichrist

A name taken from I and II John. In Daniel he is referred to as the little horn and the vile person; in II Thessalonians as the Son of Perdition; and in Revelation as the Beast out of the sea.

Satan so completely possesses the man as to amount almost to an incarnation. Scriptures appear to indicate that he, as Judas Iscariot, will become indwelt by Satan.

✓ Antichrist will oppose Christ, the saints, and the Jews. He will be first hailed as a Man of Peace and given unlimited power by the European countries, the United States and Israel. At his rise, Antichrist will be only a man, but with satanic power. His sudden, sensational rise as the saviour of a world threatened by destruction will be a mark of the beginning of the Time of the End.

His later attempt to annihilate the Jews will bring about his defeat at Jerusalem by the return of Christ. All prophecy up to the return of Christ will be fulfilled in his day.

The False Prophet

Antichrist will be the political ruler who will work the works of Satan. **The False Prophet** will be the religious ruler who will undergird the work of **Antichrist.** Both will get their power from Satan (Revelation 13:11-18; 16:13; 19:20).

The False Prophet never will attempt to promote himself. He will never become an object of worship. He will do the work of a prophet in that he directs attention away from himself to one who he says has the right to be worshipped (the Antichrist).

The False Prophet will imitate many miracles of God. He will cause fire to come down from heaven imitating the miracles of Elijah in order to convince the nation Israel that he (The False Prophet) is the Elijah whom Malachi promised was yet to come. Having achieved this deception the False Prophet will declare that since this miracle (bringing fire from heaven) shows that he is Elijah... then, therefore, the Antichrist is truly Christ and should be worshipped.

He will also build a statue and through some satanic method or miracle cause this statue (image) to talk and somehow come to life. When the people see this miracle they will fall down and worship the Antichrist believing him to be a Christ.

Mark of the Beast

During the second half of the seven year Tribulation Period the Antichrist (who previously was setting himself up as a Man of Peace) will suddenly move against the Jews and all those who have accepted Christ as Saviour during the first 3 1/2 years of this Period. In Revelation 13:16,17 we read that "...he (False Prophet) causeth all, both small and great, rich and poor, free and bond, to receive some mark in their right hand, or in their foreheads: And that no man might buy or sell, save he that had the mark..."

Therefore those who refuse to submit to the authority of this system by having this mark (the Mark of the Beast), either starve to death slowly, or else are slain by the representatives of the government, who will treat as traitors all who refuse to accept this identifying mark.

Rapture

This refers to the time, prior to the start of the 7 year Tribulation Period, when believing Christians (both dead and alive) will "in the twinkling of an eye" rise up to meet Christ in the air.

"...if we believe that Jesus died and rose again, so them also which sleep in Jesus will God bring with Him. For this we say unto you by the word of the Lord, that we which are alive and remain unto the coming of the Lord shall not precede them which are asleep.

For the Lord himself shall descend from Heaven with a shout...and the dead in Christ shall rise first: Then we which are alive and remain shall be caught up (RAPTURE) together with them in the clouds, to meet the Lord in the air: and so shall we ever be with the Lord" (I Thessalonians 4: 14-17).

The Saints

Those who accept Christ (in their heart) as both personal Saviour and Lord.

Truly, truly, I say to you, he who hears My word, and believes Him who sent Me, has eternal life, and does not come into judgment, but has passed out of death into life. (John 5:24).

For the wages of sin is death, but the free gift of God is eternal life in Christ Jesus our Lord. (Romans 6:23).

For by grace you have been saved through faith; and that not of yourselves, it is the gift of God; not as a result of works, that no one should boast. (Ephesians 2:8,9).

Blessed be the God and Father of our Lord Jesus Christ, who according to His great mercy has caused us to be born again to a living hope through the resurrection of Jesus Christ from the dead, to obtain an inheritance which is imperishable and undefiled and will not fade away, reserved in heaven for you. (I Peter 1:3,4).

Through the quoting of the above Scripture verses God's Word defines (a) how you can be a saint, (b) the rich promises that will be yours when you accept Christ as your personal Saviour, and (c) your eternal rewards in heaven.

Saved

The term "saved" and "born-again" are used interchangeably. In our terminology, one who is "saved" is one who has accepted Christ as His personal Saviour and is saved from an eternity in Hell and is assured of an eternity with Christ in Heaven.

In Acts 16:30,31 we read:

And after he brought them out, he said, "Sirs, what must I do to be saved?" And they said, Believe in the Lord Jesus, and you shall be saved, you and your household.

And the well known verses in John 3:16,17 tell us:

For God so loved the world, that He gave His only begotten Son, that whoever believes in Him should not perish, but have eternal life.

For God did not send His Son into the world to judge the world; but that the world should be saved through Him.

Second Coming of Christ

This is one of the most prominent doctrines in the Bible. In the New Testament alone it is referred to over 300 times. His first coming was over 1900 years ago when He came on earth to save man from sin. The Second Coming is an event starting at the Rapture and comprehending four phases: *First*, at the Rapture Christ takes the believers out of this world to be with Him (I Thessalonians 4). *Second*, Christ pours out His judgments on the world during the 7 year Tribulation Period. *Third*, Christ at the end of the 7 year Tribulation destroys the Antichrist and his wicked followers (Revelation 19). *Fourth*, Christ sets up His millennial Kingdom prophesied so often in the Old Testament (Matthew 25:31-46).

Tribulation

This is the term commonly given to the period also known as "Daniel's 70th Week" of years (Daniel 9:27). Precisely speaking, however, the Biblical period denoted by Jesus as that characterized by "Great Tribulation"[1] is the last half of this 7 years—from the Antichrist's committing the horrible Temple desecration called "the Abomination of Desolation" to Christ's coming to destroy the armies of Antichrist gathered in the Armageddon Valley (Esdraelon-Jezreel) of Israel.

This seven years will be a period of phenomenal world trial and suffering. It is at this time that Antichrist will reign over a federation of 10 nations which quite possibly could include the United States. See Daniel 9:27 and Matthew 24:15, 21.

OUR HOPE—CHRIST'S SECOND COMING

Behold, I tell you a mystery; we shall not all sleep, but we shall all be changed.

In a moment, in the atomas (atom age), in the twinkling of an eye, at the last trumpet; for the trumpet will sound, and the dead will be raised imperishable, and we shall be changed. (I Corinthians 15:51,52).

[1]Some scholars reserve the title "**Great Tribulation**" (Matthew 24:21), for only the latter half of this seven year period. During this latter half...the troubles of the period will reach their zenith.

An artist's conception of how the Rapture may occur. Some in your family may be left behind!

There are many mysteries found in the Scriptures. A "mystery" is a previously hidden truth, now divinely revealed in the Scriptures, but in which a supernatural element still remains even though we understand the revelation.

Full knowledge of every facet of God's word will not be revealed until we meet Christ and reign with Him. Therefore, the purpose of this book must be limited to the facts which we already know as revealed by Christ in His word.

He has told us that He will come again and that He will receive those who have accepted Him as their personal Saviour unto Himself.

> In My Father's house are many dwelling places; if it were not so, I would have told you; for I go to prepare a place for you.
>
> And if I go and prepare a place for you, I will come again, and receive you to Myself; that where I am, there you may be also. (John 14:2,3).

As you will see by the chart on page 160, the first step in God's future plan for man is the Rapture. This is when the dead in Christ will be raised and the living Christians will be caught up. You can read about this in I Thessalonians 4:16, 17.

Rapture is not a Bible word. It is an Old English word which means "to be caught up" such as I Thessalonians 4:17 declares will happen to the believer at Christ's Second Coming. He will be "caught up" (raptured) to be with Christ forever.

Christ tells us that when we see certain signs that we can be sure that the end will soon be coming to pass.

What are these signs as mentioned in the Bible?

FALSE CHRISTS

Mark 13 is a very important chapter. As you will recall. Christ was seated upon the Mount of Olives and His disciples asked Him privately "Tell us, when shall these things be? and what shall be the sign when all these things shall be fulfilled?"

> And Jesus began to say to them, "See to it that no one misleads you. (5)
>
> Many will come in My name, saying, 'I am He!' and will mislead many. (6)

There are many evidences of false Christs and false prophets in today's age.

In November, 1973, Maharaj Ji, the young Indian guru (whose followers say is God) ended a three-day event billed as "Millennium '73" at the Houston Astrodome. The guru sat atop a 14-foot-high flame shaped plexiglass throne as the scoreboard flashed verses indicating the Guru was the returned Messiah! He has since married and his mother disowned him, appointing another son as "Messiah."

The desire among many church leaders to form a United World Church is one of the most obvious examples of what Christ is talking about in verse 6 quoted on the previous page.

A few years ago in Dayton, Ohio, the Consultation on Church Union (COCU) met. The delegates were impatient at the progress of this Church Union and it was at this meeting that they drafted a plan by which the 25 million of COCU's 10 denominations can be merged into one Christian church. It is COCU's plan to merge whole denominations, property, governing boards, everything!

The idea began in 1962 with 4 denominations and has since grown to 10. It includes the Episcopal Church, the Methodist, United Church of Christ, United Presbyterian, Disciples of Christ, Evangelical United Brethren as well as others.

What in essence does this mean?

This Super Church will represent about 40% of American Protestants...and soon other denominations will be engulfed in its superstructure into one group with one governing board and one total property ownership. One of the aims of this Super Church is to establish dialogue with the Vatican with the end purpose of complete unity.

One can see that the puzzle is slowly falling in place with One Church, One Common Market, One World Government. What seemed impossible just 20 years ago is now rapidly coming into reality.

This church will compromise with the Scriptures and, in fact, rewrite the Scriptures to fulfill their own desires as to what the Bible should be. This is called the **Laodicean Church.** It is a church which is neither hot nor cold but attempts to be all things to all people and in Revelation 3:15-17 we read the following:

I know your deeds, that you are neither cold nor hot; I would that you were cold or hot. (15)

So because you are lukewarm, and neither hot nor cold, I will spit you out of My mouth. (16)

Because you say, "I am rich, and have become wealthy, and have need of nothing," and you do not know that you are wretched and miserable and poor and blind and naked. (17)

WARS, EARTHQUAKES, FAMINES

Another sign of the Coming of Christ is the sign of wars, earthquakes and famines.

Christ says in Luke 21:9 that you will hear of wars and rumors of wars. He tells us not to be terrified for these things must come to pass before the Lord comes. He then goes on to say in verse 10 and 11 the following:

> Then He continued by saying to them, "Nation will rise against nation, and kingdom against kingdom. (10)
>
> And there will be great earthquakes, and in various places plagues and famines; and there will be terrors and great signs from heaven. (11)

In previous chapters we have discussed with you the signs of increased wars and more complex wars, the evidences of famine and the dire consequences which come with an exploding population. And it is not unusual to read in the paper regarding news of tremendous earthquakes.

Let's look at earthquakes for a moment.

The recent devastating earthquakes have once again called to attention how deadly these events are and how helpless we are to combat them.

In this century alone ONE MILLION PEOPLE have died in earthquakes and their attendant floods, fires and famines. And more than 50,000 of these deaths have occurred in this decade with Iran the victim three times. Man has often strived to prevent this holocaust but without success.

In February, 1971 an earthquake struck the Los Angeles area resulting in the death of 64 people. Yet Californians ignore the fact that they are perched on top of the San

A man, wrinkled with age, holds the body of a child killed in an earthquake that shook a village in North Iran. Workmen recovered the young victim from the debris of a crumbled house in the background. ". . . there shall be . . . earthquakes, in divers places . . . all these are the beginning of sorrows" (Matthew 24:7,8).

Andreas fault that could at any time bring death and disaster.

Scientists have two theories on the causes of earthquakes. One is that the earth is still cooling down from a molten state...the other is that it is expanding. But both seem to agree that there is about 1000 tons per square inch—280 miles below the surface—which is constantly bearing on the earth's thin crust.

Most earthquakes have been confined to two main zones. One zone runs from New Zealand up through the Philippines and Japan to Alaska then down the Pacific coast of America. The other zone stretches from Morocco through Greece and Iran along the Indian side of the Himalayas and south to Java.

The worst known earthquake happened in China in January, 1556 when an estimated 830,000 people died. Other big-killer quakes this century: Japan, 1923, 150,000 dead and $2400 MILLION worth of damage. Chile, 1930, 20,000 dead. Turkey, 1940, 30,000 dead.

What does this mean: One of the first recorded earthquakes is described in I Kings 19:11,12. And one of the most remarkable is spoken about in Zechariah 14:5. Another memorable one occurred at the time of our Saviour's crucifixion (Matthew 27:51). Earthquakes are revealed with the introduction of the seven trumpets in Revelation. Earthquakes serve to remind us that God is still on the throne. They also reveal man's utter helplessness and should awaken him to his need of the Saviour.

This is very clearly outlined in Luke 21:25-28 which reads as follows:

> *And there will be signs in sun and moon and stars, and upon the earth dismay among nations, in perplexity at the roaring of the sea and the waves. (25)*
>
> *Men fainting from fear and the expectation of the things which are coming upon the world; for the powers of the heavens will be shaken. (26)*
>
> *And then will they see the Son of Man coming in a cloud with power and great glory. (27)*
>
> *But when these things begin to take place,*

JUDGMENT DAYS

REWARD JUDGMENTS FOR BELIEVERS

INCORRUPTIBLE CROWN (Victor's Crown)
". . . every man that striveth for the mastery is temperate in all things . . . they do it to obtain a corruptible crown; we an INCORRUPTIBLE." (I Corinthians 9:25)

CROWN OF REJOICING (Soul Winner's Crown)
". . . what is our hope . . . or crown of rejoicing? Are not even ye in the presence of our Lord Jesus Christ at His coming? For ye are our glory and joy." (I Thessalonians 2:19, 20)

CROWN OF RIGHTEOUSNESS
"Henceforth there is laid up for me a crown of righteousness, which the Lord, the righteous judge, shall give me at that day: and not to me only, but unto all them also that love His appearing." (II Timothy 4:8)

CROWN OF GLORY (Crown for Service)
"Feed the flock of God which is among you . . . (be) examples to the flock . . . And when the chief Shepherd shall appear, ye shall receive a crown of glory that fadeth not away." (I Peter 5:2-4)

CROWN OF LIFE (Martyr's Crown)
". . . the devil shall cast some of you into prison, that ye may be tried . . . be thou faithful unto death, and I will give thee a crown of life." (Revelation 2:10)

"Every man's work shall be made manifest . . . because it shall be revealed by fire . . . if any man's work abide . . . he shall receive a reward . . . if any man's work shall be burned, he shall suffer loss: but he himself shall be saved; yet so as by fire." (I Corinthians 3:13-15)

GOLD	
SILVER	PRECIOUS STONES

WOOD HAY STUBBLE

RAPTURE
BELIEVERS meet CHRIST in the air

1000 YEAR MILLENNIUM

JUDGMENT OF UNBELIEVERS

BOOK OF LIFE

THE BOOKS OPENED

"And whosoever was not found written in the book of life was cast into the Lake of Fire." (Rev. 20:15)

". . . the tares are the children of the wicked one. The enemy that sowed them is the devil: the harvest is the end of the world; and the reapers are the angels. As therefore the tares are gathered and burned in the fire; so shall it be in the end of this world." (Matthew 13:38-40)

LAKE OF FIRE

*straighten up and lift up your heads, because
your redemption is drawing near. (28)*

Never before has man had the power to utterly destroy the
human race.

And this is quite prophetically spoken about in Matthew
24:21,22 which reads.

*For then there will be a great tribulation, such as
has not occurred since the beginning of the world
until now, nor ever shall. (21)*

*And unless those days had been cut short, no life
would have been saved; but for the sake of the
elect those days shall be cut short. (22)*

Here Christ is telling us that unless these days be shortened
—then man, chiefly through his own creative powers, will
kill off all civilization.

And this is all summed up in Luke 21:28 which tells us:

*But when these things begin to take place,
straighten up and lift up your heads, because
your redemption is drawing near. (28)*

While these signs have occurred in other days at other
times, and while there has always been wars, rumors of
wars, famines, pestilences, earthquakes and wickedness
...it is important to note that all of these signs have never
been present before at the same time with such intensity.

In the days in which we live, all these signs are now present
simultaneously.

That's why these words in Luke 21:28 are so significant
for our day and age for the Lord tells us that when these
things begin to come to pass, we are to look up for the day
of redemption draws nigh.

In I Thessalonians 4:15-17 we are given the order in which
the events at the Coming of Christ for His church will occur.

We are told:

The Lord Himself will descend from heaven.
The Lord will shout.
The Lord will allow the archangel to speak.
He will blow a trumpet.
The dead in Christ will rise first.
The living believers will join the raised ones.

They will be reunited.
Then they will rise into the air.
They will meet the Lord.
They will remain ever with Him.

When this event does occur, every unbeliever will be left behind. Those unsaved dead (non-believers) will remain in the unseen world and they will not be raised until 1,000 years later. In the meantime, they will be in constant torment.

And the living unbelievers will remain on the earth to face the wrath of God. We will discuss this portion of Scripture in a succeeding chapter.

It might be difficult for some to believe that the Lord will come again and take away the believers.

But in Acts 1:11 we read:

> And they also said, "Men of Galilee, why do you stand looking into the sky? This Jesus, who has been taken up from you into heaven, will come in just the same way as you have watched Him go into heaven." (11)

As you may recall, as Jesus' disciples stood on Mount Olivet with Him that He was taken away from them into heaven.

This was partial fulfillment of John 14:2 & 3 which reads:

> In My Father's house are many dwelling places; if it were not so, I would have told you; for I go to prepare a place for you. (2)

> And if I go and prepare a place for you, I will come again, and receive you to Myself; that where I am, there you may be also. (3)

THE SECOND COMING...HOW IT WILL OCCUR

The Rapture, which will occur when the saints of God are taken up into heaven to be with Christ, is a joyous event. It is termed the Second Coming of Christ.

However, this should not be confused with the latter phase of His Second Coming, which will be after the Tribulation Period.

There are actually two chief phases of the Second Coming of Christ. The primary phase of the Second Coming occurs before the Tribulation and is the lifting of the saints to

Christ in which they will disappear or vanish from the earth in "the twinkling of an eye."

The latter phase of the Second Coming when Christ appears to destroy the Antichrist, occurs *after* the seven year Tribulation Period which will be discussed in another chapter.

And while we stated that the Rapture is a joyous event— this latter phase of the Second Coming will be a terrible event when the Lord takes vengeance upon the ungodly and destroys the wicked.

If you happen to be on earth after the Rapture occurs, then this book will become very important to you. For it will be a blueprint of the events that will take place in the coming days and will reveal the trials and tribulations that you will face.

It will also show you how to rise above these trials triumphantly and be assured of eternal life.

Naturally, your first step should be to read the Bible and put it in a safe place where it will not be stolen or burned for this will become your most important possession and will be your key to eternal life.

For when the Rapture (or Second Coming of Christ) does come it will not only separate believers from unbelievers but it will separate husbands from wives, brothers from sisters, and friends from friends.

In just the twinkling of an eye you might discover that your wife is no longer there in the kitchen or you might call your husband's office and discover that he has suddenly disappeared.

You might be on a picnic with your children and in just an instant realize that they have simply vanished.

You might be driving down the road on a turnpike at 55 miles an hour and suddenly see 2 or 3 cars erratically hurtling down the highway, driverless.

You might be flying in an airplane when suddenly the pilot vanishes and the co-pilot has to take over the controls.

And quite possibly, you might be sitting in church on a Sunday morning and in a congregation of 500 people, suddenly 30, 40 or 50 people simply disappear from the audience and yet you and hundreds of others are still left on earth including the minister!

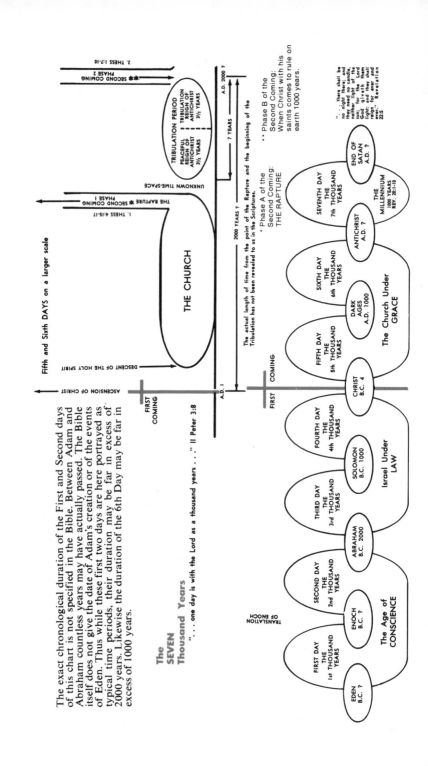

The exact chronological duration of the First and Second days of this chart is not specified in the Bible. Between Adam and Abraham countless years may have actually passed. The Bible itself does not give the date of Adam's creation or of the events of Eden. Thus while these first two days are here portrayed as typical time periods, their duration may be far in excess of 2000 years. Likewise the duration of the 6th Day may be far in excess of 1000 years.

The SEVEN Thousand Years

"... one day is with the Lord as a thousand years ..." II Peter 3:8

The actual length of time from the point of the Rapture and the beginning of the Tribulation has not been revealed to us in the Scriptures.

*Phase A of the Second Coming: THE RAPTURE

**Phase B of the Second Coming: When Christ with his saints comes to rule on earth 1000 years.

"... there shall be no night there, and they need no candle, neither light of the sun; for the Lord God giveth them light: and they shall reign for ever and ever." Revelation 22:5

Fifth and Sixth DAYS on a larger scale

2. THESS. 1:7-10

**SECOND COMING PHASE B

2. SECOND COMING PHASE 2

TRIBULATION PERIOD
PEACEFUL REIGN OF ANTICHRIST 3½ YEARS
TRIBULATION REIGN OF ANTICHRIST 3½ YEARS

A.D. 2000 ?

UNKNOWN TIME-SPACE

7 YEARS

THE RAPTURE *SECOND COMING* PHASE 1

1. THESS. 4:15-17

THE CHURCH

2000 YEARS ?

DESCENT OF THE HOLY SPIRIT

ASCENSION OF CHRIST

FIRST COMING

A.D. 1

FIRST COMING

EDEN B.C. ?

FIRST DAY THE 1st THOUSAND YEARS

TRANSLATION OF ENOCH

ENOCH B.C. ?

SECOND DAY THE 2nd THOUSAND YEARS

The Age of CONSCIENCE

ABRAHAM B.C. 2000

THIRD DAY THE 3rd THOUSAND YEARS

SOLOMON B.C. 1000

FOURTH DAY THE 4th THOUSAND YEARS

Israel Under LAW

CHRIST B.C. 4

FIFTH DAY THE 5th THOUSAND YEARS

DARK AGES A.D. 1000

SIXTH DAY THE 6th THOUSAND YEARS

The Church Under GRACE

ANTICHRIST A.D. ?

SEVENTH DAY THE 7th THOUSAND YEARS

THE MILLENNIUM 1000 YEARS REV. 20:1-10

END OF SATAN A.D. ?

This is the scene that will occur when Christ first comes back to earth to receive His saints unto Himself.

This is commonly known as the Rapture or the Second Coming of Christ.

So that you understand it more clearly, the First Coming of Christ occurred when Christ was born in Bethlehem some 1900 years ago.

The first phase of the Second Coming of Christ will occur at what is termed the Rapture, when Christ comes to meet born again believers in the air.

The latter phase of the Second Coming of Christ will actually occur AFTER the seven year Tribulation Period (i.e., seven years after the Rapture) in which Christ will come to reign on earth for a thousand years with His saints. From Revelation chapter 20 we do know that the length of the Millennium is one thousand years. As previously explained, Millennium is the time after the return of Christ when the saints reign with Christ. This Millennium period will occur immediately after the seven year Tribulation period.

THE SEVEN DAYS AND THE END OF THE WORLD

There are some that believe that the great week of human history is comprised of seven typical days—each day lasting a thousand years or more of *Recorded* Biblical history.

However, that this is true is NOWHERE taught in the Bible. It is a theory. The Bible is clear that no one knows when the Lord will come nor can they calculate it.

Nevertheless, it is interesting to note in II Peter 3:8 the following verse:

> But do not let this one fact escape your notice, beloved, that with the Lord one day is as a thousand years, and a thousand years as one day. (8)

Some people have termed this the time pattern for the great week of human history.

Following through on this belief, they state that the genealogical tables in the history of the Old Testament seem to *record* from Adam to Christ only about 4000 years of Biblical history, or 4 days (Since "one day with the Lord is as a thousand years...) II Peter 3:8. Countless years, however, may have stood between some of the ancients listed, and many believing Bible scholars such as B. B. Warfield were of this opinion. Nowhere does the Bible itself claim that 4000 years was the period between Adam and Christ.

The 5th day ended with the advent of the dark ages in 1000 A.D. (996 A.D. — since Christ was born at about 4 B.C.).

The 6th day then, according to this suggestion would end at about the year 1996. The Millennium would then be ushered in and the thousand year reign of the saints with Christ would begin.

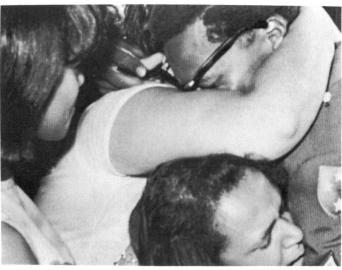

Soldier returns from dead. S/Sgt. James O. Williams is greeted by relatives as he arrived at airport in Detroit, Michigan on a 30-day leave. Williams' widowed mother had been notified by Army officers that her son had died in Vietnam. A telegram confirmed his death. But the next day Army authorities again called to report the Army had made a mistake.

What a wonderful reunion those who have accepted Christ as personal Saviour will have with their loved ones who have "gone ahead" from this earth. And what tragic sorrow and inexpressible grief awaits those who reject Christ. *"And whosoever was not found written in the book of life was cast into the lake of fire"* (*Revelation 20:15*).

If this assumption was correct, then the Rapture would take place at seven years before the Millennium. This would put the Rapture or the vanishing of the saints to meet Christ at approximately 1989.

However, nowhere in God's Word does He tell us the exact date in which He will return for the Rapture. In fact, He assures us that no mortal knows nor can any calculate this date (Matthew 24:36, 42)!

He does give us signs which we have discussed previously in this chapter.

In any event, Christ could come in 1985 or 1989 or 2010 **or some other date.**

This we do not know.

All we know is that the return of the Lord is imminent.

And that we should live as if we expected the return of the Lord at any moment—living expectantly.

Realizing this, how much more important it is for one to make sure that he has accepted Christ as his personal Saviour and to make sure that he knows he is saved from death unto life.

Noah labored for 120 years and yet only 7 other people heeded his call to repent and turn to the Lord. Only 8 persons actually believed God's message during that day.

If one would study the Old and New Testament Scriptures, he would find that there are more than 300 Scriptures which promise that Jesus will return to earth.

As the 200 Old Testament prophecies concerning Christ's virgin birth, death, burial and resurrection were fulfilled in His First Coming when He died for man's sins...So these prophecies of His Second Coming and the Great Tribulation will be fulfilled just as literally.

You will recall, we discussed earlier in this chapter that "As it was in the days of Noah, so shall it be in the days of the coming of the Son of man."

It is a sad fact to relate that a survey taken among leaders of America's largest Protestant denominations revealed that over one-third could not state they had a firm belief in God and over 40% did not believe that Jesus was divine.

One of these days the world will witness the event of the

vanishing of millions in the twinkling of an eye.

The dictionary has defined a twinkle as: "a split second action; quicker than a wink."

Just that quick, those who have accepted Christ and are alive will be caught up to meet Christ; but the dead who have accepted Christ will rise first and take part in this glorious Rapture.

In I Thessalonians 4:18 the Lord says: "Wherefore comfort one another with these words."

These words indeed, are a great comfort to those who are believers in Christ. However, they spell the beginning of great terror and tragedy for those who at this point are unbelievers and find themselves still remaining on earth.

It is to you that this book and this chapter are primarily written.

For it is my hope that you will come to know Jesus Christ as your personal Saviour and in knowing Him, will be assured of eternal life.

John 5:24 tells us:

> Truly, truly, I say to you, he who hears My word, and believes Him who sent Me, has eternal life, and does not come into judgment, but has passed out of death into life. (24)

The gospel of Christ is as simple as that. Those that believe in Him and accept Him as their personal Saviour will not come into condemnation but will pass from death unto life.

But to those who do not believe, their inheritance will be death and destruction into an everlasting hell.

It is sometimes difficult for one to imagine what will happen when the actual Rapture occurs when Christ brings His saints up from earth to meet Him in the air—prior to the seven years of tribulation for the non-believers.

Therefore, I have written the next chapter in novel form simply to show you how these things may occur to one individual.

Perhaps, in this novel form it can more graphically describe to you the vivid reality of these events.

6

I Saw The Saints Rise

Bill and I had just finished covering the Presidential conventions. And it was with a sigh of relief that we boarded our
flight in Chicago bound for the West Coast.

It seemed as though not a day passed without a major
news event and my job as a reporter on the Los Angeles
Times kept me running in circles.

There was always some cleric spouting words of peace
and some "funny people" sitting on top of mountains waiting for the destruction of the world.

One thing I hoped for and that was that my wife would
leave me alone and quit pestering me to attend church on
Sunday. It was my only day of peace . . . and I needed a rest
after those two political conventions.

As my eyes closed in a half sleep I could still hear her
saying, "George, come on, get up out of bed and come to
church with the children and me." And I would just turn
over and say, "Helen, leave me alone in peace, I see enough
hypocrites throughout the week."

And she would always reply, "All right, George, I'll leave you alone. There's a Bible by your bed and the bookmark's at I Corinthians chapter 15. Please read it and I'll see you at the Rapture."

That Helen could be a comic sometimes . . . I thought . . . half asleep . . . why is it every Sunday she had to hand me that same line . . . "I'll see you at the Rapture"? Did she really believe that stuff?

As our plane soared into the heavens and the sunlight came breaking through I glanced out over the fluffy white clouds below, stretched out in my seat, and while I slowly sipped a cocktail I mused to myself . . . Rapture . . . what a fairy tale. Why, as a reporter I knew the world was getting better and better . . . new advances in technology . . . heart transplants an|everyday occurrence . . . our first rocket ships had landed on the moon and there was talk of a regular commuter service. It looked like Pan American would get the first scheduled airline flights. Why, people were even living longer. At the medical convention I covered just a few days ago they had unveiled their first replacement bank of human parts. I remember viewing long cases of arms, legs, hearts, livers and kidneys. Doctors were talking about the success of their cancer replacement program . . . a program that made it possible to remove cancer ridden limbs and replace them with new ones from accident victims. And for the first time a serum for arresting cancer had proved 100% effective!

In my mind . . . there was no doubt about it. This old world was on the upswing. Why, even people were living longer. And there was talk of discarding old bodies and having brain transplants. This was the 21st century — not the Middle Ages. That's why I couldn't understand Helen's old fashioned concepts about God. She was one of the few I knew and her type of church was on the way out. Most churches had kept up with the times. But Helen's old church keeps singing, "The Old Rugged Cross" as though they really believed it.

I remember someone once saying . . . "in unity there is strength." And this country was sure getting unified. Helen was horrified but I was happy when I covered the United Church Fellowship. It was an

I know thy works, that thou art neither cold nor hot: I would thou wert cold or hot. So then because thou art lukewarm, and neither cold nor hot, I will spue thee out of my mouth. (Revelation 3:15,16).

historic occasion. Two very important things happened. The Protestants finally acquiesced on some silly old notions they had held on to and united with the Catholic church. And that's the way it should be. They now call it the CHURCH OF THE WORLD. Their theme was "Heaven on Earth for the World." It was a marvelous banner and a real thrill to see all the Protestant denomination leaders and all the Catholic leaders join hands on the platform singing their newly written hymn as the congregation of over 5000 clergy joined in . . .

Praise God from whom all blessings flow
God's in His heaven on earth below
Let men unite, cast out all fears
For heaven is earth for endless years!

It was a catchy tune and set the pace for the entire convention . . . and that tune spread like wildfire all over the world. Even the President adopted it as the official United States hymn in the interest of world-wide harmony. It was a brilliant gesture on his part!

The second great thing that happened at the United Church Fellowship in Rome was the election of a new world leader. And in one of the major news events of the year . . . a prominent statesman in the United States was elected honorary leader of the CHURCH OF THE WORLD. Brother Bartholomew was a dark horse. He seemed to rise up from nowhere . . . and I can't describe it . . . it was like magnetism. He had resolved the Arab-Israeli conflict and gave the Jews peace. And it was he who had almost single handedly stopped the war in China. The United States had been fighting them for 5 years and it seemed like another Vietnam.

Russia was just about ready to step in on the side of China. Brother Bartholomew secretly flew into China...and from what I heard miraculously cured Leader Chou from almost certain death. He walked unharmed through Shanghai. Some even said that he had given sight to the blind, hearing to the deaf and made crippled men walk straight.

And in the latter time of their Kingdom, when the transgressors are come to the full, a King of Fierce countenance, and understanding dark sentences, shall stand up. And his power shall be mighty, but not by his own power: and he shall destroy wonderfully, and shall prosper . . . (Daniel 8: 23,24).

China had never seen anything like it. And when he returned to the United States with a peace proposal in his hand—the Americans loved him—he could have asked for anything and got it!

And he did ask . . . and he did get it!

That's the only thing that bothers me. He seems so powerful . . . and yet as I've interviewed him . . . he seems so kind . . . so considerate . . . so dedicated to world peace which he says can only come about through a one world government.

Perhaps he may be right. Anyway he was kind enough to give me the exclusive story about his part in forming the Federated States of Europe and how he convinced our President to join the organization.

With that, the stewardess asked if I wanted another cocktail. I said no . . . which reminded me of dear old Helen again. To her, drinking was a sin. How can it be a sin . . . I reminded her . . . when the cocktail lounge at the United Church Fellowship Building was filled with high clerics all drinking. And all she would say was . . . "You'll see, George . . . just you wait . . . they're tools of the Devil."

How ridiculous I thought . . . but why argue with my wife.

It was then . . . as I was half daydreaming . . . that Bill asked me a funny question . . .

"George, do you believe in flying saucers?"

"In this modern day and age, Bill, do you still believe those fairy tales?"

Then we which are alive and remain shall be caught up together with them in the clouds, to meet the Lord in the air: and so shall we ever be with the Lord. (I Thessalonians 4:17).

"Well, not really, but I've never seen the heavens look so funny. Look way over there at that unusual formation of clouds."

"Bill, why don't you take a drink . . . maybe you'll see some more clouds!"

With that I left him to his cloud watching and I went back to my half-dozing day dreaming.

Brother Bartholomew was a man of action. And the people loved him. Our war with China, which he stopped, had seen over 250,000 of our prime young men killed in action. Oh . . . we killed over 2 million Chinese . . . but that seemed like a drop in the bucket.

So it was a real tribute to him and the United States when he was elected Honorary Leader of the CHURCH OF THE WORLD. The people were grateful. And the President in deference to his abilities had summoned us to the White House to make an announcement "of great import to the peace of the world."

I'll never forget that announcement as over 1000 reporters stood on the White House lawn on a warm, sunny day. The President was all smiles. Next to him was Brother Bartholomew. TV cameras were everywhere. This was the first time the WORLD NETWORK OF TELEVISION was telecasting. This was a new network that Brother Bartholomew had brought about. It was his belief that if all news media could be controlled to send out GOOD, then *evil* would not prevail and the world would understand each other and get better and better.

Now, why hadn't I thought of that idea? So far the Federated States of Europe had joined the WORLD NETWORK as well as the United States, Canada and South America.

And now the President was speaking:

> Ladies and Gentlemen . . . all of you know how hard I have worked for world peace. But there comes one far better than I who has achieved that which I thought would never be possible. The Bible tells us that faith can remove mountains. And with us today is one who I firmly believe is God's man for this hour—a Saint on earth—Brother Bartholomew. Through his good works he has demonstrated that he truly can remove mountains. I am happy to announce to you today that Brother Bartholomew has convinced both Russia and China to join the WORLD NETWORK of television and to work for mutual understanding of all nations. Because of his work in China in ending their war, and because I feel that the leaders of the world tomorrow will be leaders in God's church, I am directing to be built within the year a new 50 story WORLD CHURCH HEADQUARTERS building in the heart of Washington, D.C. on the Capitol grounds.

This was the most sensational news of the year! And the reporters scampered to their phones!

This convinced me that the world was getting better and better every day. I was going to really give it to Helen . . . tell her all about this fantastic new development . . . about world leaders finally recognizing God and asking a holy man to be the leader of the country . . . for the world. This was really heaven on earth . . . and I was witnessing it.

And for this cause God shall send them strong delusion, that they should believe a lie. (2 Thessalonians 2:11).

But I knew it—that day I rushed home to tell Helen the news first hand—you would think she would have been thrilled. Instead she just sat down on the couch and cried and kept repeating to me, "George, you just don't understand, you just don't understand. This is the beginning of the END!"

And I must confess, I didn't understand. How could anyone understand her and her Bible . . . especially Revelation with its trumpets and seals and horsemen . . . what a fairy tale!

How glad I was to be in on all this momentous news as it was happening—great advances in medicine, a cure for cancer, a united world church, a world leader appointed right from the United States and now a world church headquarters right in Washington, D.C.

Brother Bartholomew had confided to a few of us what his next project was and it seemed unbelievable . . . for no one thought that the Jews in Israel would ever find peace. They were constantly harrassed by enemies all around them. Russia threatened to bring their massive armies down and even their horsemen and swallow them up. It was like the perils of Egypt all over again. But over the doorway to Brother Bartholomew's office was something that was symbolic of his whole leadership.

> WORLD PEACE IS HEAVEN . . .
> WHERE PEACE ABIDES
> HEAVEN IS THERE ALSO

The turmoil of Israel was threatening world peace. And the Presidential conventions conveyed this element of unrest. It seemed that there was no suitable candidate in either party. Both parties appeared deadlocked.

Vote after vote was taken but no standard bearer was chosen. And then I remembered that grand old white haired man stand up at the Republican convention and given a standing ovation. He was one of the former leaders of the Presbyterian Church who was instrumental in bringing his church into the CHURCH OF THE WORLD at the Rome meetings.

"Gentlemen," he said, "It is evident that when man proposes, God disposes. I have watched man after man propose a leader for your party and for the Democratic party . . . and man has not succeeded.

May I be so bold to suggest that now God should have his way. Let's have a new UNITED CONVENTION of Democrats and Republicans and let's give God a chance. I move that we so do, and elect Brother Bartholomew as our DUAL representative as PRESIDENT of the United States and HONORARY HEAD of THE CHURCH OF THE WORLD!"

I'll never forget that day. The delegates went wild with excitement. And I was amazed as I watched them join hands and circle the auditorium singing ". . . let men unite, cast out all fears . . . for heaven is earth for endless years." And now that convention was over. Brother Bartholomew was elected unanimously. And I was going home. I almost missed the plane. These new supersonic jets carry 1000 people but I was the last one to get a seat. I was happy I had made the late afternoon flight. I would be home shortly. And I had a lot to tell Helen!

Just then Bill shouted excitedly, "George, look out that window . . . I tell you that's not just a cloud. I've never seen the sky so funny looking. It's as though it was opening up . . . George, IT IS OPENING UP . . . PEELING BACK LIKE A SCROLL . . . George, what's happening?"

And there shall be signs in the sun, and in the moon, and in the stars; and upon the earth distress of nations, with perplexity; with the sea and the waves roaring. (Luke 21:25)

He was shouting now . . . and I felt embarrassed. But I looked around and everyone in the plane was standing up and pointing with excitement.

And then it happened . . . Almost like a twinkling of an eye.

In a moment, in the twinkling of an eye . . . the dead shall be changed. (I Corinthians 15:52).

It seemed like the plane got much lighter . . . turned abruptly and went into a dive from 80,000 feet high.

I lost consciousness . . . I don't remember exactly what happened. There had been two stewardesses standing next to me; but when I awoke only one was there!

Then shall two be in the field; the one shall be taken, and the other left. Two women shall be grinding at the mill; the one shall be taken, and the other left. (Matthew 24: 40,41).

I picked her up off the floor and she rushed to the pilot's cabin. When she came out she was ashen white . . . and put her hand to her mouth to hold a scream.

Just then the intercom came on and we heard a voice . . .

"Ladies and Gentlemen . . . something rather unusual has happened. We are not sure what . . . but please be calm . . . everything is under control. Our pilot has vanished . . . perhaps some mysterious celestial illness. This caused the abrupt dive . . . but your co-pilot now has full control of the aircraft. Please keep your seatbelts fastened."

Why should that make the stewardess shout with fear . . . I wondered . . . and then I looked around me and she pointed with trembling hands . . .

"LOOK . . . " she screamed, "HALF OF THE PASSENGERS ARE MISSING!"

I'll never forget the chills that ran up and down my spine. HALF OF THE PASSENGERS ARE MISSING. It wasn't half . . . but it looked as though 100 or so just disappeared. And I turned to tell Bill.

BUT BILL WASN'T THERE!

And suddenly it came to me.

I WAS HERE!

When we landed, I rushed to my car. Crowds were collecting at the airport because many flights had been cancelled due to crew members not reporting for duty. I got on to the clogged highway . . . clogged with driverless cars . . . was the world going crazy? It seemed as if a multitude of sleepy drivers had all at once decided to stop no matter where they were. Most had pulled to the side of the road; but nowhere were any of these drivers to be seen. A train was halfway across a highway!

I just had to get home. Tears poured down my cheeks . . . and a cold sweat engulfed me.

I drove up the drive. Thank God, Helen's car was still there. She was home.

I rushed in the door and shouted, Honey I'm home . . . are you all right?"

No answer.

Again I shouted, "Helen, where are you? I'm home! Where are the children?"

No answer.

Frantically, I ran through every room shouting, "Helen, Helen!"

And my own voice came echoing back through the empty halls!

And then a voice of the past seemed to echo in my mind . . . "All right, George, I'll leave you alone. There's a Bible by your bed and the bookmark's at I Corinthians, chapter 15. Please read it and I'll see you at the Rapture."

For the Lord Himself shall descend from heaven with a shout, with the voice of the archangel, and with the trump of God: and the dead in Christ shall rise first: Then we which are alive and remain shall be caught up together with them in the clouds, to meet the Lord in the air: and so shall we ever be with the Lord. (I Thessalonians 4: 16,17).

"THE RAPTURE! That's it! This is the RAPTURE!

And my Helen and my children are gone!"

Quickly I ran into the bedroom and there it was—the Bible was still on the bedstand. I hurriedly opened it at the place of the bookmark.

Hurry, read, hurry, read. I must hurry. Why can't I read? The tears were flowing down my face. My eyes were so filled that the print seemed blurred . . . but I had to read what it said. Time was so precious. Why didn't I read this book before . . . when there was so much time. Why? Why?

Finally my eyes focused through the tears . . . and I read . . . I Corinthians 15:52,53.

"Behold, I show you a mystery; We shall not all sleep, but we shall be changed.

In a moment, in the twinkling of an eye, at the last trump; for the trumpet shall sound, and the dead

I got on to the clogged highway...clogged with driverless cars...was the world going crazy?...A train was halfway across a highway!

shall be raised incorruptible, and we shall be changed . . . . "

It must be true! It must be true! Everything Helen said must be true! That Bible . . . that talk about accepting Jesus Christ as personal Saviour . . . that talk of Christ dying on the cross for our sins . . . to give us eternal life . . . that talk of the Tribulation period. ALL OF IT MUST BE TRUE! I was hysterical, sobbing, kissing the picture of Helen. Then the phone rang!

That jangled, harsh ring jarred me from my hysteria. With a crying voice I answered it . . .

"Hello," I said.

"Hello, is this George?"

"Yes."

"George, this is Tom Malone at WORLD NETWORK TELEVISION. Brother Bartholomew has called a news conference for tomorrow in CHURCH OF THE WORLD Headquarters in Washington. He has some important peace moves to discuss and also will explain this weird disappearance of some heretics. I want you to be there to cover the story for us."

"OK, Tom, I'll be there. Goodbye."

And with a sigh of relief, I hung up.

The world was getting better and better. This so called Rapture must be a hoax. Why did I let myself get excited? This was God's way of punishing those who did not unite in a world church—that's why Helen disappeared and her following.

WHERE PEACE ABIDES . . .
HEAVEN IS THERE ALSO!   Revelation
Chapter 17

World peace was just around the corner.

I had many questions to ask Brother Bartholomew tomorrow.

But Brother Bartholomew would have the answers!

And that's all that mattered!   2 Thessalonians 2:1-12

IN CONCLUSION

The story you have just finished reading...I SAW THE SAINTS RISE...may appear to you to be a far-fetched novel.

> While this event has not yet happened...that is, the RAPTURE (the calling up of the Believers from earth to be with Christ), I SAW THE SAINTS RISE was written as though such an event had already occurred.

No one knows exactly how these events leading up to the Rapture will transpire. We do know that the Lord has given us certain signs to watch for...and these signs are already in evidence today.

Famine	**Luke 21:9**
Wars	**Matthew 24:6,7**
Union of Western Nations	
Union of Churches into one great Church	

And this story was written based on Scriptural promises of these Last Days. The BIBLE promises ETERNAL LIFE to all who receive Christ:

> *And the witness is this, that God has given us eternal life, and this life is in His Son.*

> *He who has the Son has the life; he who does not have the Son of God does not have the life.*

> *These things I have written to you who believe in the name of the Son of God, in order that you may know that you have eternal life. (I John 5: 11-13).*

> *For the wages of sin is death, but the free gift of God is eternal life in Christ Jesus our Lord. (Romans 6:23).*

While there is still time...
you have one choice to make...

> DEATH by rejecting Christ   **2 Thessalonians 2:11**
> LIFE by accepting Christ as your personal Saviour.

I pray you will choose LIFE!

I SAW THE SAINTS RISE is the
first chapter of a novel entitled **666.**

7
Antichrist

THE MAN OF PEACE
WHOSE AIMS ARE DESTRUCTION

His Character, A Friend to the Jew and Gentile • His First
Move • The Reign of Antichrist • The Sequence of Events
• Who is Antichrist

One of these days some great leader, admired by the world
as a man of peace will settle the Arab-Israeli dispute.

Watch out when this event happens. For this man may be
what the Scriptures term the Antichrist.

And his sweet words of peace will soon lead to the most
devastating seven years of terror, trials, and murders.

The Antichrist is a part of the Satanic Trinity just as Christ
is part of the Heavenly Trinity.

The Philadelphia Inquirer

Vol. 299, No. 81   60°   © 1978, The Philadelphia Inquirer   Monday, September 18, 1978   15 CENTS

Mideast Agreement Reached;
Israeli Withdrawals Planned

Egyptian minister resigns

By James McCartney
Inquirer Washington Bureau

WASHINGTON — Egypt and Israel
signed agreements last night out-
lining a framework for a Mideast
peace that would end their 30 years
of bloodshed.

In a dramatic breakthrough, President Anwar Sadat of Egypt, Prime
Minister Menachem Begin of Israel
and President Carter signed the documents at 10:30 p.m. before a joyous audience in the East Room of
the White House.

The nationally televised ceremony
was a sudden climax to 12 days of
secret, and evidently contentious,
Camp David summit meetings.

By one account early this morning,
Egypt's foreign minister, Mohammed Ibrahim Kamel, resigned after
Sadat agreed to concessions embod-
ied in the agreement.

The docu-

President Carter met for 12 days of secret negotiations with Israeli
Prime Minister Menachem Begin and Egyptian President Anwar
Sadat at Camp David, Maryland. The President astounded the world
by announcing a Mideast peace agreement . . . something no one else
had been able to accomplish. The agreement, reached on Sunday, September 17, 1978, was formally announced to Congress Monday evening, September 18. Most of the Arab bloc refused to honor this agreement.

Just as the Heavenly Trinity is made up of the:
1. Father
2. Son
3. Holy Spirit,

so likewise in the counterfeit Trinity the members are:

1. **Satan**—He is sometimes referred in the Scriptures as the Dragon and is known as anti-God. He imitates the work of God the Father (Revelation 12:9, 20:2).

2. **Antichrist**—He is sometimes referred in the Scriptures as the Beast. Antichrist imitates the work of God the Son (Revelation 13:1; 19:20).

3. **The False Prophet**—He is sometimes referred in the Scriptures as the Second Beast, The False Prophet imitates the work of God the Holy Spirit (Revelation 13:11; 19:20).

The word Antichrist means an enemy of Christ or one who usurps Christ's name and authority.

As you may recall, 2 Thessalonians 2:1-12 refers to the Antichrist as "that man of sin" and states that he will oppose and exalt himself above God and will actually sit in the temple of God and claim to be God.

Both the Antichrist and the False Prophet will be living during what is termed as the Tribulation Period.

This Tribulation Period will last for seven years. The second 3½ years especially will be filled with terror, death and destruction.

The False Prophet however, does not try to promote himself and should not be confused with the Antichrist.

The False Prophet never becomes an object of worship. He does the work of a prophet by directing attention away from himself and towards the Antichrist who he says has the right to be worshipped.

Both the Antichrist and the False Prophet are tools in the hands of Satan and their every move will be guided by Satan.

It is quite interesting to note that Jesus Christ in John 5:43 made a prophetic reference to the Antichrist:

> I have come in My Father's name, and you do not receive Me; if another shall come in his own name, you will receive him.

It is also sad to reflect that the Jews rejected Jesus Christ as their Messiah—but when the Antichrist comes they will be deceived by him and accept him and welcome him with open arms as their king and saviour.

In Daniel 11:36,37 we are told that the Antichrist will "...exalt himself, and magnify himself above every god...."

And in 2 Thessalonians 2:4 it is revealed, "...so that he as God sitteth in the temple of God, shewing himself that he is God."

Note the comparisons between Antichrist and Christ.

In the comparison in the chart shown on the succeeding page, we find that the Antichrist is not merely a rival of Christ, but he actually opposes Christ.

The chart on the following page clearly shows the striking contrast between the two.

There are indications in the Bible that Antichrist will become popular because of the prevailing lawlessness that occurs throughout the world and his supposed ability to resolve world problems.

HIS CHARACTER (Revelation 13)
A FRIEND TO THE JEW AND GENTILE

Antichrist will be an extremely popular individual. He will pose as a great humanitarian and the friend of men. He will appear to be a very special friend to the Jewish race. There is no doubt from the Scriptures that he will persuade the Jews that he has come to usher in the golden age for the Jewish race. In light of this they will receive him as their Messiah.

One might say that he is a "composite man" who will have an irresistible personality. Because of his versatile accomplishments, super-human wisdom, and great administrative and executive ability he will be looked upon with favor by all of the world leaders and populace.

Along with his powers as a brilliant diplomat he will be a superb strategist in the art of war.

Keep in mind that this Antichrist will come into prominence during the Tribulation Period. At the moment of the Rapture, there will not be left one single believer on this earth. So basically at the beginning of the Tribulation Period,

CHRIST

ANTICHRIST

Christ came from **Above.**
John 6:38.

Antichrist ascends from **The Pit.**
Revelation 11:7.

Christ came in His **Father's** name.
John 5:43.

Antichrist comes in his **Own** name.
John 5:43.

Christ **Humbled** Himself. Phil. 2:8

Antichrist **Exalts** himself.
2 Thessalonians 2:4.

Christ **Despised.**
Isaiah 53:3; Luke 23:18.

Antichrist **Admired.** Rev. 13:3, 4.

Christ **Exalted.**   Philippians 2:9.

Antichrist **Cast Down to Hell.**
Isaiah 14:14, 15; Rev. 19:20.

Christ to do His **Father's** will.
John 6:38.

Antichrist to do His **Own** will.
Daniel 11:36.

Christ came to **Save.**   Luke 19:10.

Antichrist comes to **Destroy.**
Daniel 8:24.

Christ is the **Good Shepherd.**
John 10:4-15.

Antichrist, the **Idol** (evil) Shepherd.
Zechariah 11:16, 17.

Christ is the **"True Vine."**
John 15:1.

Antichrist, the **"Vine of the Earth."**
Revelation 14:18.

Christ is the **"Truth."** John 14:6.

Antichrist is the **"Lie"**
2 Thessalonians 2:11.

Christ, the **"Holy One."**
Mark 1:24.

Antichrist is the **"Lawless One."**
2 Thessalonians 2:8, A.S.V.

Christ is the **"Man of Sorrows."**
Isaiah 53:3.

Antichrist is the **"Man of Sin."**
2 Thessalonians 2:3.

Christ is the **"Son of God."**
Luke 1:35.

Antichrist is the **"Son of Perdition."**
2 Thessalonians 2:3.

Christ, **"The Mystery of Godliness,"** is **God** manifest in the flesh.
1 Timothy 3:16.

Antichrist, **"The Mystery of Iniquity,"** will be **Satan** manifest in the flesh.
2 Thessalonians 2:7.

everyone on the earth will be an unbeliever and look to this Antichrist with great fascination and believe that he offers the world life-saving salvation.

One thing is certain from the many references found regarding the Antichrist in the Scriptures: He will be a counterfeit and a clever imitation of a true Christ.

His rise will be sudden.

This also will be an imitation of Christ.

You will recall that Christ for 30 years remained in obscurity in his home in Nazareth and the silence of those years is broken only once in Luke 2.

Comparatively, the Antichrist will also remain in obscurity and then suddenly his rise will be brought into prominence. He may even now be in the world and preparing for his Satan-directed work.

It is interesting that Jeanne Dixon predicted on several TV programs that a great man of peace was recently born in the Middle East who will come into prominence and have a great influence on this world.

Does it take a seer to make such a prediction? All one has to do is read the prophetic words in the Scripture and compare them with our times and it becomes very evident that the time is right for the Antichrist to be soon appearing.

HE PROMISES PEACE

As was stated before, undoubtedly one of the elements of his marvelous success in gaining the hearts of the people lies in the fact that he will come promising the very thing that is uppermost in the hearts of people all over the world today: PEACE!

Never before in history has the world been so sick of war. Several years ago the President of the United States actually announced his intention not to run and virtually abdicated his position almost a year before the end of his term.

So divided was the United States on the issues of war that this move by the late President Johnson seemed to be the only answer in his desire to heal the nation split over issues of war and peace.

One could imagine how extremely popular and what wide acclaim an individual would receive if he could deliver

---

IN EXPLANATION

1. "NOW IS THE DAY OF SALVATION" and no one should wait. The Bible does not encourage anyone to wait. Nevertheless, some disobediently do wait, and by God's grace get saved on the next day—or week—or year. This in no way detracts from God's command that all should turn to Him today. "Now is the Day of Salvation" (2 Corinthians 6:2), for the Scriptures make it clear that our life is like a vapor that vanishes away and for us tomorrow may never come (James 4:13-15).

2. A "Second Chance"? We deny that there is any "Second Chance" after death. Death, then the judgment. After Armageddon, at the Judgment of Matthew 25:31-46—when all the surviving people of the world (alive after the Tribulation) are gathered, there is no hint of a "second chance."

   At the Judgment of the Great White Throne, after the Millennium (Revelation 20), there is no Second Chance.

   However, after the Rapture (1 Thessalonians 4:13-18), those who are *not* taken up with Jesus are *still* alive on earth. They live into the *awful* Tribulation years—and many who live into this period will indeed turn to Christ (Revelation 7:13-14*).

   The vast majority of those who live past the Rapture will follow the Antichrist and *remain* lost (Revelation 13:7-8).

   Those, however, who do turn to Christ at this time will be saved (Revelation 7).

   No "Second Chance"—as long as you live you are still on that "First Chance."

*The Greek of Revelation 7:14 says that these have come out of "the Great Tribulation." Although not reflected in the King James Version translation, the definite article "the" is present in the Greek text.

---

peace to the world and resolve the great issues of the world.

This man, in the person of Antichrist, will accomplish this very thing...but what most people do not realize is that this accomplishment will be only for a little season—and then the very gates of Hell will break loose here on earth.

HIS FIRST MOVE

One of the first moves of the Antichrist will be to gain the confidence of the Jewish people and others by his diplomatically settling the then explosive Middle East situation.

Therefore, his first attempt is to gain the favor of the Jewish people.

After accomplishing this, he will help the Jewish people immeasurably in returning many of them to the land of Israel and he will show them many favors.

Actually the Tribulation Period will begin with a public appearance of Antichrist when he participates in the making of a significant seven year Middle East peace pact (Daniel 9:27). At this time, however, he will not yet be recognized as the Antichrist. This recognition awaits another 3½ years (Matthew 24:15).

This individual will eventually be the head of what may be known as the Federated States of Europe. As the head of this organization, he would be able to exert great authority and power by attempting to settle the Arab-Israeli dispute.

The Scriptures tell us that he will side with Israel in backing her claim to the land of Palestine.

Russia will be a part of a northern confederacy and will back the Arab's claim to Palestine.

The following verses in 2 Thessalonians 2 and Ezekiel 38 exhibit this prophecy.

> And then that lawless one will be revealed whom the Lord will slay with the breath of His mouth and bring to an end by the appearance of His coming;
>
> That is, the one whose coming is in accord with the activity of Satan, with all power and signs and false wonders. (2 Thessalonians 2:8,9)
>
> And you will come from your place out of the remote parts of the north, you and many peoples with you, all of them riding on horses, a great assembly and a mighty army;
>
> And you will come up against My people Israel like a cloud to cover the land. It will come about in the last days that I shall bring you against My land, in order that the nations may know Me

> *when I shall be sanctified through you before their eyes, O God.*
>
> *And in My zeal and in My blazing wrath I declare that on that day there will surely be a great earthquake in the land of Israel. (Ezekiel 38:15,16,19).*

It is estimated today that there are some 3.2 million Jews living in Israel.

To some extent they are reviving many of their distinctive historic features and customs. However, surveys show that the religious faith of the vast majority of Jews is neither Biblical Judaism nor Christianity.

Most of them hold to a liberalized Judaism religion and some of them, as in the case of so many of today's population, are even atheists.

There are very few Jews in Israel who accept Jesus Christ as the true Messiah or look to God literally to fulfill Old Testament prophecies.

In spite of this, however, they still look upon the land of Palestine as the country of great promise for them.

Why would Russia want to invade Palestine or Israel?

Scientists have discovered that all of the manufactured goods, fruits and vegetables exported from this land of Israel are nothing in comparison with the mineral wealth of the Dead Sea.

Since the days of Abraham which were four thousands of years ago, God has been pouring into this mysterious sea a fabulous amount of wealth in the form of mineral salts.

Only with the return of the Jews to this land, have attempts been made to discover the mineral content of the Dead Sea. The analysis shows that the value of the chemicals in the Dead Sea is $1,270,000,000,000. It is believed that this staggering sum is equal to the combined wealth of the United States, Great Britain, France, Germany and Italy.

THE REIGN OF ANTICHRIST

As we stated before, the Antichrist will reign seven years. This is the length of the Tribulation Period. He will be President of the 10 Federated Nations. These nations may be known as the Federated States of Europe.

While it is true that at present the great problem facing

the Western powers today is the problem of trying to bring together, under the same head, nations that were originally part of the same Roman Empire...this problem will be erased in the near future.

The 10 Federated States of Europe will probably include France, England and Germany (possibly West Germany) as well as lesser countries, and perhaps the United States.

The prophecy is revealed in Revelation 17:12-13, which shows that these nations that were once a part of the Roman Empire will gather together and are going to enter into an agreement to give their authority to one man as their head (Daniel 7:7-8,23-26 Cp. Revelation 13).

This one man will be the Antichrist.

We already see evidences of this unification movement beginning. We see it in the common market which is already in existence in Europe. We see it in the trend of religious denominations to unify as One World Church. We see it in the light of several proposals for a world monetary system as the solution for the gold crisis and the recommendation that a world banker be appointed to control all the gold and all the silver.

We also see it in the proposals made by the U.N. Secretary General for a world wide redistribution of the wealth through a United Nations graduated income tax.

In an alliance against this combined Federated States of Europe will be a Federation of Northern States, the greatest of which will be Russia.

THE SEQUENCE OF EVENTS

Now let's look at the sequence of the events. When does all of this take place?

The Antichrist will make this covenant with the nation Israel at the very beginning of the Tribulation Period. He will come claiming to be the great man of peace and he will guarantee peace for Israel. He appears to make a seven year peace pact involving Israel which he then proceeds to honor for the first 3½ years of the Tribulation (Daniel 9:27).

After the Antichrist as head of the Federated States of Europe gives the land of Palestine to Israel, Russia will start her forces working to overtake this land. Behind the scenes maneuvering will probably take between 2 and 3 years during the first 3½ year segment of this Tribulation Period.

It is the Author's opinion that Palestine will be invaded by Russia and her allies, and this invasion, it seems, will take place somewhere at or near the middle of the Tribulation Period. The exact time of this invasion, however, is not clearly revealed in Scripture—except that it will certainly be in the latter days (Ezekiel 38:8,16).

Further details on this event will be covered in a succeeding chapter entitled THE DAY RUSSIA DIES.

WHO IS ANTICHRIST

There have been many views expounded on exactly who Antichrist will be.

However, it is important to keep in mind that Antichrist will not be revealed until after the Rapture (when the saints rise to meet Christ in the air). This revelation will not be made until those who believe in Christ are first taken up from the earth. You read about this in the chapter called THE VANISHING CHRISTIANS.

After the Christians are taken up from earth to meet Christ at the Rapture—then the person of Antichrist will be identified and revealed. There have been some theologians who believe that the Antichrist will be Judas Iscariot, who was the betrayer of Jesus. He will at least be like Judas because he, like Judas, shall become Satan indwelt.

This much we do know, that he will be the master statesman of all the ages and will be the political head of the restored Roman Empire which will be a revived Federated States of Europe.

There is some indication in Scripture that the Antichrist may be active on the world scene even before the Tribulation Period begins. This is based on 2 Thessalonians 2:3:

> Let no one in any way deceive you, for it will not come unless the apostasy comes first, and the man of lawlessness is revealed, the son of destruction. (3)

Then in verse 8 of the same chapter we read:

> And then that lawless one will be revealed whom the Lord will slay with the breath of His mouth and bring to an end by the appearance of His coming. (8)

"But of the times and the seasons, brethren, ye have no need that I write unto you. For yourselves know perfectly that the day of the Lord (the awful Tribulation Period — preceded by the Rapture of believers to meet Christ) so cometh as a thief in the night. For when they shall say, Peace and safety; then sudden destruction cometh upon them (the unbelievers) . . . and they shall not escape" (1 Thessalonians 5:2,3).

From this it would appear that the Antichrist may be known to us (but not identifiable as Antichrist) before the Rapture occurs.

However, this is important. While his *identity* may be made known at this time; his real, diabolical, Satanic *character* is revealed in the middle of the Tribulation, when he demands a type of worship which can only rightly be given unto God.

It was not God's purpose to reveal everything to us in this day and age.

Some Bible scholars believe that Antichrist, taking advantage of the unsettled conditions in the Middle East, will establish himself as the ruler of Iraq, the land upon which the ancient city of Babylon once stood.

In time he will attack and subdue three member states of the Mediterranean Confederacy which from then on will be ruled by Iraq as the center of this newly acquired empire.

This would make the prophetic "Babylon" of Revelation 17 and 18 literally Babylon Rebuilt. You will recall that Babylon was the center of the nations' first rebellion against God as recorded in the Tower of Babel episode in Genesis.

What about his religion? Religiously, he will deny all authority but his own authority. He is called in Scriptures — The Lawless One.

The October, 1973 "Yom Kippur" War in the Middle East brought new problems to the world unleashing an avalanche of events that are drawing us even closer to the time of the Rapture.

The fourth Arab-Israeli war since the foundation of the Jewish state in 1948 spawned a host of perils. Not only did the combatants pay a fearsome price in blood and treasure but the conflict drew the United States and Russia into a near confrontation.

The United States, torn between whether it should support the Arab nations or Israel ... sided finally with Israel. Promptly the Arab nations stopped the flow of oil to the United States.

This sparked the famous November 7, 1973 Energy Crisis speech by President Richard Nixon. Gas stations were ordered closed on Sundays, a 55-mile per hour speed limit was enforced nationally.

"Spy on your Neighbor" programs began to rear their ugly head as some States suggested phoning a Complaint Center for those who waste energy.

Christmas tree lights were dimmed. Churches cancelled Christmas eve services. The nation and the world suddenly were caught in the mass hysteria of world trials...while a courier of peace, Henry Kissinger, flew furiously back and forth to China, to Russia and to Brussels and Geneva striving to restore peace.

These events are a prelude and a prototype of the chaos that will occur during the initial reign of Antichrist.

Time will certainly reveal the answers to these questions.

The important thing for the reader to know is not necessarily who Antichrist is but to recognize his need for the Saviour and to accept Jesus Christ as his personal Saviour and Lord.

If however, this is not done—you will recognize the Antichrist by the description we have given and by what he will do when he does come.

God alone can give genuine peace. Jesus is known as the Prince of Peace. Antichrist will try to take over this role and produce a so-called heaven on earth.

We will see the world become very enthusiastic about his reign and indeed some very marvelous things will be produced at that time. Great new cities will be built and science will make startling discoveries. Already, through heart transplants we have seen some of these modern day miracles take place.

This will be an era in which man will be exalted to the skies but in Obadiah 1:4 the Lord promises:

> Though you build high like the eagle,
> Though you set your nest among the stars,
> From there I will bring you down," declares the
>   Lord. (4)

If you live during the reign of Antichrist...don't be fooled by his message of peace...for his main purpose is to bring a reign of death and destruction.

8

The False Prophet Miracle Worker and Executioner

The Religious System of the End Times • He Imitates Elijah • The Rebirth of Jerusalem • Brings a Dead Man Back to Life • Their Day of Judgment to Come

You will recall in the previous chapter, we discussed the Satanic Trinity of which Antichrist was referred in the Scriptures as the Beast, and Satan was referred in the Scriptures as the Dragon.

We also find the **False Prophet** who is identified in the Scriptures as the **Second Beast.**

The False Prophet will cooperate traitorously with the Antichrist. They are *two distinct different individuals.*

The Antichrist will probably be known by the title of King or President and rule over the entire 10 Federated States of Europe. He will also exalt himself and claim to be this world's deity.

Now here is the difference!

The False Prophet will not be a King. He will not exalt himself as a King.

The False Prophet will not try to promote himself, nor will he ever become an object of worship.

Saturday night, November 18, 1978, self-styled Messiah, Jim Jones, led hundreds of followers in Jonestown, Guyana, in a suicide cult of death. Men, women and children drank a strawberry Flavour-aide that was mixed with painkillers, tranquilizers and cyanide. Initial reports indicated that some 300 had committed suicide. But when U.S. soldiers finally tallied the stacks of bodies piled atop each other at the campsite, the total count soared over 900! Jones, a false prophet, headed the People's Temple in San Francisco. It was reported assets turned over to him by his followers totaled over $7 Million.

This tragedy equalled the mass suicide of Jewish Zealots who defended the fortress of Masada against besieging Roman legions in 73 A.D. Here 960 men, women and children died in self-slaughter; however, for a righteous cause. Events such as the Jonestown cult suicide may eventually cause a backlash against any faith that is not within the "conventional, organized religions" of denominations in the World Council of Churches. This will bring on persecution of Bible believers and the rise of the False Prophet during the Tribulation Period.

Actually the False Prophet will do the work of a prophet, in that he directs attention away from himself to one who he says has the right to be worshipped, and that one will be the Antichrist.

To redefine what we have previously said: **Satan** imitates the work of God the Father; the **Antichrist** imitates the work of the Son in subjecting the world to himself; and **the False Prophet** imitates the work of the Holy Spirit in magnifying the False King (the Antichrist) who will reign on the world's throne.

Three times in the book of Revelation the False Prophet is mentioned by name.

> And I saw coming out of the mouth of the dragon and out of the mouth of the beast and out of the mouth of the false prophet, three unclean spirits like frogs. (Revelation 16:13)

> And the beast was seized, and with him the false prophet who performed the signs in his presence, by which he deceived those who had received the mark of the beast and those who worshiped his image; these two were thrown alive into the lake of fire which burns with brimstone. (Revelation 19:20).

> And the devil who deceived them was thrown into the lake of fire and brimstone, where the beast and the false prophet are also; and they will be tormented day and night forever and ever. (Revelation 20:10).

You will note that twice the False Prompet is associated with the Antichrist and once he is associated with Satan. Note also their final doom in the last Scripture verse quoted above.

THE RELIGIOUS SYSTEM OF THE END TIMES

When the 10 kings surrender all their mighty power into the hands of one man (Antichrist; Rev. 17:12,13), there must be a most compelling reason. The reason will be, that, within the confines of what was once the Roman Empire, a belief in God and a form of religion will still prevail. And a religious system, typified by "the great harlot" of Revelation 17, will dominate this federation and its head.

Perhaps partially to save this religious system, the ten nations will clash with Russia, and give power to the Beast (Antichrist) to be their leader. Revelation, chapter 17 is a very important chapter for here you will read a complete description of the religious system of the end-time. Eventually, at the middle of the 7 year Tribulation period, the False Prophet and the Antichrist turn against the religious system called The Great Harlot and "they destroy it" (Revelation 17:16). From hence forth all worship will be directed by the False Prophet towards the Antichrist alone!

HE IMITATES ELIJAH

Just for a moment, let's turn in the Bible to 2 Kings 1:10 where we read:

> And Elijah answered and said to the captain of fifty, "If I am a man of God, let fire come down from heaven and consume you and your fifty." Then fire came down from heaven and consumed him and his fifty.

Now if you will look at verses 12 and 14 you will find that this miracle happened again and again.

By causing fire to come down from heaven, Elijah validated himself as a representative from God to the nation, Israel.

Now if you will look to the last two verses of the Old Testament—Malachi 4:5 & 6 we read:

> Behold, I am going to send you Elijah the prophet before the coming of the great and terrible day of the Lord. (5)

> And he will restore the hearts of the fathers to their children, and the hearts of the children to their fathers, lest I come and smite the land with a curse. (6)

Now here is the interesting part of this revelation. This was the last spoken word from God before the 400 silent years. These last spoken words were the promise that Elijah would come *before* the Lord returns to make God's Kingdom on earth after the Tribulation Period.

Now let's look at Revelation 13:13:

> And he performs great signs, so that he even
> makes fire come down out of heaven to the earth
> in the presence of men.

Here we find that the False Prophet is calling fire down from heaven. This seems unusual but it isn't for this reason. Satan knows the Scriptures and the False Prophet is one of Satan's representatives.

Throughout the Tribulation Period you will find Satan imitating the miracles of God.

In this particular instance, he is imitating the miracles of Elijah by bringing down fire from heaven to convince the nation of Israel that he (the False Prophet) is truly an Elijah.

You can see how cleverly Satan will be working in the Last Days to convince the world that he and his other counterparts in the Satanic Trinity—the Antichrist and the False Prophet are truly the real authentic Heavenly Trinity.

Is it no wonder that the Scriptures tell us

> And with all the deception of wickedness for
> those who perish, because they did not receive
> the love of the truth so as to be saved.
> And for this reason God will send upon them a
> deluding influence so that they might believe
> what is false. (2 Thessalonians 2:10, 11).

There will be one way that you can tell the difference between the miracles that the Lord Jesus did and those which are created by the False Prophet. The difference is this... the Lord Jesus never worked a miracle just to be spectacular. There was always a lesson in each miracle which he wrought.

But when the False Prophet works a miracle, his Satanic miracles are incidental to the message and you will find that they are spectacular simply for the purpose of being spectacular and creating attention.

In Revelation 13:14 we read:

> And he deceives those who dwell on the earth be-
> cause of the signs which it was given him to
> perform in the presence of the beast, telling
> those who dwell on the earth to make an image to
> the beast who had the wound of the sword and
> has come to life.

This refers to the time when Satan will cause the False Prophet to set up a great image in Jerusalem and make Jerusalem the center of world-wide religion (The author has first-hand information from one of the three top leaders of Israel that this *latter* goal is already underway for Jerusalem).

MAKES THE DEAD SPEAK

The False Prophet will indeed be a miracle worker. In fact, his greatest miracle is described in Revelation 13:14 when he somehow causes a statue to come to life and speak.

Sometime during the reign of the first 3½ year period of the Tribulation, the Antichrist will be killed—perhaps in a battle—then he will reappear alive. The False Prophet will make an image or a statue of this Antichrist in the city of Jerusalem.

He will have the power somehow to make this image come to life and to speak and demand that all who will not worship it be put to death.

Actually this statue will not only arouse fear but will seem to be a living, speaking automaton.

It is amazing how many comparisons there are of events in prophecy with events that have occurred in the Old Testament.

You will recall when the children of Israel were delivered from Egypt under Moses' leadership and that, thinking Moses had forsaken them, they called Aaron to make them a god and Aaron made the Golden Calf.

In Exodus 32:1-6 we read the description of this event and how the Jews worshipped the Golden Calf.

So the False Prophet will have the people worshipping the "image of the beast" who will be the Antichrist.

The amazing thing will be that this image or statue will suddenly come to life and speak!

In the ensuing terror and executions that will take place during this Tribulation Period, people will realize that the False Prophet who sets himself up as a shepherd of his flock, really has no care for the lives of others. He will cause them to bow down and worship Antichrist. If they refuse to do so, they will be killed or they will starve to death.

We will discuss this in future chapters of this book.

God foretold in Zechariah 11:15-17 the following:

> And the Lord said to me, "Take again for yourself the equipment of a foolish shepherd. (15).
>
> "For behold, I am going to raise up a shepherd in the land who will not care for the perishing, seek the scattered, heal the broken, or sustain the one standing, but will devour the flesh of the fat sheep and tear off their hoofs. (16).
>
> "Woe to the worthless shepherd
> Who leaves the flock!
> A sword will be on his arm
> And on his right eye!
> His arm will be totally withered,
> And his right eye will be blind." (17)

In this passage, the arm is a sign of strength and the eye a sign of wisdom. What God is saying is that the power and wisdom of the False Prophet will come to no avail.

Both the False Prophet and the Antichrist will have their day of glory on the earth.

THEIR DAY OF JUDGMENT TO COME

But the Bible also tells that a day of judgment will be coming for them in which they will be cast alive into a lake of fire burning with brimstone. This is found in Revelation 19:20:

> And the beast was seized, and with him the false prophet who performed the signs in his presence, by which he deceived those who had received the mark of the beast and those who worshiped his image; these two were thrown alive into the lake of fire which burns with brimstone.

However, before that takes place, they will have had the opportunity to impose their Satanic rule and destruction upon millions of people on the earth during the seven year Tribulation Period.

This is the Period which immediately follows what is termed "the Rapture of the Saints" or when those who have accepted Christ rise up to meet Him in the air.

Sometime after the Rapture, the Tribulation Period begins and the awesome leadership of the Antichrist with the collaboration of the False Prophet also begins.

If this event has not yet occurred while you are reading this book—then by all means you should get yourself a Bible and read the Scriptures diligently and accept Christ as your personal Saviour.

In I Thessalonians 1:9,10, we are admonished to turn "...to God from idols to serve the living and true God; And to wait for his Son from heaven, whom He raised from the dead, even Jesus, which delivered us from the wrath to come."

There is only one way to God and salvation for the Jew or the Gentile—and that is by believing the Gospel.

In Romans 1:16 we read:

> For I am not ashamed of the gospel, for it is the power of God for salvation to every one who believes, to the Jew first and also to the Greek.

If the Rapture has not occurred then there is still time for you to be included in this wonderful event and to escape the Tribulation Period.

However, if the Rapture has occurred and you are reading this during the Tribulation Period, the succeeding chapters will tell you more of the events to come and how you still can be assured of eternal life.

In the event that you are reading this during the Tribulation Period, you will have no trouble identifying the Antichrist and the False Prophet.

Watch out for the False Prophet for he will create many great convincing miracles and yet, though he will be a man of miracles, he may also be your executioner.

9
False Security

In an issue of the Saturday Evening Post, there appeared an
article titled: "The Government Has the Right to Lie."

It was written by Arthur Sylvester who was Assistant
Secretary of Defense from 1961 until 1968.

His article begins: "If I had been living in the early 19th
Century in what was then our country's West, and had
been a religious man, I am sure I would have taken my
stand with the Lying Baptists against the Truthful Baptists."

He was referring to an incident in 1804 in Kentucky when
some Baptists were disputing whether they should tell
the truth and possibly sacrifice the life of a child in so
doing, or whether they should lie to the marauding Indians
and possibly save the child.

THE RIGHT TO LIE

Further on in his article, Mr. Sylvester states: "...that on occasions when the nation's security was at stake, the government had the right, indeed the duty, to lie if necessary to mislead an enemy and protect the people it represented."

October 19, 1962, the government of the United States released one of these lies to the American public in a release which stated: "A Pentagon spokesman denied tonight that any alert had been ordered or that any emergency military measures have been set in motion against Communist-ruled Cuba." Further, the spokesman said, "the Pentagon has no information indicating the presence of offensive weapons in Cuba."

In reality, the second sentence was completely untrue.

Many of you will recall the U-2 incident in which the government of the United States denied to the Russians that they had any knowledge of spy planes flying over Russia.

They continued to perpetuate this lie until the Russians actually produced the captured pilot and placed him on trial.

It was then that their barefaced lie was brought into the open.

More recently the scandal of Watergate showed how lies and intrigue worked hand in hand to achieve a dictator-like leadership.

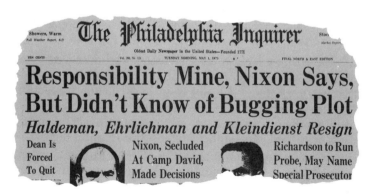

Undoubtedly, there are many convincing arguments that would support the fact that when the national security of the United States is in jeopardy the government has the right to lie.

The purpose of this chapter is not to challenge this fact or accept this fact. This is a decision you personally must make.

The purpose is simply to show you that the government of the United States has accepted this policy and that the government of the United States not only has exercised the right to lie but has on occasion purposely lied to its citizens.

This is a fact which has appeared in print several times and which even government spokesmen will not deny.

Having accepted this as an acknowledged fact, you can see how much easier it will be for you to understand that in the Last Days, there will appear on the earth, a man whom everyone will respect as a man of peace.

But he will be the greatest deceiver and the greatest liar in the world. His lies will be so eloquent that people will believe them and worship him as indeed, the saviour of mankind.

As we mentioned in previous chapters, this man is called the Antichrist. He will not be known by that name, however. He might be known as a President or a King.

This Antichrist will imitate the work of the Son in subjecting the world to himself.

People will actually believe that he is a Christ because he will be able to work many miracles and will accomplish peace on the earth for a time.

This chapter deals with the beginning of the Tribulation Period. As we previously mentioned, the Tribulation Period will last 7 years. The first 3½ years will be years of distress, but yet there will arise in them hopes for peace throughout the world.

These accomplishments will be heralded as being the direct accomplishments of Antichrist.

You will recall we stated, that if one could amicably settle the Arab-Israeli dispute, his wisdom would probably be recognized as the wisdom of Solomon. And as such, he would be considered a diplomat without an equal in the history of the world.

The Antichrist will settle the Arab-Israeli dispute and because of this he will be hailed as the greatest leader of all times.

Perhaps while you are reading this you find it difficult to believe that in the near future there will be one man whom all the nations of the world will bow down to and unanimously select as their leader (Revelation 13:8).

But the Bible says that this will happen and if you study Scriptures and compare them with current events you can see how such conditions are already being set up for this very thing to occur.

TOWARD WORLD GOVERNMENT

It may surprise you that several years ago, Belgium's Premier, P. H. Spock made a statement in his country's newspaper, LaSeur, which stated:

> "The truth is that the method of international committees has failed. What we need is a person, someone of the highest order of great experience, of great authority, of wide influence, of great energy.
>
> Let him come and let him come quickly. Either a civilian or a military man, no matter what his nationality, who will cut all the red tape, shove out of the way all the committees, wake up all the people and galvanize all governments into action. Let him come quickly. This man we need and for whom we wait will take charge of the defense of the West. Once more I say, it is not too late, but it is high time."

A CLEVER IMITATION

Remember, previously that we pointed out that Satan's triumvirate, which includes Satan, Antichrist and the False Prophet, will attempt to duplicate the life and miracles of the Heavenly Trinity which is Father, Son and Holy Spirit.

Therefore, when we read in the Bible

> The next day he saw Jesus coming to him, and said, "Behold the Lamb of God who takes away the sin of the world!" (John 1:29).

we find that Satan introduces his masterpiece of religious deception—Antichrist—as coming as a lamb.

The difference is, however, that Christ came as a lamb to take away the sin of the world. The Antichrist, who follows the message of Satan himself, comes not to bring man a revelation from God nor salvation from God.

The Antichrist comes actually to blind men and to deceive men through the workings of a lie.

This is described quite graphically in 2 Thessalonians 2:8-11 which says:

> And then that lawless one will be revealed whom the Lord will slay with the breath of His mouth and bring to an end by the appearance of His coming; (8)
>
> that is, the one whose coming is in accord with the activity of Satan, with all power and signs and false wonders, (9)
>
> and with all the deception of wickedness for those who perish, because they did not receive the love of the truth so as to be saved. (10)
>
> And for this reason God will send upon them a deluding influence so that they might believe what is false. (11)

THE FIRST 3 1/2 YEARS
OF THE TRIBULATION PERIOD

Sometime after the Rapture (which is when the believers are caught up to meet Christ in the air) the 7 year Tribulation Period will begin.

This tribulation is spoken of in Matthew 24:21,22 as follows:

> For then there will be a great tribulation, such as has not occurred since the beginning of the world until now, nor ever shall. (21)
>
> And unless those days had been cut short, no life would have been saved; but for the sake of the elect those days shall be cut short. (22)

As we previously stated, the Antichrist will be the head of the Federated States of Europe and will make his appearance at the beginning of the Tribulation Period.

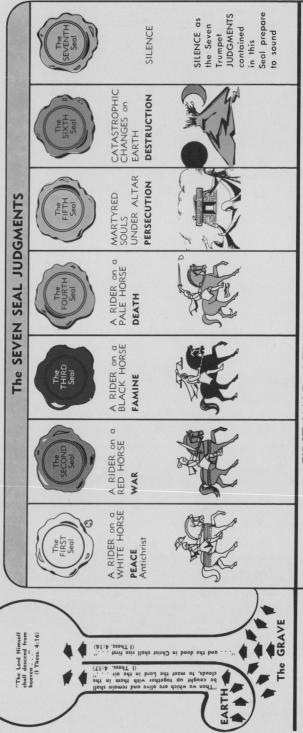

The RAPTURE

"The Lord Himself shall descend from heaven . . ." (I Thess. 4:16)

"Then we which are alive and remain shall be caught up together with them in the clouds, to meet the Lord in the air . . ." (I Thess. 4:17)

". . . and the dead in Christ shall rise first . . ." (I Thess. 4:16)

The GRAVE

EARTH

Copyright © 1968 Salem Kirban, Inc.

The SEVEN SEAL JUDGMENTS

| The FIRST Seal | The SECOND Seal | The THIRD Seal | The FOURTH Seal | The FIFTH Seal | The SIXTH Seal | The SEVENTH Seal |

A RIDER on a WHITE HORSE

PEACE
Antichrist

A RIDER on a RED HORSE

WAR

A RIDER on a BLACK HORSE

FAMINE

A RIDER on a PALE HORSE

DEATH

MARTYRED SOULS UNDER ALTAR

PERSECUTION

CATASTROPHIC CHANGES on EARTH

DESTRUCTION

SILENCE

SILENCE as the Seven Trumpet JUDGMENTS contained in this Seal prepare to sound

FIRST HALF of TRIBULATION PERIOD—3½ Years

This is 7 years before the Lord Jesus Christ comes back on this earth to establish His Kingdom and to reign at the time of the Millennium.

It is not until the middle of the Tribulation Period that Satan fully moves in and terror and tragedy begin (Daniel 9:27).

It may seem to you that we are repeating facts on several occasions throughout these chapters, but it is necessary in order that you understand the sequence of events properly.

In discussing the Tribulation Period, we do not want to burden the reader with a great many Old Testament and New Testament Scriptures.

Once you understand the sequence of events and see the panorama of what will occur, we would recommend that you get other books on the subject which deal more fully with the theological explanations. You will find this recommended reading list at the back of this book.

THE MYSTERY NUMBER—666

In Revelation 13:18 we read:

> Here is wisdom. Let him who has understanding calculate the number of the beast, for the number is that of a man; and his number is six hundred and sixty-six.

For years scholars have been trying to discover what 666 means.

And for years they have been unable to fathom this particular part of the prophetic Scriptures as found in the book of Revelation.

This verse was written for the benefit of those who will be alive in the Tribulation Period.

For during that time, the figure 666 will have a very significant meaning. And if you are living in that time it will indicate to you that the man who has this number is the Antichrist.

In today's day and age, there are still some things in the Scriptures that remain a mystery to us. The Lord did not intend to divulge every aspect of His master plan to us.

As an example, if you were living 50 years ago, think how

difficult it would be for you to comprehend the verse which in part states: "And every eye shall see Him" (Revelation 1:7).

Now in today's technological age, through the miracle of TV satellites which circle the globe, it is even humanly possible for "every eye to see Him." By watching their television screen, every person in the world can simultaneously see one event as it is occurring! It would have been also impossible for anyone to believe 50 years ago that there could be such elements of destruction that could literally wipe out the earth.

Now with the advent of the atomic bomb and the hydrogen bomb, statements of great destruction as found in the Bible become very possible to us who are living in this day and age.

And as we understand the events just noted, so those living during the Tribulation Period will understand what the figure 666 means and in understanding this they will be able to identify the individual who will be the Antichrist.

THE INITIAL 3 1/2 YEARS

At this point it would be well for you to look at the chart on page 160 which outlines the sequence of events that will occur during the first 3½ year period of the Tribulation.

Chapters 6-19 of the book of Revelation in the Bible constitute the fullest description of the Tribulation Period in the entire Bible.

God's judgment is poured out upon an unbelieving and wicked world, first in the seven seals, then in the seven trumpets, and last of all in the seven vials.

Again it is important to realize that it apparently is not the will of God to reveal to us the exact time in which each of these judgments will occur.

However, Bible scholars generally agree that the seven seals will cover the first 3½ years of the Tribulation and that the seven trumpets come somewhere in the midst of this period and that the vial judgments will come near the end of the last 3½ years of tribulation.

MATTHEW and REVELATION COMPARISON
ON FIRST 6 SEALS OF JUDGMENT

Matthew 24	Revelation 6
"Many shall come in my name saying, I am Christ; and shall deceive many."	"And I saw, and behold a **white** horse: and he that sat on him had a bow; and a crown was given unto him; and he went forth conquering, and to conquer."
"And ye shall hear of wars and rumours of wars . . . for nation shall rise against nation, and kingdom against kingdom."	"And there went out another horse that was **red:** and power was given to him that sat thereon to take peace from the earth, and that they should kill one another and there was given unto him a great sword."
"and there shall be famines"	"And I beheld, and lo a **black** horse; and he that sat on him had a pair of balances in his hand."
"and pestilences"	"And I looked, and behold a **pale** horse: and his name that sat on him was Death."
"Then shall they deliver you up to be afflicted, and shall kill you, and ye shall be hated of all nations for my name's sake."	"And when he had opened the **fifth seal,** I saw under the altar the souls of them that were slain for the word of God, and for the testimony which they held."
"and earthquakes in divers places."	"And I beheld when he had opened the **sixth seal** and, lo, there was a great earthquake; and the sun became black as sackcloth of hair, and the moon became as blood."

This chapter will deal with the first 3½ years of the Tribulation in which the seven seal judgments will be evident on the earth.

For a moment let's compare Matthew 24 and Revelation 6 and see how identical they are in describing the first 6 seals of judgment that will come to the earth during this first 3½ year period of the Tribulation.

In Revelation 6 we see Christ seated on a throne and holding in His hands a scroll.

Words have been written on this scroll and it is rolled up and sealed.

The writer of the book of Revelation, John, inspired to write this book by the Lord, tells how he watches the Lord Jesus Christ open this seven sealed book (scroll).

In this scroll are contained the first series of judgments which God will pour out upon the earth.

These judgments are referred to as the Seven Seal judgments of God.

THE SEVEN SEALS

*And I saw when the Lamb broke **one** of the seven seals, and I heard one of the four living creatures saying as with a voice of thunder, "Come."*

And I looked, and behold, a white horse, and he who sat on it had a bow; and a crown was given to him; and he went out conquering, and to conquer. (Revelation 6:1-2).

The first judgment is that Christ allows a man to appear on earth who will pose as a "saviour of the world."

He will be the Antichrist. He is mentioned in this Scripture as the rider on the White Horse. Notice that he is described as carrying a bow but no arrow. This may indicate that he will be a man supposedly coming on a mission of peace. Certainly the color of this mount, white, portrays his supposedly holy, pure, and peaceful pretensions.

How will he become so popular?

This is how it will happen. There will be a great peace movement throughout the world. People will be tired of war and will be seeking peace.

Actually the Tribulation Period will begin with a public appearance by Antichrist. This individual will eventually become the head of the Federated States of Europe. To those living at that time he will not be revealed to them as the Antichrist nor will the name of the cooperating countries necessarily be known exactly as the "Federated States of Europe."

In fact, the Antichrist will be looked on with great admiration.

This is described quite fully in 2 Thessalonians, chapter 2.

Antichrist will assert his great authority and power by attempting to settle the Arab-Israeli dispute. He will side with Israel in backing her claim to the land of Palestine against Russia which in Scriptures is mentioned as the Northern Confederacy.

It will be the Northern Confederacy that backs the Arabs' claim to Palestine. This is described in Ezekiel 38:1 to 39:16.

Though God has not chosen to reveal all of the details on how exactly these things will come to pass, it **seems** that when the Federated States of Europe announce their support for Israel in the coming Arab-Israeli dispute (in order to prevent the Russian invasion) you will then know that we are near the Rapture (if it hasn't already occurred) when the saints will rise from the earth to be with Christ.

And therefore, if we are near the Rapture then the events of the Tribulation Period will soon be unfolding.

The SECOND Seal

A RIDER on a RED HORSE

WAR

*And when He broke the **second seal**, I heard the second living creature saying, "Come."*

And another, a red horse, went out; and to him who sat on it, it was granted to take peace from the earth, and that men should slay one another; and a great sword was given to him. (Revelation 6:3-4).

Now let's set the scene for you and show you how these events are now beginning to occur and will shape up to the events of the Tribulation Period.

You will recall we have already discussed the First Seal on which the White Horse (Antichrist) will appear on the earth.

We now want to explain the Second Seal which is defined as a Red Horse which means WAR.

* * * * *

Without getting deep into the prophetic teaching of the book of Daniel, it is important that we understand some of the background to give us proper perspective on the future for the nation Israel.

You will recall in Daniel 2 that Nebuchadnezzar, King of Babylon saw a great image in his dream.

When he woke up he could not recall the dream and he called on his wisemen and magicians to reveal to him his forgotten dream. They could not.

Finally Daniel revealed both the dream and the interpretation of it and prefaced this revelation with these words:

> *However, there is a God in heaven who reveals mysteries, and He has made known to King Nebuchadnezzar what will take place in the latter days. This was your dream and the visions in your mind while on your bed. (Daniel 2:28).*

In this verse, we find that Daniel first gives glory to God for revealing this secret and then points out that it was God who is revealing to the king what should take place in the latter days (which are the days in which we now live). Daniel talked about a great image which had:

A head of gold
chest and arms of silver
abdomen and thighs of brass
legs of iron
feet part of iron and part of clay

These four metals represent the four great world empires that were to rule over the Jews and were to control the land and have authority over Jerusalem.

The first world empire to do so is described as the empire with the *head of gold*. This was the Neo-Babylonian empire in which King Nebuchadnezzar was the head of state (606 B.C.).

The Babylonian empire was the first of these four empires to rule over the Jews.

The second empire to rule over the Jews is described as an empire with a *chest and arms of silver*. This we know to be the Medo-Persian empire for Medes united with the Persians to form a second great world empire, and then conquered the Babylonians in 536 B.C.

The Image of Daniel 2

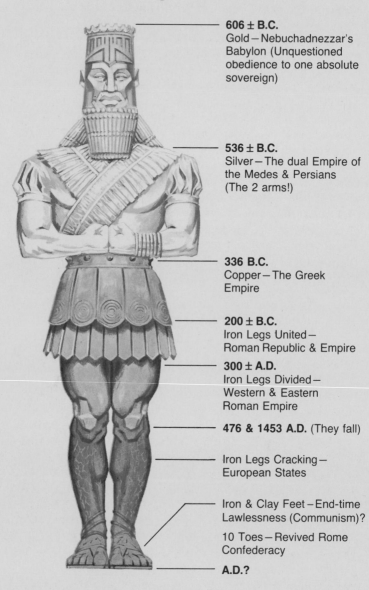

606 ± B.C.
Gold – Nebuchadnezzar's Babylon (Unquestioned obedience to one absolute sovereign)

536 ± B.C.
Silver – The dual Empire of the Medes & Persians (The 2 arms!)

336 B.C.
Copper – The Greek Empire

200 ± B.C.
Iron Legs United – Roman Republic & Empire

300 ± A.D.
Iron Legs Divided – Western & Eastern Roman Empire

476 & 1453 A.D. (They fall)

Iron Legs Cracking – European States

Iron & Clay Feet – End-time Lawlessness (Communism)?

10 Toes – Revived Rome Confederacy

A.D.?

In doing so, the rule over Palestine passed from the Babylonians to the Medo-Persians.

Verse 39 tells us of another third kingdom of *brass* which shall rule over all the earth.

Again history tells us how Alexander was victorious over the Medo-Persian coalition (336-323 B.C.) and Alexander's Greek empire then ruled over the territory formerly controlled by the Babylonians and the Medo-Persians.

The fourth kingdom is described in verse 30 of Daniel 2. It is described as a kingdom that "shall be strong as *iron.*" This was the Roman Empire that was successful in replacing the Greek empire. It was Rome that became the fourth world empire.

What Daniel is giving us here in the interpretation of his vision is the succession of four world empires that would reign over the Jews in Palestine.

Daniel tells us that the fourth Kingdom, the Roman Empire, would be as strong as iron.

History has shown us that Rome exerted the most powerful and dominating influence of any empire that has existed in the course of world history.

THE FEET OF IRON AND CLAY

You may then ask, well, what about the feet of this great image which are described as part iron and part clay? What does this mean?

What Daniel is saying here is that the longer the Roman empire existed, the weaker it would become until finally when you come down to the toes (which is that last form of that Gentile world power) it is divided into 10 toes representing 10 separate kingdoms (Daniel 2:41-44).

In reality, he is indicating that when you divide an empire into 10 separate kingdoms the inevitable result is a weakness and although Rome was a strong empire initially—strong as iron—this empire is now diminishing because of its division and he likens it to the frailty of clay.

This is a description (the 10 nations) of how the Roman Empire will appear in the latter days.

We are rapidly seeing this formation of the 10 kingdoms taking place.

In fact, the great problem facing western powers today is the problem of trying to bring together under the same head, nations that were originally part of the same empire.

France won't get together with Germany and Germany won't get together with Britain...France tried to keep Britain out of the Common Market...France recently ejected the NATO headquarters, etc.

This indicates to us that we are living in the days that we have seen predicted in the book of Daniel.

Please keep this in mind. Palestine has never been ruled over by any power outside of the territorial bounds of the ancient Roman Empire from the time of the Roman conquest (63 B.C.) until the present. Even Palestine's moslem rulers during the Middle Ages, the Seljuk Turks, ruled from within the ancient land bounds of the Roman Empire of 117 A.D.

And we have already discussed that the time is going to come when these 10 nations that were once part of the Roman Empire will get together and enter into an agreement to give their authority to one man as their head. This man will be the Antichrist (Revelation 17:12).

It is important to understand that this federation will be by *mutual consent of all of the nations involved.*

The cementing force between the union of these 10 nations is the rise of Russian Communism as a voracious beast to their East.

Russian Communism is so strong and powerful that we have already created the North Atlantic Treaty Organization (NATO) and the European Common Market.

These are the first steps towards unification of United States and European powers.

Therefore, we see that the Roman Empire in the Last Days is revived and restored under these 10 rulers.

* * * * *

All the above is said to give you a further background on the Second Seal which is broken and revealed in the book of Revelation as the Red Horse.

And another, a red horse, went out; and to him who sat on it had a bow; and a crown was given

> to him; and he went out conquering, and to con-
> quer. (Revelation 6:4).

What will be the event that will cause Russia to be against the European states?

The answer of course, is Palestine, known today as Israel.

WHY RUSSIA WANTS ISRAEL

Why would Russia want to invade Israel?

The prophet Ezekiel anticipated this question.

> And you will say, 'I will go up against the land of
> unwalled villages. I will go against those who are
> at rest, that live securely, all of them living with-
> out walls, and having no bars or gates; (Ezekiel
> 38:11).

> to capture spoil and to seize plunder, to turn your
> hand against the waste places which are now in-
> habited, and against the people who are gathered
> from the nations, who have acquired cattle and
> goods, who live at the center of the world. (Ezekiel
> 38:12).

The great prize which Russia wants is the vast mineral deposits in the Dead Sea. It is calculated that there is enough potash to provide the needs of the entire world for 2,000 years.

You might wonder what in the world potash is and why is it so valuable.

Potash is used as a fertilizer and one must keep in mind that vegetation and, consequently, animal life including human life desperately requires it. An end-time famine-filled world will thirst for potash's life-giving properties.

It also has another important use and that is in the making of explosives.

One estimate of the potential value of the potash, bromine and other chemical salts in the Dead Sea is 1 trillion, 270 billion dollars—$1,270,000,000,000.

In a succeeding chapter titled "The Day Russia Dies" we will get more into the details of Russia's part in its attempts to overtake Israel.

Suffice it now to say that—although again Scripture does not here specify all of the details—within the pale of the

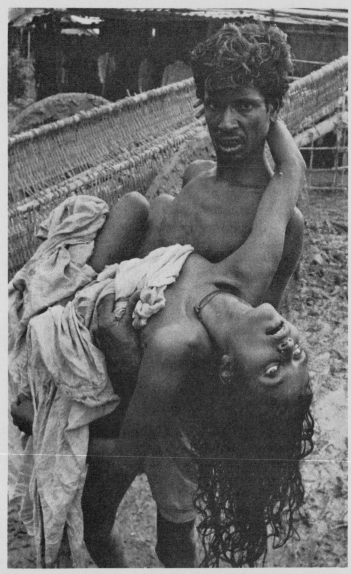

Famine and disease has already hit Third World nations. African prepares to bury his wife.

war of the Second Seal which is the Red Horse, we seem to see the first attempt of Russia to march into Israel and take it by force.

When this great army of occupation moves into Israel to take possession of the land, no battle, as such, will be fought.

The Western Powers will only make a protest. But God will intervene and cause great earthquakes and disasters which will kill all of the enemy forces and throw the Russian forces into utter confusion in which "every man's sword shall be against his brother" (Ezekiel 38:18-22 and Ezekiel 39:2-4).

The THIRD Seal

A RIDER on a BLACK HORSE

FAMINE

*And when He broke the **third seal,** I heard the third living creature saying, "Come." And I looked, and behold, a black horse; and he who sat on it had a pair of scales in his hand. (Revelation 6:5).*

The third seal which is broken reveals a Black Horse with a rider holding a pair of scales.

This tells us that during the first part of the Tribulation there will be a famine.

Able-bodied men everywhere will have been drafted for war and many fields will remain untilled. Further, during conditions of hostilities farmers are universally unwilling to plant and labor for months, only to see marauding armies come and take away their crops.

Because of this, famine will follow just as Christ prophesied (Matthew 24:7).

*And when He broke the **fourth seal**, I heard the voice of the fourth living creature saying, "Come."*

And I looked, and behold, an ashen horse; and he who sat on it had the name "Death"; and Hades was following with him. And authority was given to them over a fourth of·the earth, to kill with sword and with famine and with pestilence and by the wild beasts of the earth. (Revelation 6:7-8).

The rider on the First Horse, which is a White Horse, is the Antichrist but his present identity is unknown.

The rider on the Second Horse, which is a Red Horse, is the one who will attempt to take peace from the earth and we described this in the breaking of the second seal.

The Rider on the Third Horse, which is the Black Horse, will cause famine to fall upon the world.

The Fourth Seal, which is a Pale Horse, has a rider which is called "Death."

This follows the warfare and famine of the former seals.

What is described here is the worldwide suffering of the first 3½ years of the Tribulation period which because of war and famine bring about death.

One-fourth of the population of the earth will be destroyed with the opening of this fourth seal. This is revealed in Revelation 6:8 previously quoted right after the title "The Fourth Seal."

Actually during the Tribulation, the world will experience its most grievous time in history.

> **If we went on the basis of our present population ...this would mean that some 750 million people will die through various judgments during this Tribulation Period.**

If Revelation 6:8 with its death upon "one-fourth of the earth" refers *not* to one quarter of the earth's population dying, but rather to an area of one quarter of the globe being saturated with death, then the toll will also be frightful indeed.

*And when He broke the **fifth seal,** I saw underneath the altar the souls of those who had been slain because of the word of God, and because of the testimony which they had maintained. (Revelation 6:9).*

When the Fifth Seal is opened, this will reveal the persecution that results in the deaths of many thousands of Christian martyrs who will be killed for their Christian testimony during the Tribulation.

These will be those who have accepted Christ as their personal Saviour during the first 3½ year Tribulation Period. They are martyred now as scapegoats for the troubles which have arisen in this first half of the seven awful judgment years.

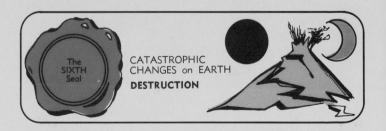

CATASTROPHIC
CHANGES on EARTH
DESTRUCTION

And I looked when He broke the **sixth seal,** and there was a great earthquake; and the sun became black as sackcloth made of hair, and the whole moon became like blood;

and the stars of the sky fell to the earth, as a fig tree casts its unripe figs when shaken by a great wind.

And the sky was split apart like a scroll when it is rolled up; and every mountain and island were moved out of their places.

And the kings of the earth and the great men and the commanders and the rich and the strong and every slave and free man, hid themselves in the caves and among the rocks of the mountains;

and they said to the mountains and to the rocks, "Fall on us and hide us from the presence of Him who sits on the throne, and from the wrath of the Lamb. (Revelation 6:12-16).

When the Sixth Seal is broken, there will be great physical changes occurring on the earth.

So drastic will be these changes that men will run to the caves of mountains and beg for death in order to be spared the terrible disasters that await them.

They will hide under the rocks and in caves.

There will be a great earthquake and the sun will become "dark like black cloth" and the moon will be "blood-red."

Stars (meteors) from heaven will fall to earth. The mountains will move around like checkers on a checkerboard.

THE 144,000 WITNESSES

Between the breaking of the Sixth Seal and the Seventh Seal we see an interval. This will be a time in which 144,000 of the children of Israel, 12,000 from each of the 12 tribes will be "sealed."

This seal will be in their foreheads.

> *And I saw another angel ascending from the rising of the sun, having the seal of the living God; and he cried out with a loud voice to the four angels to whom it was granted to harm the earth and the sea, (Revelation 7:2).*

> *saying, "Do not harm the earth or the sea or the trees, until we have sealed the bond-servants of our God on their foreheads." (Revelation 7:3).*

Do not confuse this seal with the mark of the beast (Antichrist) which is put on the hands or foreheads of the unbelievers.

This seal, described in the Scripture verse above, will be the mark of God and will identify them as God's chosen witnesses during the Tribulation Period. Neither Antichrist nor Satan will be able to stop them from witnessing to their faith in Christ.

There will not be one Gentile in these 144,000.

Their identity, as far as the present is concerned, is lost. But God will know who they are, scattered among the nations.

God is ready for them. He will bring them together to be a witness during this Tribulation Period.

Revelation 7:4-8 tells us the names of these 12 tribes.

> *And I heard the number of those who were sealed, one hundred and forty-four thousand sealed from every tribe of the sons of Israel: (Revelation 7:4).*

Then they are listed as follows:

Judah	12,000
Reuben	12,000
Gad	12,000
Asher	12,000
Naphtali	12,000
Manasseh	12,000

Simeon	12,000
Levi	12,000
Issachar	12,000
Zebulun	12,000
Joseph	12,000
Benjamin	12,000

God supernaturally protects these 144,000 Jews and they boldly proclaim His message. As a result of their ministry, and the ministry of God's two witnesses of Revelation 11, a great multitude from every nation, kindred and tongue are saved (Revelation 7:9).

The SEVENTH Seal

SILENCE

*And when He broke the **seventh seal**, there was silence in heaven for about half an hour. (Revelation 8:1).*

At the breaking of the seventh seal, there is an interval of silence which takes place before the next judgment which falls on earth.

The Seventh Seal seems to end the first 3½ years of the Tribulation Period and ushers in the second 3½ years which appears to begin with the sounding of the Seven Trumpets.

The first 3½ year period just described will have its moments of comparative calm in which there is an era of peace and the unsuspecting Jews look up with great admiration to their "saviour," the Antichrist, who has protected them and preserved their land, Israel.

However, this time of relative peace is short-lived and great terror and destruction awaits those who still remain on the earth during the second half of the Tribulation which is the next 3½ years.

For in the first 3½ years, Israel has been living under a false security that soon will end with terror and tragedy.

10
Terror and Tragedy

Why God Allows the Tribulation Period to Occur • Satan's Role in the Tribulation Period • What Action Reveals the Antichrist's True Objectives? • The Role of the Social Church • The Mark of the Beast (Antichrist) • America and the Mark of the Beast • What is the Identifying Mark • The First Trumpet • The Second Trumpet • The Third Trumpet • The Next Three Trumpets Bring Forth Greater Wrath • The Fifth Trumpet • The Sixth Trumpet • The Two Witnesses • The Seventh Trumpet • The First Vial • The Second Vial • The Third Vial • The Fourth Vial • The Fifth Vial • The Sixth Vial • The Seventh Vial • Four Purposes for Tribulation

To those in Israel, the first 3½ years will seem like a heaven on earth.

They are back in their land. The Antichrist has fulfilled his promises in bringing peace to the land and protecting the Jews from the onrushing armies of Russia and her allies.

Jerusalem is looked up to as one of the most elite cities of the world and is the hub of business activity, fashion and world culture.

It would appear that Utopia had arrived. At last the world could now settle down to a world of peace under the protectorate of a great world leader who has amassed under him the cooperation of the 10 powerful states known as the European Federation of States.

But the honeymoon is over and the next 3½ years of the last half of the Tribulation Period ushers in a most horrible period of death and destruction for both the Jews and those who then will turn to Christ.

How does this all begin and why does it occur?

WHY GOD ALLOWS THE TRIBULATION PERIOD TO OCCUR

Israel had been warned that this Tribulation event would occur. In the Old Testament, these prophecies were predicted in Isaiah, Daniel, and Jeremiah.

Even the Lord Jesus, Himself, had told what was coming and what the Jews should do at that time.

> I have come in My Father's name, and you do not receive Me; if another shall come in his own name, you will receive him. (John 5:43).

Let's look at the comparison. Jesus had come without deception, claiming to be sent by His Father.

> For I have come down from heaven, not to do My own will, but the will of Him who sent Me. (John 6:38).

> And this is the will of Him who sent Me, that of all that He has given Me I lose nothing, but raise it up on the last day. (John 6:39).

He gave all the glory to His Father.

> And behold, one came to Him and said, "Teacher, what good thing shall I do that I may obtain eternal life?" (Matthew 19:16).

> And He said to him, "Why are you asking Me about what is good? There is only One who is good; but if you wish to enter into life, keep the commandments." (Matthew 19:17).

> But if I do them, though you do not believe Me, believe the works; that you may know and understand that the Father is in Me, and I in the Father." (John 10:38).

And yet, Jesus warned the Jews that there would be one coming who would claim to be God and demand worship as such.

It is during this second 3½ year period of the Tribulation, this man of sin, Antichrist, will be revealed.

He is the incarnation of Satan himself.

> And his power will be mighty, but not by his own
>   power,
> And he will destroy to an extraordinary degree
> And prosper and perform his will;
> He will destroy mighty men and the holy people.
> (Daniel 8:24).

This will be Satan's supreme effort.

> "For this reason, rejoice, O heavens and you who dwell in them. Woe to the earth and the sea; because the devil has come down to you, having great wrath, knowing that he has only a short time." (Revelation 12:12).

And for this he had schemed thousands of years.

> How you have fallen from heaven,
> O star of the morning, son of the dawn!
> You have been cut down to the earth,
> You who have weakened the nations!
>   (Isaiah 14:12)

> But you said in your heart,
> 'I will ascend to heaven;
> I will raise my throne above the stars of God,
> And I will sit on the mount of assembly
> In the recesses of the north. (Isaiah 14:13)

> 'I will ascend above the heights of the clouds;
> I will make myself like the Most High.'
>   (Isaiah 14:14)

You will recall that under God's direction Solomon's Temple had been erected upon Mount Moriah. And at the time of dedication, the glory of God had filled this temple with a cloud. It was here that Jehovah had put His name and received worship as the one true God of Israel.

Actually it was to Israel alone that God had revealed Himself in a special way.

> "We have become like those over whom Thou
>   hast never ruled,
> Like those who were not called by Thy name.
>   (Isaiah 63:19)

There will be cries of disappointment and sorrow as Israeli's witness Antichrist placing his image in the Temple during the middle of the Tribulation Period. Their leader of peace has betrayed them. Ahead of them lies 3½ years of unrelenting persecution.

Since Satan is the great imitator of God...during the first half of the Tribulation Period, or before, Satan permits Israel to rebuild this temple that he might at this place and in the temple erected to God, transfer worship from God to himself.

And where Jehovah had put His name...Satan in turn sets up his image and working through the False Prophet, who directs worship to the Antichrist, leads the Jews astray and fulfills that part of prophecy which was quoted before as saying:

> I have come in My Father's name, and you do not receive Me; if another shall come in his own name, you will receive him (John 5:43).

So here we find the Jews welcoming and worshipping Antichrist thinking that he is God.

The sad fact is that the prophet of the Old Testament had prophesied of this day and Jesus, too had warned Israel, more than 1900 years ago, about this coming event.

Jeremiah spoke of this in the Old Testament, referring to it as the time of Jacob's trouble, when he said in Jeremiah 30:7:

> Alas! for that day is great,
> There is none like it;
> And it is the time of Jacob's distress,
> But he will be saved from it.

And we are fast approaching the day which Jeremiah, Isaiah, Daniel and the Lord Jesus and others had prophesied.

Now Satan will be fulfilling these prophecies exactly as they had been written. Antichrist will assume power and the temple will be erected. And because Israel refuses to worship Satan as God, there will follow one of the greatest slaughters in history as Jacob's trouble begins.

This shows the power of sin! God has given both the Jews and the Gentiles signs in the heaven and earth, but these are mocked by the people of this day. Is it no wonder that the Bible tells us:

> For the coming of the Son of Man will be just like the days of Noah (Matthew 24:37).

The tragedy is that even under these new judgments which redouble with intensity, the world will still continue to worship Satan and not believe in the true God.

This will be the condition of the world at the close of the first 3½ years of the Tribulation Period.

What is now left for God to do when He is rejected of men?

The only thing left for Him to do is to follow His plan for the development of His kingdom during this closing period when there are false teachers and false preachers and people believing and worshipping a lie.

Therefore, He allows the second 3½ years of the Tribulation Period to occur in which this trial by fire awakens many thousands to accepting Christ as their personal Saviour and brings the Jew back to the fold into acknowledging Christ as Messiah, Saviour, Redeemer and Lord.

This is why the second half of the Tribulation Period, commonly known as "Jacob's trouble," must come to pass.

Will the Dome of the Rock be destroyed by an earthquake or by a war? Only time will tell. It is in this area that the people of Israel want to build their Temple.

SATAN'S ROLE IN
THE TRIBULATION PERIOD

During the first 3½ years Antichrist (the world ruler) and the False Prophet (the world church leader) have so fooled the world into believing that they are truly called of God and have truly brought peace to the earth...that now Satan can move into the next phase of his program and cause the people of the world to bow down and worship him.

To those who refuse, their refusal will heap on their heads terror and tragedy.

Jerusalem, the city of Peace, has been the scene of many bloody conflicts.

But God promised that the time would come when that city would be rebuilt and extended according to His blueprint. He also promised that after this the city would not be destroyed again.

We find this in Jeremiah 31:38-40:

> *"Behold, days are coming,"* declares the Lord, *"when the city shall be rebuilt for the Lord from the tower of Hananeel to the Corner Gate. (38)*
> *"And the measuring line shall go out farther straight ahead to the hill Gareb, then it will turn to Goah. (39)*
> *"And the whole valley of the dead bodies and of the ashes, and all the fields as far as the brook Kidron, to the corner of the Horse Gate toward the east, shall be holy to the Lord; it shall not be plucked up, or overthrown any more forever."*
> *(40)*

Politically, Jerusalem is a modern city of over 300,000 inhabitants spread over several hills.

But the spiritual image of Jerusalem is of the Biblical city within the walled area.

On the East, occupying about a fifth of the old city area is the site of Solomon's Temple and its courts. The lower stones of the Western Wall (Wailing Wall) which border this Temple Area are believed to be the relics of a wall surrounding the Solomonic Temple. The layers of stone above come from the time of Herod's rebuilding of the Temple. Above these are stones set by the Turkish rulers of Jerusalem in the Middle Ages. At the center of this entire Temple Area square there now stands the Mosque of Omar built to worship Mohammed.

It is hard to envision the changes that will have to come in the Middle East to once again make possible the building of a Jewish Temple. This Jewish Temple will be built right on the spot now occupied by the Moslem Dome of the Rock, sometimes called the Mosque of Omar—or at the very least it will be constructed near it, somewhere in the now chiefly vacant Temple Area which occupies the most sacred 1/5th of the walled city of Old Jerusalem.

This Mosque is the third most sacred Mohammedan shrine.

THE REBIRTH OF JERUSALEM

Immediately after the Six Day War, Mayor Teddy Kollek centered all his energies into rebuilding Jerusalem.

Teddy Kollek is the first Jewish mayor that the whole city of Jerusalem has had since the Romans destroyed it 19 centuries ago.

Teddy Kollek loves Jerusalem and he has dreams for this "City of God."

One of his dreams is to bring more visitors to this city of some 240,000 Jews and 80,000 Arabs. He plans to stage "sound and light" productions from the Mount of Olives and rebuild the ancient Jewish Quarter.

In a recent magazine article he states: "I would suggest the United Nations move here. This is the place where the idea of peace was expressed best...."

His pet dream is to raise a "World Synagogue" in the Jewish Quarter near the Wailing Wall.

A magazine article on Jerusalem indicated that already an architect has been commissioned to build the most magnificent synagogue in the world, right in the city of Jerusalem.

That architect is located in the city of Philadelphia, Pennsylvania.

In an interview with Mr. Yigal Allon, Prime Minister of Israel, he personally told me that it was the desire of Israel to make Jerusalem a holy place for all faiths to worship.

Seventeen times the city of Jerusalem has been razed to the ground. But now in our day, we are seeing the city once again being rebuilt and following a pattern of prophecy as set forth in the Scriptures.

In Isaiah 17:10,11 which says:

> For you have forgotten the God of your salvation
> And have not remembered the rock of your refuge.
> Therefore you plant delightful plants
> And set them with vine slips of a strange god. (10)
> In the day that you plant it you carefully fence it in,
> And in the morning you bring your seed to blossom;
> But the harvest will be a heap
> In a day of sickliness and incurable pain. (11)

God reminds Israel that the day will come when their land will blossom as a rose, but because they have forgotten God, they will first reap a bitter harvest.

This harvest is the "time of Jacob's trouble" which we will refer to as the last 3½ years of the Tribulation Period.

WHAT ACTION REVEALS THE ANTICHRIST'S TRUE OBJECTIVES?

Here again many of the details have not been given to us, yet the following reconstruction of the events to come seems to fit the prophecies given:

As we previously stated, there will appear on the scene the Antichrist who will be head of the Federated States of Europe.

In attempting to settle the Arab-Israeli dispute, he will side with Israel and back her claim to the land of Palestine against Russia.

Russia will back the Arabs' claim to Palestine (Ezekiel 38).

Because the Antichrist will make a pledge to protect Israel the Jews will flock back to Israel in unprecedented numbers.

The Scriptures seem to give us some indication that in this time Russia will part with her Jews and allow them to return to Israel. It is estimated that there are over 2 million Jews in Russia at present.

After this occurs, Russia, feeling she is all powerful, will move into the land of Israel.

God will allow this to happen because He will not tolerate His people looking to the Antichrist as their saviour. Therefore, the Jews will again be driven out of their land and many will flee from Israel and the two thirds of those left behind will be slain so that, alas, the soil of Israel will again be drenched with the blood of the children of Abraham.

> *"And it will come about in all the land,"*
> *Declares the Lord,*
>
> *"That two parts in it will be cut off and perish;*
> *But the third will be left in it." (Zechariah 13:8)*
>
> *"And among these nations you shall find no rest, and there shall be no resting place for the sole of your foot; but there the Lord will give you a trembling heart, failing of eyes, and despair of soul. (Deuteronomy 28:65)*
>
> *"So your life shall hang in doubt before you; and you shall be in dread night and day, and shall have no assurance of your life. (Deuteronomy 28: 66)*
>
> *"In the morning you shall say, 'Would that it were evening!' And at evening you shall say, 'Would that it were morning!' because of the dread of your heart which you dread, and for the sight of your eyes which you shall see. (Deuteronomy 28:67)*

After this occurs may be the time when God will step in and devastate Russia and Russian Communism, including her allies as He has prophesied in Ezekiel 38:1-39:16. (This will be explained in Chapter 11, **The Day Russia Dies).**

It seems that this is the time that the Federated States of Europe will move into this vacuum created by the defeat of Russia. It is at this time that Antichrist will rule over all the earth.

THE ROLE OF A SOCIAL CHURCH

It is important to remember that after the Rapture the

false church which is left behind (which we will call, "The Social Church,") will unite under the authority of Rome. This is a Church "having a form of godliness but denying the power thereof:..." (2 Timothy 3:5).

As discussed in previous chapters, we already see evidences where Protestant churches are already exerting every effort to bring about a one world church.

Their efforts will be successful.

This unified church may be instrumental in bringing about the union of the Western Democratic Powers (Federated States of Europe). These powers will be greatly influenced by the end-time World Church which will have its headquarters in Rome (Revelation 17:3,9).

This will leave one great political-religious system now in control. This system will have worldwide influence and bring all things under its control.

However, the Democratic coalition of nations which we are calling the Federated States of Europe, will rise up and destroy the apostate world church.

Revelation 17:16 vividly describes this destruction.

Therefore we first have the destruction of a huge Russian Communist army and second the destruction of the False World Church.

This clears the way so that the Antichrist and the False Prophet can come to worldwide power and under Satan, cause all nations to worship him (Antichrist...Rev. 13:7-8).

This then brings us to what is commonly known as the "Great Tribulation" of the Seven Trumpets and the Seven Vials (Bowls) which is God's wrath being poured out upon the earth. The figure of Trumpets that blow are to sound an alarm. The pouring out of the Seven Vials portray a special release of stored up divine judgment and wrath.

We will soon briefly describe the Seven Trumpets and Seven Vials and what will occur when they are introduced.

THE MARK OF THE BEAST
(Antichrist)

You will recall in a previous chapter how we discussed how the False Prophet (religious leader) caused the statue to somehow come alive and to speak.

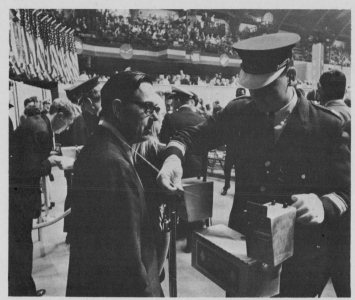

Guard inserts Identification Tag of delegate into security machine at 1968 Democratic Presidential Convention in Chicago.

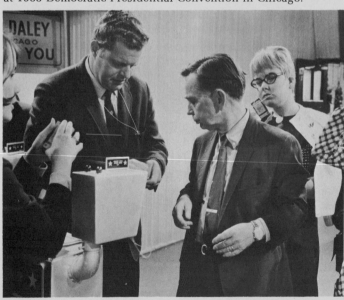

Delegates line up at security machine. Identification Tags were generally worn around neck. Note girl in background holding tag to cheek. Will this innovation become commonplace? Are the vertical line markings on supermarket products the beginning of the computer age that will witness the emergence of Antichrist?

The individual brought to life is the Antichrist, and the statue is of him.

It is at this time that in Revelation 13:15 we read that the False Prophet decrees "...that as many as would not worship the image of the beast (Antichrist) should be killed."

If you look back at verse 5 of this same chapter you will read:

> And it was given to him to make war with the saints and to overcome them; and authority over every tribe and people and tongue and nation was given to him. (Revelation 13:7)

It is then further revealed how the Antichrist will try to overcome the saints.

And this is how it will happen. He sets up this great religious system with himself (Antichrist) as its god. And in Revelation 13:16-17 we are told:

> And He who sat on the cloud swung His sickle over the earth; and the earth was reaped. (16)
>
> And another angel came out of the temple which is in heaven, and he also had a sharp sickle. (17)

Therefore, in that day it will be impossible to buy or sell without this identifying sign either on the back of your hand or on your forehead. When an individual refuses to submit to the authority of the Antichrist and will not allow this mark to be put on his body, he faces the consequences of either starving to death slowly or else being slain by a representative of the then existing government.

AMERICA AND THE MARK OF THE BEAST

You may recall that Sunday evening, August 25, 1968 on prime time television, CBS reporter Walter Cronkite was describing to a television audience of millions—preparations for the Democratic political convention.

Graphically he told of the over 8000 police, national guard and army units that ringed the convention center to keep unauthorized personnel at least a mile away from the site. He showed the elaborate security precautions that made it even difficult for delegates to enter.

Their bags and their pockets were subject to close search. Each delegate carried two means of identification—one a badge and the other a special tag.

A fig tree at Jerusalem in full leaf, before invasion of locusts. The same tree 15 minutes later, completely denuded of every leaf by a locust swarm. Huge swarms of locusts are becoming increasingly prevalent today. Locusts can devour 8500 tons or crops a day and have forced thousands of Africans into starvation. This is a prelude of the Tribulation judgments.

This identifying tag was to be placed in a computer upon entering the building. If the tag was in order a green light went on. If the tag was not in order a red light flashed and an alarm sounded.

So distressed was commentator Cronkite by the wall of tight security that he ended his program with the following:

> **"So tight is delegate security in Chicago that it allows only one more security precaution—that of placing a tattoo on the arm of each delegate. A Democratic convention is about to begin in a police state. There's just no other way of saying it."**

What does this mean: It is a sad commentary on free democratic America when it becomes necessary to arm to the teeth to protect its own people. This is part of the fruits of barring prayers from school and opening the doors to pornography. More important what seemed a fairy tale to many—the book of Revelation—is sooner than expected becoming a reality. But who would think indications of the Last Days would be revealed here in America. Revelation 13:16 tells us that "he (False Prophet) causeth all, both small and great, rich and poor, free and bond, to receive a mark in their right hand, or in their foreheads."

WHAT IS THE IDENTIFYING MARK

What this identifying mark will be...the Lord has not desired to make clear to us at this time.

It may be the number "**666**" which is the number of MAN and stops short of the perfect number 7. Thus "**666**" may well represent the humanistic and sinful counterfeit Satanic Trinity falling short of the divine 777, and catering to lost and fallen man. You will recall man was created on the *sixth* day, and in Daniel 3:1-7 we read where Nebuchadnezzar's image to be worshipped was sixty cubits in height, six cubits wide and six instruments of music summoned the worshippers to worship him.

The Number 666

Ever since Henry Kissinger's rise to prominence in world affairs, I have been flooded with phone calls and letters concerning this man.

Some people have called me claiming to have special visions. Others have met me personally, and in confidential terms expressed that they had the key to the answer of who Antichrist was.

In each case, the individual was certain that Antichrist was Henry Kissinger. Some have constructed elaborate number-letter charts based on the Bible verse, Revelation 13:18 which reads:

> Here is wisdom. Let him who has understanding calculate the number of the beast, for the number is that of a man; and his number is six hundred and sixty-six.

Some have come up with the following numerical chart to buttress their conclusion that Henry Kissinger is the Antichrist.

It, however, would be both unfair and unwise for any Christian at this time to label Henry Kissinger as Antichrist —for who knows, perhaps your name too adds up to 666?

The chart starts at A and increases each letter by 6

		The Name & Number
A - 6	N - 84	
B - 12	O - 90	
C - 18	P - 96	**K** - 66
D - 24	Q - 102	**I** - 54
E - 30	R - 108	**S** - 114
F - 36	S - 114	**S** - 114
G - 42	T - 120	**I** - 54
H - 48	U - 126	**N** - 84
I - 54	V - 132	**G** - 42
J - 60	W - 138	**E** - 30
K - 66	X - 144	**R** - 108
L - 72	Y - 150	**666**
M - 78	Z - 156	

However it must be kept in mind that this same type of numbering system has been used in the past to show that others, including the Pope of Rome, is to be the Antichrist.

One title of the Pope of Rome is Vicarivs Filii Dei. If you take the letters of his title which represent Latin numerals (printed large) and add them together, they come to **666** as per the computation listed below.

V	-	5	F	-	0
I	-	1	I	-	1
C	-	100	L	-	50
A	-	0	I	-	1
R	-	0	I	-	1
I	-	1		
V	-	5	D	-	500
S	-	0	E	-	0
			I	-	1

666

Others have said that **666** applies to Pope Paul VI:

PAUL VI = 6 letters in his name
Paul in latin is Paulus. This is also 6 letters.
He was the 6th Pope named Paul

Thus, **666**

His ELECTION was on 6/21/63
(This involves 2 6's and 2 + 1 + 3 = 6)

Thus, **666**

At age 66, he was the 6th Pope elected in the 20th century.

Therefore, **666**

His crowning took place on 6/30/63
(Again, 2 6's and 3 + 3 = 6)

Therefore, **666**

While Pope Paul VI was in office, the traditional mass of the Catholic Church was changed to a "new order of Mass." This change brought a split in the church.

The important thing to remember is that at this present time, **nobody knows who Antichrist is,** and certainly no Christian will know.

The Antichrist will not be known for certain as the Antichrist until the middle of the Tribulation Period (after the Rapture) when his human identity will at last be revealed. Matthew 24:15 shows this to be so.

Ancient Number Code Possible*

Or, it may be that Antichrist's name or title may add up to a total equalling "**666**" using the following ancient number code (this code could be applied to any alphabetical language):

$$A = 1$$
$$B = 2$$
$$C = 3$$
$$D = 4$$
$$E = 5$$
$$F = 6$$
$$G = 7$$
$$H = 8$$
$$I = 9$$
$$J = 10$$
$$K = 20$$
$$L = 30$$
$$M = 40$$
$$N = 50$$
$$O = 60$$
$$P = 70$$
$$Q = 80$$
$$R = 90$$
$$S = 100$$
$$T = 200$$
$$U = 300$$
$$V = 400$$
$$W = 500$$
$$X = 600$$
$$Y = 700$$
$$Z = 800$$

Those people who do carry this mark will most likely prefer to have it on the back of their right hand so that it can readily be seen in the act of signing checks and buying.

It is conceivable that the daily papers will contain a list of the names of those who have been killed the day before who have refused to have this mark imprinted on their forehead or on their hand.

---

*The above is an excerpt from pp. 32-35 of **KISSINGER: MAN OF PEACE**, Salem Kirban, 1974, 64 pages, $1.50.

According to Revelation 20:4, the instrument of death will be the guillotine, or some similar beheading agent.

Will the guillotine soon become the standard method of execution again? Read Revelation 20:4.

THE 7 TRUMPET JUDGMENTS

1st
TRUMPET

HAIL
FIRE
BLOOD

⅓ Earth
on fire
⅓ Trees
burned
All Grass
burned

2nd
TRUMPET

FALLING
METEOR

Destroys
⅓ Ships
⅓ Fish
⅓ Sea filled
with Blood

3rd
TRUMPET

FALLING
STAR

Poisons
⅓ of all
Water on
Earth

4th
TRUMPET

SUN,
MOON &
STARS

⅓ of Sun,
Moon
& Stars
Darkened

5th
TRUMPET

LOCUSTS

5 Months
of Torture
by Scorpion
Stings

6th
TRUMPET

SATAN'S
ARMY

200 Million
Warriors
Kill ⅓
of Mankind

INTERVAL

CHRIST
Takes
Control
of Earth

Two
Witnesses
Testify of
Christ's
Soon
Coming

7th
TRUMPET

EARTH-
QUAKE

7000
Die in
Jerusalem
People run
to mountains

LAST 3½ YEARS OF 7 YEAR TRIBULATION PERIOD

(Continues on to next chart)

With the reign of terror which demands that everyone wear the identifying mark of the Antichrist, and with plague judgments of the Lord, there will be a mass exodus in which the Jews will try to flee from this destruction into what to them will be unfamiliar and unfriendly territory.

Some Bible scholars believe the area they will flee to is the city of Petra. Others suggest a flight into the wilderness of the nations of the world.

THE SEVEN TRUMPETS

What are these plagues that will come at this time?

The first is a series of Seven Trumpets which are sounded to blow an alarm.

THE
FIRST
TRUMPET

HAIL, FIRE, BLOOD

⅓ Earth on Fire
⅓ Trees Burned
All Grass Burned

*And the **first** sounded, and there came hail and fire, mixed with blood, and they were thrown to the earth; and a third of the earth was burnt up, and a third of the trees were burnt up, and all the green grass was burnt up. (Revelation 8:7).*

Here we find that hail and fire mingled with blood are cast upon the earth and a third of all the trees on the earth will be burned up and all the green grass will be burned up.

This is God's judgment upon nature. God is cursing the earth because it is the scene of man's display of lawlessness.

FALLING METEOR

Destroys
1/3 Ships
1/3 Fish
1/3 Sea filled with

THE
SECOND
TRUMPET

*And the **second angel** sounded, and something like a great mountain burning with fire was thrown into the sea; and a third of the sea became blood; and a third of the creatures, which were in the sea and had life, died; and a third of the ships were destroyed. (Revelation 8:8-9).*

When the second angel blows his trumpet, what appears to be a huge burning mountain is thrown into the sea.

There are some that believe that this refers to a huge meteor falling from the sky.

When this does occur, it will destroy a third of all the ships on earth and a third of the sea will be turned blood red and a third of all the fish will be killed.

THE
THIRD
TRUMPET

FALLING STAR

Poisons
⅓ of all
Water on Earth

*And the **third angel** sounded, and a great star fell from heaven, burning like a torch, and it fell on a third of the rivers and on the springs of waters; and the name of the star is called Wormwood; and a third of the waters became wormwood; and many men died from the waters, because they were made bitter. (Revelation 8:10-11).*

Here we see an unusual phenomenon. A great flaming star falls from the heaven. This may be another meteor.

This star will be referred to as bitterness or "wormwood" because it will poison a third of all water on the earth and many people will die from the poisonous rivers and springs.

SUN, MOON & STARS

THE
FOURTH
TRUMPET

⅓ of Sun, Moon
& Stars DARKENED

And the ***fourth angel*** *sounded, and a third of the sun and a third of the moon and a third of the stars were smitten, so that a third of them might be darkened and the day might not shine for a third of it, and the night in the same way. (Revelation 8:12).*

With the blowing of the fourth trumpet by the fourth angel, one third of the sun and the moon and the stars are darkened.

Now just for a moment look back to Luke 21:25-26. Here we read these very prophecies which have not yet occurred and yet which will occur in the last half of the Tribulation Period.

> And there will be signs in sun and moon and stars, and upon the earth dismay among nations, in perplexity at the roaring of the sea and the waves. (25)
>
> Men fainting from fear and the expectation of the things which are coming upon the world; for the powers of the heavens will be shaken. (26)

THE NEXT THREE TRUMPETS BRING FORTH GREATER WRATH

> And I looked, and I heard an eagle flying in mid-heaven, saying with a loud voice, Woe, woe, woe, to those who dwell on the earth; because of the remaining blasts of the trumpet of the three angels who are about to sound! (Revelation 8:13)

The people living on earth during this Tribulation Period will have seen hail and fire mixed with blood thrown down upon the earth.

They will have seen one-third of the trees burned. They will have seen all the green grass burned up.

They will have seen what may be a meteor thrown into the sea and a third of all the ships destroyed and a third of all the sea turned into blood with a third of all the fish being killed.

They will see another great flaming star fall from heaven upon one-third of all the rivers and springs of the world. This star will poison these waters and cause thousands of people to die.

They will also see a third of the sun and the moon and the stars darkened. This will cause the daylight to be very dim and the nighttime to be very dark. It will be a supernatural darkness over the face of the earth.

But as terrible as all this is, the Lord warns that the next three trumpets that will be sounded will bring even greater wrath upon those people still remaining on earth. Thus these last trumpet judgments the 5th, 6th, and 7th, are called **"Woes"** (Revelation 8:13; 9:12; 11:14).

THE FIRST WOE

**THE
FIFTH
TRUMPET**

LOCUSTS
5 Months of
Torture by
Scorpion Stings

And out of the smoke came forth locusts upon the earth; and power was given them, as the scorpions of the earth have power. (3)

And they were told that they should not hurt the grass of the earth, nor any green thing, nor any tree, but only the men who do not have the seal of God on their foreheads. (4)

And they were not permitted to kill anyone, but to torment for five months; and their torment was like the torment of a scorpion when it stings a man. (5)

And in those days men will seek death and will not find it; and they will long to die and death flees from them. (6)

And the appearance of the locusts was like horses prepared for battle; and on their heads, as it were, crowns like gold, and their faces were like the faces of men. (7)

And they had hair like the hair of women, and their teeth were like the teeth of lions. (8)

And they had breastplates like breastplates of iron; and the sound of their wings was like the sound of chariots, of many horses rushing to battle. (9)

And they have tails like scorpions, and stings; and in their tails is their power to hurt men for five months. (10)

They have a king over them, the angel of the abyss; his name in Hebrew is Abaddon, and in the Greek he has the name Apollyon. (11)

The **first Woe** is past; behold, two Woes are still coming after these things. (12) (Revelation 9:3-12).

From reading the description on the previous page it may be difficult for the reader to visualize the terrible wrath of God that will be poured out upon those people who do not have the mark of God.

Notice in verse 4 that the locusts are going to attack those people who did not have the seal of GOD on their foreheads.

While it might seem like a science fiction story to you, it is an actual fact that these locusts, or whatever they represent, will be much larger than ordinary locusts and they will not look like the locust of today.

Ordinary locusts feed on vegetation. But you will note that these locusts, as mentioned in the Scriptures just quoted, are forbidden to eat the grass or the trees or any green thing.

They will not be permitted to kill, but only to torment.

They will be a combination in appearance of a horse, man, woman, lion and scorpion and undoubtedly will be very frightful in appearance. It is difficult for us to visualize or understand their exact nature, but that day will declare it.

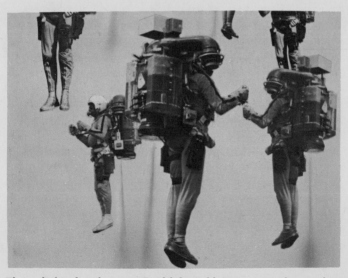

Flying belts already exist! Could the Fifth Trumpet judgment be an army of flying men equipped with poisonous sprays that can be released over wide areas?

THE SECOND WOE

THE
SIXTH
TRUMPET

SATAN'S ARMY
200 Million
Warriors
Kill ⅓ of
Mankind

And the **sixth angel** sounded, and I heard a voice from the four horns of the golden-altar which is before God. *(13)*

One saying to the sixth angel who had the trumpet, "Release the four angels who are bound at the great river Euphrates." *(14)*

And the four angels, who had been prepared for the hour and day and month and year, were released, so that they might kill a third of mankind. *(15)*

And the number of the armies of the horsemen was two hundred million; I heard the number of them. *(16)*

And this is how I saw in the vision the horses and those who sat on them; the riders had breastplates the color of fire and of hyacinth and of brimstone; and the heads of the horses are like the heads of lions; and out of their mouths proceed fire and smoke and brimstone. *(17)*

A third of mankind was killed by these three plagues, by the fire and the smoke and the brimstone, which proceeded out of their mouths. *(18)*

For the power of the horses is in their mouth and in their tails; for their tails are like serpents and have heads; and with them they do harm. *(19)*

And the rest of mankind, who were not killed by these plagues, did not repent of THE WORKS OF THEIR HANDS, so as not to worship DEMONS, AND THE IDOLS OF GOLD AND OF SILVER AND OF BRASS AND OF STONE AND OF WOOD, WHICH CAN NEITHER SEE NOR HEAR NOR WALK. *(20)*

And they did not repent of their murders nor of their sorceries nor of their immortality nor of their thefts. *(21)* *(Revelation 9:13-21).*

The sixth trumpet reveals what seems to be a marching army of 200,000,000 men (200 million). This army will destroy one-third of the world's population as it travels across the world. Read verse 15 just quoted.

Some may doubt that there could be such an army of 200 million warriors. However, in view of the world population of 3 1/2 billion you can see that this is altogether possible even now.

In China alone in 1961 (population of over 760 million) there were an estimated 200 million armed and organized militiamen (Associated Press release, April 24, 1964). It is said that the largest army ever to go into a field of battle was under Xerxes. This was when he invaded Greece.

For four years Xerxes collected troops and war materials for his invasion. Then in 481 B.C. he set forth to war with an army that Herodotus estimated to be 2,641,000 fighting men. There were an equal number of engineers, slaves, merchants and food suppliers.

The army was made up of Persians, Medes, Babylonians, Assyrians, Scyths, Phoenicians, Syrians, Egyptians, Ethiopians, Libyans and a host of other nationalities. There were chariots, cavalrymen and footmen. There were even elephants! Over 1200 ships were needed to transport this army.

When the Persian fleet entered the Bay of Salamis, it found its 1200 hundred strong ships no match for the 300 Greek boats with skilled oarsmen. The Persian fleet made up of so many nationalities could not cope with the confusion of tongues, minds and superfluous ships and the Greeks won the battle!

The four Satanic angels will loose 200 million troops against the earth. It may be difficult to think in such terms, particularly since during World War II at the height of the conflict, America had only 12 million men under arms.

These warriors will ride on horses and may in some sense be super-human. Those on earth will not be able to stop them nor will they be able to conquer them.

While the army of locusts did not kill any men—only tormented them—this army of horsemen will leave in its wake, one-third of the earth's population—dead.

But although one-third of the earth's population will be killed by these horsemen, the other two-thirds will still refuse to repent or turn towards God.

On December 15, 1978, President Jimmy Carter announced the rejection of Free Taiwan and the beginning of full diplomatic relations with the People's Republic of China (Red China). Senator Barry Goldwater called this step by President Carter "a cowardly act." In effect, we abandoned our god-fearing friends (Taiwan) in favor of atheistic Communism. This move strengthens the hand of the Asiatic army for its eventual invasion attempt of Israel.

One would think that after this terrible slaughtering there would be a season of turning to God.

You may recall, we previously mentioned 2 Thessalonians 2:8-12. This passage shows that the mass of people at this time, as before, will prefer to believe a lie.

> And then that lawless one will be revealed whom the Lord will slay with the breath of His mouth and bring to an end by the appearance of His coming; (8)
>
> That is, the one whose coming is in accord with the activity of Satan, with all power and signs and false wonders, (9)
>
> And with all the deception of wickedness for those who perish, because they did not receive the love of the truth so as to be saved. (10)
>
> And for this reason God will send upon them a deluding influence so that they might believe what is false, (11)
>
> In order that they all may be judged who did not believe the truth, but took pleasure in wickedness. (12)

If we were to compare the death rate of judgments just described on the basis of the current population of the earth which is approximately 3,500,000,000 people (3½ billion*)—the sixth trumpet with its army of horsemen will kill one-third of the world population. By today's figures this would be over ONE BILLION PEOPLE KILLED! (*source, Statistical Office, United Nations). Even if the killing should *only* involve the slaying of a third of the people in one continent the number would still be staggering—in the millions.

THE TWO WITNESSES

In Revelation 11:3-5 we read the following:

> *"And I will grant authority to my two witnesses, and they will prophesy for twelve hundred and sixty days, clothed in sackcloth." (3)*

> *These are the two olive trees and the two lampstands that stand before the Lord of the earth. (4)*

> *And if any one desires to harm them, fire proceeds out of their mouth and devours their enemies; and if any one would desire to harm them, in this manner he must be killed. (5)*

Here is the prophecy that the Lord will send Two Witnesses to prophesy during half of the Tribulation Period.

Note that in verse 6 "They have power to shut the skies so that no rain will fall during the three and a half years they prophesy."

This seems to indicate that one of the two will be Elijah or Elijah-like. It is worthy to note that Elijah was translated and that he might therefore come again during this day of Tribulation since he has never died. He will shut up the heavens for 42 months or 3½ years—which is exactly the same length of time as he did in the days of Ahab.

> *These have the power to shut up the sky, in order that rain may not fall during the days of their prophesying; and they have power over the waters to turn them into blood, and to smite the earth with every plague, as often as they desire. (Revelation 11:6)*

This would identify the other witness as Moses. For Moses is the only person mentioned in the Scriptures who had such power and it may be that for this purpose his body was saved from desecration.

> *But Michael the archangel, when he disputed with the devil and argued about the body of Moses did not dare pronounce against him a railing judgment, but said, "The Lord rebuke you." (Jude 1:9)*

During their period of witnessing, the two witnesses will have the power to destroy their enemies with fire. But this power will end 1260 days (3½ years) after they will appear. At that time they will be killed and their bodies will lie exposed in the streets of Jerusalem for 3½ days. At the end of the 3½ days, they will rise and ascend to heaven to the amazement of everyone. Read Revelation 11:11.

THE THIRD WOE

THE
SEVENTH
TRUMPET

EARTHQUAKE
7000 Die in
Jerusalem
People Run
to Mountains

*And the **seventh angel** sounded; and there arose loud voices in heaven, saying, "The kingdom of the world has become the kingdom of our Lord, and of His Christ; and He will reign forever and ever."*

And the temple of God which is in heaven was opened; and the ark of His covenant appeared in His temple, and there were flashes of lightning and sounds and peals of thunder and an earthquake and a great hailstorm (Revelation 11:15, 19).

Before the sounding of the Seventh Trumpet by the seventh angel, the Two Witnesses are caught up in the heaven. At this time there will be a terrible earthquake that levels a tenth of the city of Jerusalem, leaving 7,000 dead. Those left in the city will give glory to God for this occurrence (Revelation 11:13).

With the sounding of the Seventh Trumpet, voices from heaven announce that the kingdom of this world now belongs to our Lord and Saviour and that He will reign forever and ever.

At that time, the heavens open, lightning flashes, thunder crashes and there is a great hailstorm and the world is shaken by a mighty earthquake.

Then begins the final and awful portion of the Tribulation Period in which the Seven Vials are opened. These portray a special manifestation of God's divine judgment and wrath.

THE 7 VIAL JUDGMENTS

1st VIAL	2nd VIAL	3rd VIAL	4th VIAL	5th VIAL	6th VIAL	7th VIAL
BOILS	SEA of BLOOD	RIVERS of BLOOD	OPPRESSIVE HEAT	DARKNESS	River Euphrates DRIED UP	HAIL
Malignant Sores affect those with Mark of Antichrist	Everything in Ocean Dies	Rivers and Springs turn to Blood	Sun Scorches ALL Mankind	Earth Plunged into Darkness	Army Marches on Israel	Cities Crumble

CHRIST RETURNS to Earth with Believers

The 1000 Year Millenium Period for Believers BEGINS

BATTLE of ARMA-GEDDON

SATAN cast into BOTTOMLESS PIT.

FALSE PROPHET and ANTI-CHRIST in LAKE OF FIRE

CONTINUATION OF LAST 3½ YEARS OF TRIBULATION PERIOD

THE POURING OF
THE SEVEN VIALS OF WRATH

BOILS

Malignant
Sores affect
those with
Mark of Antichrist

THE
FIRST
VIAL

And I heard a loud voice from the temple, saying to the seven angels, "Go and pour out the seven bowls of the wrath of God into the earth."

And the **first angel** went and poured out his **bowl** into the earth; and it became a loathsome and malignant sore upon the men who had the mark of the beast and who worshiped his image (Revelation 16:1-2).

With the judgment of the First Vial, there comes a great running festering sore upon the body of every man who gave allegiance to the Antichrist and to the False Prophet. These malignant sores will be horrible in appearance. It may be that the mark of the Beast upon them is a tattoo, and for some reason there is a disease which breaks out in connection with an infection of these tattoos.

THE
SECOND
VIAL

SEA of BLOOD

Everything in
Ocean Dies

*And the **second angel** poured out his **bowl** into the sea, and it became blood like that of a dead man; and every living thing in the sea died (Revelation 16:3).*

Once again the sea is turned to blood with the announcement of the opening of the Second Vial. As the waters turned to blood in Egypt in Moses' day by a miracle of God so shall it be again—only here on a worldwide level.

It brings worldwide death. Every living creature in the sea will die. And the sea will become as the "blood of a dead man."

 THE THIRD VIAL — RIVERS of BLOOD — Rivers and Springs Turn to Blood

And the **third angel** poured out his **bowl** into the rivers and the springs of waters; and they became blood.

And I heard the angel of the waters saying, "Righteous art Thou, who are and who wast, O Holy One, because Thou didst judge these things;

For they poured out the blood of saints and prophets, and Thou has given them blood to drink. They deserve it."

And I heard the altar saying, "Yes, O Lord God, the Almighty, true and righteous are Thy judgments" (Revelation 16:4-7).

With this judgment, all of the rivers will become blood (or bloodlike). These will be terrible times when there will be nothing to quench the thirst but to drink the blood that exists in the waterways throughout the earth. It will be a time of great famine and thirst.

THE FOURTH VIAL

OPPRESSIVE HEAT

Sun Scorches all Mankind

*And the **fourth angel** poured out his **bowl** upon the sun; and it was given to it to scorch men with fire.*

And men were scorched with fierce heat; and they blasphemed the name of God who has the power over these plagues; and they did not repent, so as to give Him glory (Revelation 16:8-9).

The relationship between the sun and the earth will be, in some way, at this time, so altered that the sun will burn all that live upon the face of the earth, scorching them like fire.

Instead of turning to God, this judgment will cause men to curse God.

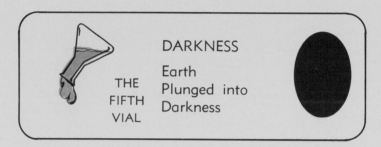

DARKNESS

Earth
Plunged into
Darkness

THE
FIFTH
VIAL

*And the **fifth angel** poured out his **bowl** upon the throne of the beast; and his kingdom became darkened; and they gnawed their tongues because of pain.*

And they blasphemed the God of heaven because of their pains and their sores; and they did not repent of their deeds (Revelation 16:10-11).

In the Fifth Vial we have the judgment upon all those who are in the kingdom of the Antichrist. We are told that they will gnaw their tongues in pain and they will curse the God of the Heaven because of their pain and suffering.

Notice that this follows the plague of scorching heat as mentioned in the Fourth Vial. This Fifth Vial will bring darkness over the entire earth and cause even greater suffering. As in Egypt was the darkness of the Mosaic plague, so here it shall be again.

RIVER Euphrates
DRIED UP

THE
SIXTH
VIAL

Army Marches
on Israel

And the **sixth angel** poured out his **bowl** upon the great river, the Euphrates; and its water was dried up, that the way might be prepared for the kings from the east.

And I saw coming out of the mouth of the dragon and out of the mouth of the beast and out of the mouth of the false prophet, three unclean spirits like frogs;

For they are spirits of demons, performing signs, which go out to the kings of the whole world, to gather them together for the war of the great day of God, the Almighty.

(Behold, I am coming like a thief. Blessed is the one who stays awake and keeps his garments, lest he walk about naked and men see his shame.)

And they gathered them together to the place which in Hebrew is called Har-Magedon (Revelation 16:12-16).

At the opening of the Sixth Vial, we see the River Euphrates completely dried up so that the kings of the east (India, China and Japan) and their armies can cross over and gather for the soon coming Battle of Armageddon.

The prophet, Isaiah foretells this someday occurring in Isaiah 11:15:

> And the Lord will utterly destroy
> The tongue of the Sea of Egypt;
> And He will wave His hand over the River
> With His scorching wind;
> And He will strike it into seven streams,
> And make men walk over dry-shod.

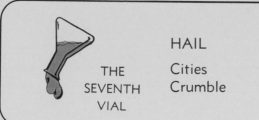

THE SEVENTH VIAL

HAIL
Cities Crumble

*And the **seventh angel** poured out his **bowl** upon the air; and a loud voice came out of the temple from the throne, saying, "It is done."*

And there were flashes of lightning and sounds of peals of thunder; and there was a great earthquake, such as there had not been since man came to be upon the earth, so great an earthquake was it, and so mighty.

And the great city was split into three parts, and the cities of the nations fell. And Babylon the great was remembered before God, to give her the cup of the wine of His fierce wrath.

And every island fled away, and the mountains were not found.

And huge hailstones, about one hundred pounds each, came down from heaven upon men; and men blasphemed God because of the plague of the hail, because its plague was extremely severe (Revelation 16:17-21).

God's final display of wrath is shown when he empties the Seventh Vial.

Undoubtedly, in reading these horrible judgments that God inflicts, one can appreciate something of God's hatred for sin and God's judgment on sinners and upon the scene of man's sins.

FOUR PURPOSES FOR THE
TRIBULATION

Amid God's all embracing purposes for bringing the Tribulation upon the earth, we can see four items clearly:

1. **Israel:** The nation Israel watched with interest the Lord Jesus Christ when he lived on earth. They avidly followed His miracles. But when He asked them to turn to Himself, they would not have fellowship with Him and they rejected Him.

   Because of this rejection wrath is poured out upon them in the form of a Tribulation Period. This will finally cause Israel to turn to her Christ (Zechariah 12:10).

2. **The Gentile Nations:** God is going to judge the Gentile Nations because they have turned to sin and unbelief and have been the oppressors of Israel.

   After the Tribulation judgments there will be a judgment on living Gentiles. The Lord will separate the Gentiles in two classes when He returns—the saved (those who have been born again and are Believers) and the unsaved (those who reject Him as Christ: Matthew 25:31-46).

3. **To reveal the true program of Satan:** A third purpose of God in allowing the Tribulation to occur is to reveal once and for all to everyone the real program of Satan in all of its true sinister character and demonism.

   From the time Satan rebelled against God before man was created until the present, he has always desired to be the head of the kingdom. Antichrist will, in some measure, fulfill this hope of Satan but in the end will be cast into the Lake of Fire for everlasting destruction.

4. **Judgment upon those who reject Him:** To those who reject Christ as their personal Saviour and do not honor Him as their Lord, God is going to inflict them in the Tribulation Period with His wrath because of their lawlessness and their rejection of the Gospel.

   The Bible tells us that so great will be their suffering that they will seek physical death and will not be able to find it.

> And they said to the mountains and to the rocks,
> "Fall on us and hide us from the presence of Him
> who sits on the throne, and from the wrath of the
> Lamb (Revelation 6:16).

The amazing thing is that in spite of this suffering, they will not only continue in their rejection of Christ but will also curse Him.

Here then is much of God's purpose in the Tribulation. First, for Israel, it is to clean this nation and bring a remnant to Himself; then for the Gentiles, it is to punish them because of sin and unbelief shown in their disgraceful treatment of the Jews; then for Satan, it is to reveal the true identity of his kingdom and his sinister motives; and to the unbelievers it is to punish them for rejecting Christ as their Lord and Saviour.

So we see, what briefly appeared to be (in the first 3½ years of the Tribulation) a world at peace with a safe and satisfied Israel suddenly becoming in the last 3½ years an era of terror and tragedy.

But the worst is still to come!

11
The Day Russia Dies

The Russian Desire to "Save" the World • Russia's Growing Influence • The Growing Russian Empire • Religion • Its Warpower • Why Russia Will Invade Israel • Russia in the Scriptures • The Plan of Attack • The Conquest • A Miracle Occurs

The Russian astronaut, Gherman Titoy said after his return from space...

> "Some people say there is a God out there...but in my travels around the earth all day long, I looked around and didn't see Him...I saw no God nor angels. The rocket was made by our own people. I don't believe in God. I believe in man, his strength, his possibilities, his reason."

The Lord anticipated this type of unbelief and we read in 2 Peter 3:3-4:

> Know this first of all, that in the last days mockers will come with their mocking, following after their own lusts, (3)

> And saying, "Where is the promise of His coming? For ever since the fathers fell asleep, all continues just as it was from the beginning of creation." (4)

THE RUSSIAN DESIRE TO "SAVE" THE WORLD

It was five o'clock in the morning in Prague. The city was asleep.

Suddenly a young man raced through the street outside the Prague radio station—a modern day Paul Revere—bellowing his warning plea through his car window.

The beginning of sorrows. A Czechoslovakian woman cries in anguish as she holds photo of her country's leaders in defiance of invading Russian troops. ". . . ye shall hear of wars . . . all these things must come to pass . . . nation shall rise up against nation . . . kingdom against kingdom . . . all these are the beginning of sorrows . . . and many false prophets shall rise, and shall deceive many" (Matthew 24:6-8, 11).

His face was contorted with anguish and anger.

With all the volume left within him he shouted...

> "Blow your claxon (horn). Drive through the streets. Wake everybody up. They've come. They've come!"

And within a few short hours they did come and covered all of Czechoslovakia with their half million men.

Once again the Russians had arrived and made a new conquest.

This time they had come much to the embarrassing surprise of the United States government.

To help them in the invasion of Czechoslovakia were troops from Hungary, Bulgaria, Poland and East Germany.

This invasion plan was carried out with such stealth and speed that it took the world by surprise. U.S. Intelligence included.

Ironically, it came less than 24 hours before President Johnson was to announce his own surprise ... a summit meeting with Soviet Premier Alexei Kosygin to discuss limiting nuclear arms.

What made the Russians invade Czechoslovakia and why did they accomplish it with no resistance from western powers?

To justify the invasion of its Warsaw Pact ally by four of the five other members, Moscow offered this specious explanation: Czech government and Communist Party officials—whom it never named—had requested armed intervention to prevent counter revolution.

Because humanity is hanging on to one small thread of existence and because any movement by western powers might result in a nuclear holocaust that would sever that thread—the United States and its allies believed the only recourse would be through formal diplomatic protest.

Besides, from a practical standpoint, Russia had tipped the balance in central Europe in troop capacities ready for war.

While NATO forces had a total of some 778,000 troops in central Europe including the 210,000 from the United States ...Russia and her allies had 790,000 troops from their Warsaw Pact of nations.

3 DECISIVE WARS

War	Participants	Occurs	Reason for War	Outcome	Scripture References
1	Russia and Allies (Arab nations, Iran, Germany) vs. Israel	Before or during first 3½ years of Tribulation Period (This could happen at any time!)	Russia desires Israel's vast mineral wealth.	God will intervene and through an earthquake in Israel plus rain and hail, the Russian army will be wiped out. It will take the Israelites 7 years to collect the debris. It will also take them 7 months to bury the dead!	Ezekiel 38:1-39:16
2 Battle of Armageddon	Armies from All Nations vs. God at Jerusalem	At End of 7 year Tribulation Period	Flushed with power Antichrist will defy God, seek to destroy the 144,000 witnessing Jews and Jerusalem.	The Lord Jesus Christ comes down from heaven and wipes out the combined armies of more than 200 million men. The blood bath covers over 185 miles of Israel and is "even unto the horse bridles." (Revelation 14:20) Antichrist and the False Prophet are cast alive into the Lake of Fire. (Revelation 19:20) Satan is bound in the bottomless pit for 1000 years. (Revelation 20:1-3)	Joel 3:9, 12 Zechariah 14:1-4 Revelation 16:13-16 Revelation 19:11-21 Ezekiel 39:17-29
3 The Final Rebellion	Satan vs. God	At End of 1000 year Millennium Period	God allows Satan one more opportunity on earth to preach his deceiving message.	Satan will be successful in deceiving vast multitudes (out of those born during the millennial period) to turn away from Christ. This horde of perhaps millions of people will completely circle the Believers in Jerusalem in a state of siege. When this occurs, God brings FIRE down from Heaven killing the millions in Satan's army. Satan is then cast into the Lake of Fire, where the False Prophet and Antichrist are, and they will be tormented day and night for ever and ever.	Revelation 20:7-10

It is interesting to note at this point that in the NATO forces of 778,000 are included 425,000 West Germans or more than half of this group.

Prophecy seems to indicate to us in the Book of Revelation that Germany (possibly East Germany) in the Last Days will side with Russia and her armies in the Middle East war in which Russia is a major contender (Ezekiel 38:6).

RUSSIA'S GROWING INFLUENCE

U.S. News and World Report in its August 26, 1968 issue commented on the fact that suddenly the Russians are emerging as the "Hot new salesmen in Asia."

The Soviets have sold over 2 billion board feet of Siberian lumber to Japan. And Japan in turn will pay for this five year deal with $133 million of bulldozers and other logging equipment plus $33 million in consumer goods.

There are indications that Japanese businessmen will soon be getting shipments of natural gas from Russia's island of Sakhianto, Japan. Japanese businessmen also are looking forward to a joint development of Siberian oil and minerals such as iron ore.

Russia is already Malaysia's biggest customer for rubber. Even President Marcos of the Philippines is talking of trade with Russia.

THE GROWING RUSSIAN EMPIRE

In the last 75 years there have been over 140 armed conflicts throughout the world; 25 of these have taken place in the Middle East.

But the Middle East has never seen such wars and such slaughter as will occur during the Last Days and during the Tribulation Period.

And the instigator of the first Great War will be none other than Russia and her allies.

However, this war will bring a virtual end to Soviet Communism in the Middle East for this will be the day that Russia dies.

Russia—the Union of Soviet Socialist Republics—in area the largest country in the world—stretches across two continents from the North Pacific to the Baltic Sea. It occupies the northern part of Asia and the eastern half of Europe. Its western borders brush against Finland, the Baltic, Poland, Czechoslovakia, Hungary, and Romania. On the south it is bounded by Romania, the Black Sea, Turkey, Iran, Afghanistan, China, Mongolian Peoples Republic and North Korea. In the far northeast, the Bering Strait separates it from Alaska.

This vast territory of the U.S.S.R. occupies 1/6th of the earth's land surface.

In land area it covers 8,647,172 square miles and has a population of about 260 million people. Comparative estimated population of the United States is 215 million people.

The U.S.S.R. is extremely rich in natural resources. It claims to possess 57% of the world's coal deposits, 58% of its oil, 41% of iron ore, 88% of the manganese, 54% of potassium salts, 30% of phosphates and 25% of all timberland. Gold production is estimated at more than 50% of the production of the rest of the world.

The U.S.S.R. produces about 25% of world iron ore output, 19.5% of steel.

In education it has universal compulsory education and this education is free. Recent figures indicate that there are over 200,000 primary, secondary and technical schools with enrollment of over 50 million students. The U.S.S.R. annually graduates more than 432,000 students from higher education establishments. This includes an estimated 240,000 engineers and scientists. Illiteracy has been reduced to 1.5%.

RELIGION

In 1918 Russia passed a law effecting a separation of church and state.

While nine branches of Christianity are represented in the U.S.S.R.—from reports coming out of Russia—it is certain that there is no true freedom of worship in this country. This is particularly true since its leaders are atheists and its government has persecuted Jews and Gentiles alike.

It is estimated that there are 2 million Jews in Russia.

In the Last Days, it seems that Russia will permit these Jews to leave their country and return to Israel.

ITS WARPOWER

It is difficult to arrive at any firm numbers regarding the power of its armed force both in people and equipment. It is believed that the Soviet armed forces number somewhere between 3½ million and 4½ million.

At that time it was estimated that their air force had approximately 25,000 first-line planes including a possible 300 heavy bombers and 500 medium bombers.

The total Soviet budget for strategic forces approximates 25% of Russia's national security budget—in contrast to 12% for the United States. By 1985, the Soviets will be spending at *twice* our level.

Recent reports on Russia's race to the moon and its missiles race indicate that they may be ahead in their outer space achievements. And they could well use these achievements to cause devastating destruction on their opponents.

WHY RUSSIA WILL INVADE ISRAEL

Now that we've set the background for you on Russia, perhaps you can better understand how Russia, built up as it is in self-confidence, will finally gather her armies and march into Israel. There is one important fact that warring nations seem to forget. It is this:

God does avenge Himself of all who persecute the Jew.

And when Russia (which is referred to as Gog in Ezekiel 38 and 39) leads her forces down into Israel against the defenseless Jews, God's wrath will be kindled...for He declares:

> "And it will come about on that day, when Gog comes against the land of Israel," declares the Lord God, "that My fury will mount up in My anger." (Ezekiel 38:18)

Many prophetic Bible scholars identify Gog with Russia and the author makes the following observations based on this premise.

No one can do an injustice to the Hebrew people—or for that matter to an individual of that race—because he is a Jew, and go unpunished. God distinctly declares to Abraham and his seed (the Jew),

Adolf Hitler marching before admirers in 1934 Nazi rally.

> And I will bless those who bless you,
> And the one who curses you I will curse.
> And in you all the families of the earth shall be
> blessed. *(Genesis 12:3)*

God warned men against mistreating His people when through His prophet, Zechariah, He said:

> For thus says the Lord of hosts, "After glory He has sent Me against the nations which plunder you, for he who touches you, touches the apple of His eye." *(Zechariah 2:8)*

If you would care to make a study of history you will find that every time nations have come in contact with Israel or her people and mistreated her, God has avenged Himself on these who have persecuted the Jew.

Just briefly, Egypt, which was the mightiest empire of that day, was cast down into the dust of humiliation and reduced to the basest of all kingdoms because of her persecution of Israel. The same is true for 15th century Spain.

The Assyrians adopted the same attitude towards the Jew and God in His anger cast that cruel empire into the oblivion of annihilation. All that remains of her empire of ancient power and glory are the rubbish heaps of Mesopotamia in the regions around about the Tigris River. This is also true of once mighty and triumphant Babylon.

More recently we have seen what happened in Germany when Hitler sought to wipe the Jews from the face of the earth.

It is also interesting to note that while God imposes punishment on all those who persecute the Jews, He also imparts special blessings to all those who will bless Abraham and his seed.

And the Lord is just as faithful in the fulfillment of this promise as He is in carrying out His threat against the Anti-Semites.

Too many times people think that God is only a God of love. This is not true.

While God is a God of love, He is also a God of vengeance and expresses righteous indignation every day.

In Psalm 7:11 we read:

> God is a righteous judge,
> And a God who has indignation every day. (11).

In Exodus 34:6-7 we find God's own statement on His character, which is:

> Then the Lord passed by in front of him and proclaimed, "The Lord, the Lord God, compassionate and gracious, slow to anger, and abounding in lovingkindness and truth; (6).

> Who keeps lovingkindness for thousands, who forgives iniquity, transgression and sin; yet He will by no means leave the guilty unpunished, visiting the iniquity of fathers on the children and on the grandchildren to the third and fourth generations." (7).

Since there is unrighteousness and injustice practiced every day, the God of holiness and justice of necessity has anger every day.

RUSSIA IN THE SCRIPTURES

Both Russia and her allies who will take part in this great invasion in Israel are mentioned in the Scriptures.

However, it is not the purpose of this book to get into the fine points of theology but simply relate the facts concerning the Last Days so that the ordinary layman can understand it.

If you would like to further determine for yourself how these countries are specifically mentioned in the Word of God we would recommend two books for your reading. They are:

ISRAEL AND THE NATIONS IN PROPHECY by Richard W. DeHaan, chapter 9

PROPHECY FOR TODAY, by Dr. J. Dwight Pentecost, chapter 10

To find complete information on these books look to the back of this book under the "Recommended Reading" section.

Who are these Russian allies?

The basic Russian allies that are to take part in this coalition of nations that will invade Israel appear to be: Iran, Germany, Turkey, and the other Arab states.

This coalition will come about because the Federated States of Europe will back the Jewish claims to Israel and guarantee their rights in the land of Palestine.

Because of this the Arab states will turn to Russia because it will be their only avenue to seek aid to accomplish their desires in the regaining of their land.

This war of Russia and her allies against Israel is very graphically described in Ezekiel 38:1 — 39:16.

We are quoting below Ezekiel 38:14-16,22-23, which very prophetically outlines the events to come.

> "Therefore, prophesy, son of man, and say to Gog, 'Thus says the Lord God, "On that day when My people Israel are living securely, will you not know it? (14)

> "And you will come from your place out of the remote parts of the north, you and many peoples with you, all of them riding on horses, a great assembly and a mighty army; (15)

And you will come up against My people Israel
like a cloud to cover the land. It will come about
in the last days that I shall bring you against My
land, in order that the nations may know Me
when I shall be sanctified through you before
their eyes, O Gog." (16)

"And with pestilence and with blood I shall enter
into judgment with him; and I shall rain on him,
and on his troops, and on the many peoples who
are with him, a torrential rain, with hailstones,
fire, and brimstone. (22)

"And I shall magnify Myself, sanctify Myself, and
make Myself known in the sight of many nations;
and they will know that I am the Lord." (23)

On the basis of the Scriptures just quoted, it is possible
to make the following statements:

1. The invasion of Israel will occur in the Last Days.

After many days you will be summoned; in the
latter years you will come into the land that is
restored from the sword, whose inhabitants have
been gathered from many nations to the mountains of Israel which had been a continual waste;
but its people were brought out from the nations,
and they are living securely, all of them. (Ezekiel
38:8)

And you will come up against My people Israel
like a cloud to cover the land. It will come about
in the last days that I shall bring you against My
land, in order that the nations may know Me when
I shall be sanctified through you before their
eyes, O Gog. (Ezekiel 38:16)

**2. The invasion of Israel will occur when Israel is dwelling
in safety and feeling secure in their land.**

Thus says the Lord God, "It will come about on
that day, that thoughts will come into your mind,
and you will devise an evil plan, (Ezekiel 38:10)

And you will say, 'I will go up against the land
of unwalled villages. I will go against those who
are at rest, that live securely, all of them living
without walls, and having no bars or gates. (Ezekiel 38:11)

Israeli women lay barb wire in preparation for coming invasion.

"Therefore, prophesy, son of man, and say to Gog, 'Thus says the Lord God, "On that day when My people Israel are living securely, will you not know it?" (Ezekiel 38:14)

3. The invasion will come from the "north parts."

"And you will come from your place out of the remote parts of the north, you and many peoples with you, all of them riding on horses, a great assembly and a mighty army." (Ezekiel 38:15)

Gomer with all its troops; Beth-togarmah from the remote parts of the north with all its troops — many peoples with you. (Ezekiel 38:6)

And I shall turn you around, drive you on, take you up from the remotest parts of the north, and bring you against the mountains of Israel. (Ezekiel 39:2)

If you look at your map, you will find that Russia is the nation which meets this qualification.

In reading Scripture, it is always important to remember that Palestine is the hub of all prophetic Scriptures and therefore, any points of the compass that are given in Scripture are generally given in relation to Israel. Israel is rightly regarded as the geographic center of the earth's surface. So when the Bible speaks of south, it means south of Palestine...when it speaks of the north, it means north of Palestine, etc.

If you will draw a straight line from Jerusalem to the North Pole on your map, you will find that this line will pass right near the city of Moscow. Both Moscow and Jerusalem are located near the same meridian, Jerusalem 35° 10' and Moscow 37° 40' east of Greenwich.

Thus we see that the northern armies will be Russian and they will meet a crushing defeat when they invade Israel in the Last Days.

In these Last Days we will find 4 great kingdoms as follows:

1. Russia and her allies
2. Egypt and the Arab countries
3. Europe in the Western Federation of States
4. Oriental or Asiatic powers.

THE PLAN OF ATTACK

In other chapters of this book we discussed how Israel will finally be in peace in her land. The European western states, which may be called the Federated States of Europe, will guarantee her safety.

Because of this short period of safety, many people will temporarily think that at last the world has conquered war and from now on there will be peace and we will have a "heaven on earth."

However, this period of safety for Israel will be short lived. It is possible that during this time, Russia will allow the 2 million Jews in her country to return to Israel.

Naturally she will have ulterior motives in allowing this to happen, but it will be looked on with favor from the other states.

However, Russia cannot sit idle too long, particularly when she views the vast natural wealth in Palestine and the tremendous financial resources that can be hers as well as the great mineral wealth that is in this area.

Just as quickly as she moved into Czechoslovakia—Russia and her allies, which will include many of the Arab states as well as Iran and Germany (perhaps East Germany only), will move into the land of Israel.

And just as in the case of Czechoslovakia, where the western nations did not interfere but simply voiced a diplomatic protest...the same western powers will again simply voice a protest for fear of causing a far greater war and decide not to interfere at this point.

Parade of tanks in Jerusalem on alert in preparation for war.

THE CONQUEST

The threat of Russian Communism hangs as a spectre over the world. Some scoff at the topic, while others dwell on it continually.

What a tragedy that many of our youth leaders of today—without God—blindly seek some answer to today's problems but turn everywhere except to God. They neglect the unsearchable riches of Christ for the stubble of human schemes to save the world—Communism, education, world law....

Perhaps some of this tragedy lies with us as parents and leaders of our churches throughout the land...for we have failed to preach very plainly and clearly, the Gospel of Jesus Christ and how an individual, by accepting Christ as their personal Saviour can be redeemed for a life in eternity with Christ.

Dr. J. Dwight Pentecost in his book PROPHECY FOR TODAY makes this statement which I would like to quote exactly because it has such great meaning. It is this:

> "Russian Communism is absolutely under the authority and the control of God and cannot go one step beyond that which God proposes. No matter how dark this world situation looks, it has not gotten out from under God's sovereign authority, but God is letting all things progress according to His will. While men think they are developing their plans and purposes, it is all according to God's plans, so that He may demonstrate that He is God without an equal."

Therefore, we find that the Russian forces move into Israel and cover that land completely. They do so overriding the vigorous objections of the West. And with their invasion they bring death and desolation and bloodshed These armies will come to rob, plunder and spoil the land that previously has been resting so safely under the supposed protection of the Western powers.

But God has a purpose in allowing Russia to come to Israel. God will use Russia as the greatest object lesson this world has ever seen—and that object lesson is that no nation can persecute His people and succeed.

Soviet leader General Leonid Brezhnev gestures with his fist as he makes a point with former Secretary of State, Henry Kissinger. One day Russia will substitute weapons for words as she strives to conquer Israel.

A MIRACLE OCCURS

"And in My zeal and in My blazing wrath I declare that on that day there will surely be a great earthquake in the land of Israel. (Ezekiel 38:19)

"And the fish of the sea, the birds of the heavens, the beasts of the field, all the creeping things that creep on the earth, and all the men who are on the face of the earth will shake at My presence; the mountains also will be thrown down, the steep pathways will collapse, and every wall will fall to the ground. (Ezekiel 38:20)

"And I shall call for a sword against him on all My mountains," declares the Lord God. "Every man's sword will be against his brother. (Ezekiel 38:21)

"And with pestilence and with blood I shall enter into judgment with him; and I shall rain on him, and on his troops, and on the many peoples who are with him, a torrential rain, with hailstones, fire, and brimstone. (Ezekiel 38:22)

"And I shall magnify Myself, sanctify Myself, and make Myself known in the sight of many nations; and they will know that I am the Lord." (Ezekiel 38:23)

Here the Lord tells us quite plainly how the Russian invasion of Israel will end.

The heavens will open and God will pour out a judgment from heaven that will wipe out the Russian military might and the power of the Russian Confederacy.

There will be a severe earthquake and the earth around Israel will tremble severely.

This earthquake will throw the soldiers into such a panic that in confusion they will kill one another (Verse 21).

In addition to this, sudden diseases will strike them and very violent rain and hail will fall down on them.

And if this were not enough—fire and brimstone will explode right in their very midst (Verse 22).

Through this righteous indignation of God we will find that the Russian armies with their allies will be destroyed without even being attacked by any other nation.

Now look at Ezekiel 39:2-4 which states:

> And I shall turn you around, drive you on, take
> you up from the remotest parts of the north, and
> bring you against the mountains of Israel. (2)
>
> And I shall strike your bow from your left hand,
> and dash down your arrows from your right hand.
> (3)
>
> You shall fall on the mountains of Israel, you and
> all your troops, and the peoples who are with
> you; I shall give you as food to every kind of preda-
> tory bird and beast of the field. (4)

Here we find that the Russian forces will be destroyed.
What is the extent of this vast judgment?

It is described in verses 9 thru 12 of Ezekiel 39 as follows:

> "Then those who inhabit the cities of Israel will go
> out, and make fires with the weapons and burn
> both the shields and bucklers, the bows and
> arrows, war clubs and spears and for seven years
> they will make fires of them. (9)
>
> "And they will not take wood from the field or
> gather firewood from the forests, for they will
> make fires with the weapons; and they will take
> the spoil of those who despoiled them, and seize
> the plunder of those who plundered them," de-
> clares the Lord God. (10)
>
> "And it will come about on that day that I shall
> give Gog a burial ground there in Israel, the valley
> of those who pass by east of the sea, and it will
> block off the passers-by. So they will bury Gog
> there with all his multitude, and they will call it
> The Valley of Hamon-Gog. (11)
>
> "For seven months the house of Israel will be
> burying them in order to cleanse the land." (12)

Here we see that seven years later the Israelites are yet
collecting the debris that has been caused by this war.
(Verse 9)

And according to verses 11 and 12, the casualties are going
to be so extensive (almost all the Russian armed forces will
be killed) that it will take seven months to bury the dead.

So horrible will be the battlefields in Israel that those
traveling to the north of Israel will have to "stop their
noses" because of the stench of decaying bodies.

WHEN DOES THIS END-TIME BATTLE OCCUR?

Although the Bible does not give exact specifications on this—except that it will be in the "latter days" when Israel is dwelling in seeming peace—allow me to suggest the following:

You will recall we mentioned before that Antichrist will come on the world scene to unite Europe under him...just after the believers are called to meet Christ in the air at the Rapture.

At the beginning of the Tribulation Period, Antichrist will make a peace pact with Israel and guarantee her protection and peace in her land. After this occurs, Russia is going to want this land, but she probably will not make any moves in this direction for about 3 years.

Then at about the middle of the Tribulation Period, as I view the picture, Israel will be invaded by Russia and her allies.

When God steps in and wipes out the military machine of Russia and Russian Communism—this will leave a vacuum of power because of Russia's overthrow.

It is at this time that the Antichrist will assume even greater power and turn on Israel and the Jewish people and inflict on them, great terror and tragedy.

At this time many people in the nation Israel will turn to God and accept Him as their personal Saviour. In fact, many people of the nations of the world—seeing this miraculous power of Christ in the destruction of Russia—will acknowledge Jesus Christ as Lord and Saviour.

The Bible gives and indication of this in Ezekiel 38:23 when the Lord says:

> "And I shall magnify Myself, sanctify Myself, and make Myself known in the sight of many nations; and they will know that I am the Lord." (23)

At the time this book is being written, Russia is at her peak.

And through her space accomplishments, she feels not only that there is no God—but that if there is, that God is Russia in her might.

In her efforts to conquer the world, if Russia would spend less time flooding the world with an intricate spy system—

and more time in studying what her destiny will be as found in God's Word—the Bible...and in so doing if she would turn to God...the coming events might be completely different.

However, Russia will continue on her disaster course and in so doing will attempt the Waterloo of history when she invades the land of Israel.

For when this event occurs, it will be THE DAY RUSSIA DIES.

The Philadelphia Inquirer

Vol. 299, No. 109 · · · · · · © 1978 The Philadelphia Inquirer · Tuesday, October 17, 1978 · 15 CENTS

Polish Cardinal Is Pope

Michener: Pope has wit, humor

By Mike Leary
Inquirer Staff Writer

The dinner conversation was convivial one night last week in Rome, ranging across topics and touching only momentarily on the matter that was uppermost, the choice of a new pope.

"We did mention that," author James Michener recalled yesterday.

But Michener and his Polish dinner partner — a prelate named Cardinal Wojtyla of Krakow — quickly dismissed the matter and, over stuffed cabbage, crisp white wine from Poland and tasty cake, they went on with a reunion of good friends.

"The idea had positively not occurred to him," Michener said, that Cardinal Wojtyla might himself become the Pope. And, so far as the author was concerned, "I personally did not think he had a chance."

So when the news was announced that Cardinal Wojtyla had been elected Pope, and had taken the name of John Paul II, Michener said he was "very surprised" and "very pleased." He predicted that the new Pope would be friendly and outgoing like his predecessor, paying special attention to pastoral affairs.

"He is quite suave," Michener said. "He is a brilliant man. He laughs easily. He has a very nice wit."

By way of illustration, Michener recalled an incident that occurred last July, moments after the author had concluded taping an interview with the cardinal for a documentary to be shown next month on American public television.

"He smiled and said to me, 'Now if this goes well, I will expect a call from Hollywood,' and we all laughed robustly at that. And then he took me by the arm and said, 'You know, Michener, I trained for the stage as
(See MICHENER on 4-A)

455 years of Italian rule ends

By Rod Nordland
Inquirer Staff Writer

ROME — The leaders of the Roman Catholic Church yesterday elected Karol Cardinal Wojtyla of Poland to become the 264th pope and the first from outside Italy in 455 years.

He chose the papal name John Paul II in honor of his predecessor, whose pontificate lasted only 34 days.

Wojtyla, attaining the highest eminence of any prelate from an Iron Curtain nation, is the first Pole to be chosen pope and, at 58, the youngest elected in the 20th century.

A doctrinal moderate, he was chosen by the 110 other cardinals of the church on the second day — and the seventh or eighth secret ballot — of the papal conclave.

About 200,000 people were in St. Peter's Square when white smoke issued from the chimney atop the Sistine Chapel to signal the selection at 6:18 p.m. (1:18 p.m. Philadelphia time).

Within 15 minutes, Pericle Cardinal Felici of Italy appeared on the balcony of the Basilica of St. Peter's. The choirs that began when he pronounced the famous words, "habemus papam," — "We have a pope" — did not subside when Romans learned that for the first time since the reign of Adrian VI of Holland in 1523, the pope was not an Italian.

Pope John Paul II, staying behind the pastoral cross that always precedes the pope, was presented briefly on the balcony, dressed in white vestments with the scarlet and gold stole that had belonged to Pope John Paul I. He reappeared within half an hour, to the delight of the crowd, and gave the acceptance speech that popes customarily reserve for the following day.

"Dear brothers and sisters," he said, "we are all still sorrowful after the death of the very beloved John Paul I, and here the very eminent cardinals have elected a new Bishop of Rome."

By first referring to himself in his subsidiary role rather than as pontiff, he drew wild cheers from the mostly Roman audience.

"They called me from a distant country," he said. He paused and appeared to be trying to correct

Karol Cardinal Wojtyla greets crowds at the Vatican after becoming the first non-Italian Pope in 455 years

On Monday, October 16, 1978 the leaders of the Roman Church elected Karol Cardinal Wojtyla of Communist Poland to become the first Pope outside Italy in its 455 year history! Time will tell what part this surprise move will play in God's prophetic plan!

12
The Great War

Armageddon—a strange sounding name—will be the battle
ground for the greatest blood bath that the world has ever
seen.

In a previous chapter, we discussed the last 3½ year Tribulation Period and showed how God would pour out His
judgments on the world through the Seven Trumpets and
the Seven Vials. We also showed how Russia would be
defeated by God destroying the threat of Russian Communism. This power vacuum will then make ANTICHRIST
and the FALSE PROPHET more venturesome in their defiance of God.

During this time the False Prophet, with Antichrist, will
have disposed of the Great World Religious System, and
will command tremendous power to work his evil deeds.

The Antichrist, who will be the head of the Federated
States of Europe, will have succeeded in becoming the
most powerful man on earth (Revelation 13:3,4).

Now at the end of this 7 year Tribulation Period, all the
events of the past focus together into one tremendous
battle between the forces of good and the forces of evil.

This is called the Battle of Armageddon.

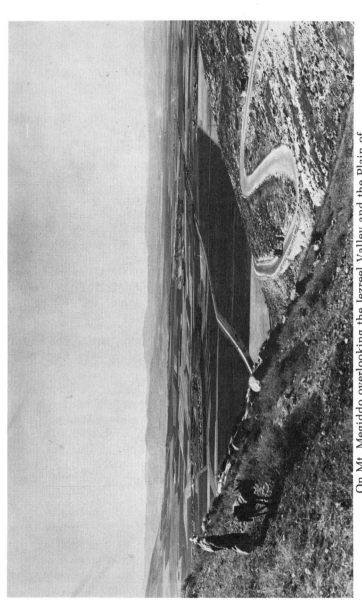

On Mt. Megiddo overlooking the Jezreel Valley and the Plain of Esdraelon it is easy to see how an army of 200 million could

Let's look at the following verse:

> And they gathered them together to the place
> which in Hebrew is called Har-Magedon. (Reve-
> lation 16:16).

This area was the scene of many decisive battles in the history of Israel. Since Mt. Megiddo commands the Jezreel Valley and the Plain of Esdraelon the name Armageddon (Hebrew for: "Mount Megiddo") represents this entire strategic valley area in North Israel. It is the gateway through the mountains from the North to Jerusalem.

It was here that Gideon defeated Midian.

> Then all the Midianites and the Amalekites and
> the sons of the east assembled themselves; and
> they crossed over and camped in the valley of
> Jezreel. (Judges 6:33).

It was here that Saul died in a battle with the Philistines. Saul and Jonathan perished on Mt. Gilboa which is in the Eastern portion of this Armageddon-Jezreel Valley (I Samuel 31:1; II Samuel 1:6,21).

It was here Josiah was slain in battle with Pharaoh-nechoh.

> In his days Pharaoh Neco king of Egypt went up
> to the king of Assyria to the river Euphrates. And
> King Josiah went to meet him, and when Pharaoh
> Neco saw him he killed him at Megiddo. (II Kings
> 23:29).

> And his servants drove his body in a chariot
> from Megiddo, and brought him to Jerusalem
> and buried him in his own tomb. Then the people
> of the land took Jehoahaz the son of Josiah and
> anointed him and made him king in place of his
> father. (II Kings 23:30).

The town of Megiddo guarded the northwest to southeast pass which formed the easiest caravan route between the Plain of Sharon and the Valley of Jezreel. It has been stated that the low mountains around were silent witnesses of perhaps more bloody encounters than any other spot on earth, continuing down through recent times. Hence the appropriateness of this place for the vast conflict as pictured in Revelation chapters 14, 16 and 19; Joel 3; and Isaiah 63 (Zondervan Bible Dictionary, Merrill C. Tenney).

Where is this Mountain of Megiddo?

Megiddo lies east of Mount Carmel in the northern part of Israel.

From this site, a vast plain stretches from the Mediterranean Sea eastward across the northern part of Israel.

It was Napoleon who called this area "the world's greatest natural battlefield" because there was sufficient room for the armies of the world to maneuver.

To get a little background as to how this Battle of Armageddon begins it is necessary to examine some of the people and countries that will play a role in this battle.

ECCLESIASTICAL BABYLON

Dr. J. Dwight Pentecost in his book PROPHECY FOR TODAY (Zondervan Publishing Co.) states the following:

> Revelation 17:1-18:
>
> "I do not know of any theme of prophecy of the Word of God that is as difficult to speak about today as this theme to which we are directing attention in this chapter. For we are growing up in an atmosphere in which to speak about any system or religion is to invite accusations of being narrow, conceited, or bigoted. And yet, because the Word of God devotes a considerable portion to it, I trust that the Spirit of God will give you a hearing ear and an understanding heart. Understand that we are not speaking to be bigoted, nor are we speaking against individuals who may be enmeshed in a system. But we are speaking to declare, as God gives us wisdom and ability, that end to which the visible Church is steadily moving. It is our desire that you should understand those Scriptures that reveal the consummation and culmination of the ecumenical movement in a great world-wide religious system that is under the curse and wrath of God. If we do not speak in accordance with the Word of God, do not give credence to what we say. But if that which we share with you is based upon the truth of the Word of God, we ask you to consider it carefully, for the truth of God is unalterable and invincible."

The ecclesiastical Babylon refers to the religious system of the apostate World Church in the Last Days.

This world church will be very rich and very powerful.

It basically exists today.

It is important that you read chapter 17 of Revelation for here we have the greatest description of what the Lord calls the "Great Harlot."

In modern day English this would be termed "the Great Prostitute."

The Lord is saying that this great World Church system, which claims to be the Bride of Christ and the only true church...is, in actuality, an adulteress who has been unfaithful to the very one to whom she professes to be joined in marriage.

It is with this frame of reference that this church is referred to as an "adulterer," the "Great Harlot" and the "Mother of Prostitutes."

This is very strong language but it is the language which God Himself gives in the Scriptures. It is during this Tribulation Period that His judgment is poured out on a church which had a form of godliness but denied the power thereof. And because it was an imitation church, it incurs the full wrath of God by the end of the Tribulation Period.

Let us look at chapter 17 from the book of Revelation in greater detail so that you can understand the description of the Great Harlot, which is known as the False Church.

> And one of the seven angels who had the seven bowls came and spoke with me, saying, "Come here, I shall show you the judgment of the great harlot who sits on many waters, (1)
>
> With whom the kings of the earth committed acts of immorality, and those who dwell on the earth were made drunk with the wine of her immorality." (2)

It is at this time that the Great Harlot (or Notorious Prostitute), is revealed in all her wickedness in the Scriptures above.

The Lord is stating here that the kings and rulers of the world have sacrificed their Christian ideals and have compromised with the Word of God in uniting with the Great

Harlot and in this fellowship have been made drunk through cooperating in communion with this great religious system.

> *And he carried me away in the Spirit into a wilderness; and I saw a woman sitting on a scarlet beast, full of blasphemous names, having seven heads and ten horns. (Revelation 17:3)*

> *And the woman was clothed in purple and scarlet, and adorned with gold and precious stones and pearls, having in her hand a gold cup full of abominations and of the unclean things of her immorality, (Revelations 17:4).*

> *And upon her forehead a name was written, a mystery, "BABYLON THE GREAT, THE MOTHER OF HARLOTS AND OF THE ABOMINATIONS OF THE EARTH." (Revelation 17:5).*

Here we see the head of the great End Time church, having power over the Federated States of Europe (or what may be known as the New Roman Empire) and since the rider is sitting on this animal which depicts these countries—it is evident that the rider has some control of these countries.

Yet since she is astride the Beast, (the "scarlet animal"—vs. 3), it is his (the United Federated Europe's) power which is also moving her forward.

We find that the rider is described as wearing purple and scarlet clothing and beautiful jewelry with a great deal of wealth and precious stones. And yet in her hand she holds a cup filled with obscenities or filthiness.

This poisonous cup, because of its imitation of Christ's message, is poured out on additional peoples through the world to subject them to the Harlot Church's power and authority.

Note that she is called Babylon the Great.

CITY OF BABYLON

The original city of Babylon was built by Nimrod (Genesis 10:8-10). This was the seat of the first great imitation of God. It was here that the so-called "Babylonian Cult" was created.

You will recall that Nimrod called his city Babel. He tried

to build a great tower—(a large ziggurat or stepped pyramid)—that would reach up into heaven.

This was the way, he thought, Man would approach God. The word "Babel" means confusion. And it was here at Babel that we find introduced the first recorded organized adulterous religious system in the world (Genesis 11:1-9).

This was a system that claimed to possess the highest wisdom and to reveal the most divine secrets. It was in the latter days of the Neo-Babylonian Empire (6th and 7th Century B.C.) that the Babylonian Cult reached its height. A member, to be initiated, had to confess to the Priest. It was the Priest then who had the individual in his power.

Once the men were admitted into this order, they were no longer Babylonians, or Egyptians or from any other country. They were then members of a "mystical brotherhood." Over this brotherhood was placed a Pontiff or "high Priest" whose word was the law.

The tower of Babel must have been a tremendous structure. It may have consisted possibly, like its later Babylonian counterparts, of eight towers, each 75 feet high, rising one upon the other.

There was a chapel on the top which made the total height over 600 feet. This is equivalent to almost a 60 story building and it is as high as the modern 3½ million dollar Space Needle of Seattle, Washington.

The upper chapel typically had very expensive furniture. It is estimated that one golden image alone of Neo-Babylonian times which was 45 feet high was valued at $17,500,000. It was also estimated that sacred utensils which were used were worth approximately $200 million.

In later (c. 600 B.C.) Babylon the towers with their hanging gardens were one of the Seven Wonders of the ancient World.

In this city of Babylon were 25 avenues, 150 feet wide which ran across the city from north to south. The same number crossed them at right angles from east to west. This made 676 great squares...each nearly three fifths of a mile on a side.

The city was divided into two equal parts by the River Euphrates. This city of Babylon reached its greatest glory during the reign of Nebuchadnezzar, B.C. 604-562.

It was an exact square of 15 miles on a side or 60 miles around.

There is a great background of history on the city of Babel (Babylon) which traces this false religion step by step down to the present apostate churches and councils.

Those interested in pursuing this further, will find the book PROPHECY FOR TODAY by Dr. J. Dwight Pentecost, pages 125 to 138 of extreme interest.

> *And I saw the woman drunk with the blood of the saints, and with the blood of the witnesses of Jesus. And when I saw her, I wondered greatly. (Revelation 17:6)*

While the so-called Catholic-Christian church in the Middle Ages has already been a participant in many persecutions in which thousands of people have become martyrs—this particular verse refers to the martyrs who will be killed during the Tribulation Period because they will not fall down and worship the Antichrist or follow the religious teachings of the final apostate ecclesiastical system, the World Church.

Pope Paul VI, M.M. Thomas of Indian Church, the Rev. Eugene Carson Blake of World Council of Churches and Miss Pauline Mary Webb, United Kingdom (Methodist), pray together in chapel at Ecumenical Center at Geneva, Switzerland.

> And the angel said to me, "Why do you wonder? I shall tell you the mystery of the woman and of the beast that carries her, which has the seven heads and the ten horns. (Revelation 17:7)
>
> "The beast that you saw was and is not, and is about to come up out of the abyss and to go to destruction. And those who dwell on the earth will wonder, whose name has not been written in the book of life from the foundation of the world, when they see the beast, that he was and is not and will come. (Revelation 17:8)
>
> Here is the mind which has wisdom. The seven heads are seven mountains on which the woman sits. (Revelation 17:9)

Some authors have stated that more than two-thirds of the earth's population today are worshippers of some type of idols.

This most likely is true when one sees the idol worship that goes on not only in foreign countries but right here in the United States.

The Bible tells us that our worship must be to God and to God alone and to no other individual or being.

> "Thus says the Lord, the King of Israel
> And his Redeemer, the Lord of hosts:
> 'I am the first and I am the last,
> And there is no God besides Me. (Isaiah 44:6)
>
> 'Do not tremble and do not be afraid;
> Have I not long since announced it to you and
>   declared it?
> And you are My witnesses.
> Is there any God besides Me,
> Or is there any other Rock?
> I know of none.'" (Isaiah 44:8)
>
> Those who fashion a graven image are all of them futile, and their precious things are of no profit; even their own witnesses fail to see or know, so that they will be put to shame. (Isaiah 44:9)

FALSE CHURCH IDENTIFIED

In Revelation 17:9 we are told the identity of the False Church. We are told that his seven heads represent a certain city built on seven hills.

Anyone with a knowledge of history and geography will know that this city is the city of ROME! Thus the end-time apostate world church, be it called a Church or a Council of Churches, will have as its head the City of Rome. If the time of the end is near, as we believe, we may expect the links of church union to be more and more forged between the apostate Protestant bodies and Rome. This United World Church will be the Great Harlot of Revelation 17.

> *And they are seven kings; five have fallen, one is the other has not yet come; and when he comes, he must remain a little while. (Revelation 17:10)*

> *And the beast which was and is not, is himself also an eighth, and is one of the seven, and he goes to destruction. (Revelation 17:11)*

> *And the ten horns which you saw are ten kings, who have not yet received a kingdom, but they receive authority as kings with the beast for one hour. (Revelation 17:12)*

Here we read that this city represents seven kings of which five have already fallen, the sixth now reigns and the seventh is yet to come.

Ecumenical cross displayed in service in Philadelphia.

What this means is that five kingdoms have already fallen. These were past forms of government which no longer exist.

"The sixth now reigns" refers to the kingdom that was reigning at the time John wrote the book of Revelation under the inspiration of the Holy Spirit.

"The seventh is yet to come, but his reign will be brief" refers to the Revived Roman Empire that will reign during the seven year Tribulation Period.

"The scarlet animal who died is the eighth king" refers to the Antichrist who "will go to his doom."

The ten horns represent the ten kings who are the ten Federated Powers of Europe who will invest all of their powers into the hands of Antichrist.

> "These have one purpose and they give their power and authority to the beast. (Revelation 17: 13)
>
> "These will wage war against the Lamb, and the Lamb will overcome them, because He is Lord of lords and King of kings, and those who are with Him are the called and chosen and faithful." (Revelation 17:14)
>
> And he said to me, "The waters which you saw where the harlot sits, are peoples and multitudes and nations and tongues. (Revelation 17:15)
>
> "And the ten horns which you saw, and the beast, these will hate the harlot and will make her desolate and naked, and will eat her flesh and will burn her up with fire. (Revelation 17:16)
>
> "For God has put it in their hearts to execute His purpose by having a common purpose, and by giving their kingdom to the beast, until the words of God should be fulfilled. (Revelation 17:17)
>
> "And the woman whom you saw is the great city, which reigns over the kings of the earth." (Revelation 17:18)

Verse 13 tells us that these ten powers of the Federated States of Europe will sign a treaty turning over their power to Antichrist.

Verse 14 tells us that together these powers will become involved in a war with Christ and that Christ will conquer them.

This is the war which is called the Battle of Armageddon.

In verse 17, God is telling us that the end-time kings will believe in a Satanic plan and will put all of their power into the hands of Antichrist who in actuality will be fulfilling the destined purposes of God.

This then is the background of what God describes as "The Great Harlot" which is the all powerful end-time apostate church that has set up her own religious system, imitating true churches found in Christ Jesus.

And her power and her wealth will grow steadily until the last days of the Tribulation. It will be the most powerful religious system on earth.

And it is her power, coupled with the sinister political powers of Antichrist, which together will war against Christ and in so doing will cause the greatest blood bath in history.

ANTICHRIST BECOMES JEALOUS

Rome, as the headquarters of the final united-world religious system, becomes so powerful that it becomes embarrassing to Antichrist who is the head of the ten Federated States of Europe and the most powerful figure on earth at that time.

The power of the world religious confederation will be like a chicken bone caught in the throat of Antichrist and will be a cause of great irritation.

It will suddenly dawn on this coalition of nations and the head of this coalition (Antichrist) that they are nothing but puppets and that the one who really rules over them is the end-time false world church system led by its headquarters in the city of seven hills, Rome.

As we near the end of the Tribulation Period this coalition of nations under the leadership of Antichrist will rise up and wipe out the Harlot Church (Revelation 17:12, 16). The False Prophet will then emerge as the world religious leader and he will direct all worship only to the Antichrist.

This is the destruction of Babylon (Rome) and is fully described in Revelation, chapter 17 and 18. Chapter 17 speaks of the destruction of the apostate (unfaithful) religious system and 18 tells of the ruination of its commercial capital, the city itself.

Here again we see God's purposes fulfilled as He allows the False Church to continue its ungodly system until it has gotten a strangle hold on the world. Then God allows these puppet nations, who are subservient to it, to finally rise up and destroy it.

To give you the proper sequence of events—first we find that in the Last Days the war machine of Russian Communism will be destroyed. Then the united-world (apostate) church will be destroyed.

With the destruction of these two major forces in the world, Antichrist and the False Prophet can now rise to world-wide power and world-wide authority having complete rule over all the nations.

THE SEVEN HILLED CITY'S FINAL DESTRUCTION

Let us look at Revelation 18 from the New American Standard Bible for it graphically portrays how this 7 hilled city of Revelation 17:9 (which is referred to as Babylon) is finally destroyed. Do you know the name of this 7 hilled city?

> After these things I saw another angel coming down from heaven, having great authority, and the earth was illumined with his glory. (1)
>
> And he cried out with a mighty voice, saying, "Fallen, fallen is Babylon the great! And she has become a dwelling place of demons and a prison of every unclean spirit, and a prison of every unclean and hateful bird. (2)
>
> For all the nations have drunk of the wine of the passion of her immorality, and the kings of the earth have committed acts of immorality with her, and the merchants of the earth have become rich by the wealth of her sensuality. (3)
>
> And I heard another voice from heaven, saying, Come out of her, my people, that you may not participate in her sins and that you may not receive of her plagues. (4)
>
> For her sins have piled up as high as heaven, and God has remembered her iniquities. (5)

Pay her back even as she has paid, and give back to her double according to her deeds; in the cup which she has mixed, mix twice as much for her. *(6)*

To the degree that she glorified herself and lived sensuously, to the same degree give her torment and mourning; for she says in her heart, I sit as a queen and I am not a widow, and will never see mourning. *(7)*

For this reason in one day her plagues will come, pestilence and mourning and famine, and she will be burned up with fire; for the Lord God who judges her is strong. *(8)*

And the kings of the earth, who committed acts of immorality and lived sensuously with her, will sweep and lament over her when they see the smoke of her burning. *(9)*

Standing at a distance because of the fear of her torment, saying, Woe, woe, the great city, Babylon, the strong city! For in one hour your judgment has come. *(10)*

And the merchants of the earth weep and mourn over her, because no one buys their cargoes any more. *(11)*

Cargoes of gold and silver and precious stones and pearls and fine linen and purple and silk and scarlet, and every kind of citron wood and every article of ivory and every article made from very costly wood and bronze and iron and marble. *(12)*

And cinnamon and spice and incense and perfume and frankincense and wine and olive oil and fine flour and wheat and cattle and sheep, and cargoes of horses and chariots and slaves, and human lives. *(13)*

And the fruit you long for has gone from you, and all things that were luxurious and splendid have passed away from you and men will no longer find them. *(14)*

The merchants of these things who became rich from her, will stand at a distance because of the fear of her torment, weeping and mourning. *(15)*

Saying, Woe, woe, the great city, she who was clothed in fine linen and purple and scarlet, and adorned with gold and precious stones and pearls. (16)

For in one hour such great wealth has been laid waste. And every shipmaster and every passenger and sailor, and as many as make their living by the sea, stood at a distance. (17)

And were crying out as they saw the smoke of her burning, saying, What city is like the great city? (18)

And they threw dust on their heads and were crying out, weeping and mourning, saying, Woe, woe, the great city, in which all who had ships at sea became rich by her wealth, for in one hour she has been laid waste. (19)

Rejoice over her, O heaven, and you saints and apostles and prophets, because God has pronounced judgment for you against her. (20)

And a strong angel took up a stone like a great millstone and threw it into the sea, saying, Thus with Babylon, the great city, be thrown down with violence, and will not be found any longer. (21)

And the sound of harpists and musicians and flute-players and trumpeters will not be heard in you any longer; and no craftsman of any craft will be found in you any longer; and the sound of a mill will not be heard in you any longer. (22)

And the light of a lamp will not shine in you any longer; and the voice of the bridegroom and bride will not be heard in you any longer; for your merchants were the great men of the earth, because all the nations were deceived by your sorcery. (23)

And in her was found the blood of prophets and of saints and of all who have been slain on the earth. (24) (Revelation 18:1-24)

Look again at verse 8 of this chapter and you will notice that this city will be destroyed in a very short span of time —in a single day.

It also states that she will be destroyed completely by fire.

This is in exact harmony with the words of Isaiah 13:19 which speaks of ancient Babylon which is the antitype of the endtime Babylon:

> And Babylon, the beauty of kingdoms, the glory of the Chaldeans' pride, Will be as when God overthrew Sodom and Gomorrah.

If you will refer to Revelation 16:19, you will find even greater description of how this destruction will take place as quoted below:

> And the great city was split into three parts, and the cities of the nations fell. And Babylon the great was remembered before God, to give her the cup of the wine of His fierce wrath. (19)

> And every island fled away, and the mountains were not found. (20)

> And huge hailstones, about one hundred pounds each, came down from heaven upon men; and men blasphemed God because of the plague of the hail, because its plague was extremely severe. (21) (Revelation 16:19-21)

MARCHING TO ARMAGEDDON!

Now that we have set the scene for you showing how the final apostate (unfaithful) world Church which has its headquarters in Rome will be destroyed, leaving Antichrist and the False Prophet as the supreme leaders of the world, you can better understand the events that will next occur.

It is clear from the Bible that at the end of the 7 year Tribulation period there will occur the end-time Battle of Armageddon when evil armies from all over the world come up against Jerusalem for a diabolical purpose (Joel 3, Revelation 14 and 19). While this is clear, yet the exact synthesis of all of the details leading up to this battle is not completely revealed. Those alive at the time will see these details unfold before their eyes. With this in mind, nevertheless, using those details revealed in the Scriptures as my guide, permit me to suggest that it will take place as follows:

Antichrist, under the great coalition of western nations, will set up his headquarters in Jerusalem and reign over Israel. Not only will he reign over Israel and Europe but will also control the entire world.

It will be at the close of the Tribulation Period that Israel will find itself under an invasion by an Army numbering 200 million men.

This army will come from the east to contest the right of the Federated States of Europe to have world-wide dominion.

You will recall we discussed this figure of 200 million warriors in a previous chapter. We showed that since there are 3 1/2 billion people in the world at present and 200 million organized militiamen in China alone, such a figure is not out of line with our current day thinking.

Here we find 200 million troops marching towards Israel with the intent of destroying the city and taking over world rulership.

Naturally, Antichrist is alarmed and decides that he is going to meet this 200 million man army.

However, his intent is to fight them on a battleground which will be to his advantage. Therefore, he will set himself up in the Mountains of Judea where he will have the advantage of some natural defenses.

Suddenly something unusual happens. We read about it in Revelation 19:11-18. We are going to quote the entire 8 verses because they are so important.

> And I saw heaven opened; and behold, a white horse, and He who sat upon it is called Faithful and True; and in righteousness He judges and wages war. (11)
>
> And His eyes are a flame of fire, and upon His head are many diadems; and He has a name written upon Him which no one knows except Himself. (12)
>
> And He is clothed with a robe dipped in blood; and His name is called The Word of God. (13)
>
> And the armies which are in heaven, clothed in fine linen, white and clean, were following Him on white horses. (14)

Artist's view of Battle of Armageddon as tanks fire wildly in the sky at approaching army riding on stately white horses.

> And from His mouth comes a sharp sword, so that
> with it He may smite the nations; and He will rule
> them with a rod of iron; and He treads the wine
> press of the fierce wrath of God, the Almighty. (15)
>
> And on His robe and on His thigh He has a name
> written, KING OF KINGS, AND LORD OF LORDS.
> (16)
>
> And I saw an angel standing in the sun; and he
> cried out with a loud voice, saying to all the birds
> which fly in midheaven, Come, assemble for the
> great supper of God. (17)
>
> In order that you may eat the flesh of kings and
> the flesh of commanders and the flesh of mighty
> men and the flesh of horses and of those who sit
> on them and the flesh of all men, both free men
> and slaves, and small and great. (18)
>
> (Revelation 19:11-18)

Notice that verse 11 tells us that the heavens are open and
verse 18 gives us an indication of a great holocaust that
will occur when God comes to earth for the Battle of
Armageddon.

When Antichrist with his western confederacy prepares
to battle with the invading Asiatic force—suddenly the
heavens open and the two opposing sides realize that some
unusual occurrence is taking place directed by God. It is
at this time that they unite forces in order to devote all
their energies into fighting the Lord Jesus Christ.

Therefore we find the Lord Jesus Christ coming down
from heaven seated on a white horse with the armies of
heaven following Him dressed in finest linen and also
riding on white horses.

On His robe and thigh is written the title "KING OF KINGS
AND LORD OF LORDS."

At last the Antichrist realizes that all his armies and the
armies of the world are no match for the power of the Son
of God and the prophecy predicted in Matthew 24:30 becomes a reality.

> And then the sign of the Son of Man will appear
> in the sky, and then all the tribes of the earth
> will mourn, and they will see the Son of Man com-
> ing on the clouds of the sky with power and great
> glory.

It is interesting to note that one of the fullest descriptions of what will occur at that time is found in the Second Psalm.

Spoken centuries before the actual occurrence of the Battle of Armageddon, the Prophet David sees the nations of the earth in rebellion against God which reaches its climax under the rulership of Antichrist. Here the world powers finalized in Antichrist declare that they will not permit God to set up his King on David's throne to reign over the world.

God actually laughs at the vain boasting of Antichrist and we read in Psalm 2:4-6 that He quietly sits on His throne in heaven and chuckles.

From God's prophetic Scripture, it is evident that the Middle East will be the focal point of the world. And pouring into the land of Israel from every side will be millions of soldiers...and blood will be flowing like water.

The Battle of Armageddon which describes the final siege of Jerusalem, is described not only in Revelation 16:12-16 but also in Zechariah 14, Joel 3, and Isaiah 63. These combined armed forces will be destroyed by a direct judgment from God.

One of the great miracles of God which occurs at this time is a tremendous earthquake which splits the great city of Babylon into three sections (Revelation 16:19). Cities around the world also will crumble into heaps of rubble. Islands will vanish and mountains will crumble into plains.

We find here also a tremendous hailstorm where hailstones weighing over a hundred pounds fall from the sky.

> And I saw the beast and the kings of the earth and their armies, assembled to make war against Him who sat upon the horse, and against His army. (19)
>
> And the beast was seized, and with him the false prophet who performed the signs in his presence, by which he deceived those who had received the mark of the beast and those who worshiped his image; these two were thrown alive into the lake of fire which burns with brimstone. (20)
>
> And the rest were killed with the sword which came from the mouth of him who sat upon the horse, and all the birds were filled with their flesh. (21). (Revelation 19:19-21)

In the verses on the previous page we see Antichrist (the beast) who had gathered his government together to fight against Christ and His army.

The Antichrist is captured and with him the False Prophet. While the False Prophet could do mighty miracles when Antichrist was present, now, with Antichrist captured, the False Prophet's power is gone.

Both of them are thrown alive into the Lake of Fire that burns forever and ever.

This is a literal place and not merely a meaningless symbol.

Note in verse 21 that the entire army is killed by the Lord Jesus Christ alone and that the birds of heaven eat the flesh of this army.

Can you imagine what vast destruction this is?

This adds up to almost 200 miles of blood that the Scripture tells us will splash upwards "...even unto the horse bridles...."

Isaiah speaks of this time when the land of Israel will be soaked with blood (Isaiah 34:1-8).

In Revelation 14:18-20 we also read of this prophecy.

So we find the Antichrist and False Prophet forever in the Lake of Fire. They will experience continual suffering forever and ever.

With the Battle of Armageddon coming to an end, this brings to a close the great 7 year Tribulation Period and heralds in the time when Christ will return to earth *with* his believers (those who are born again or saved).

THE MILLENNIUM AND AFTER

Those believers in Christ will then reign with Christ on this physical earth for 1000 years.

This is called the Millennial Period (the word Millennium meaning "1000 years").

During this Millennial Period, Satan will be bound in the bottomless pit which is his prison for the entire 1000 year period.

> And I saw an angel coming down from heaven, having the key of the abyss and a great chain in his hand. (1)

> And he laid hold of the dragon, the serpent of old, who is the Devil and Satan, and bound him for a thousand years. (2)

> And threw him into the abyss, and shut it and sealed it over him, so that he should not deceive the nations any longer, until the thousand years were completed; after these things he must be released for a short time. (3) (Revelation 20:1-3)

With Satan bound, the 1000 years begins with the reign of Christ and His saints on earth.

At the end of the 1000 year Millennial Period, Christ allows Satan to be "loosened for a season" to make one final test of those who are born during the Millennial Period.

This is his last drive to attempt to conquer the world and overthrow God.

However, his attempt comes to utter defeat and he meets his eternal doom.

> And when the thousand years are completed, Satan will be released from his prison. (7)

> And will come out to deceive the nations which are in the four corners of the earth, Gog and Magog, to gather them together for the war; the number of them is like the sand of the seashore. (8)

> And they came up on the broad plain of the earth and surrounded the camp of the saints and the beloved city, and fire came down from heaven and devoured them. (9)

> And the devil who deceived them was thrown into the lake of fire and brimstone, where the beast and the false prophet are also; and they will be tormented day and night forever and ever. (10) (Revelation 20:7-10)

If you will get your Bible and read the last part of Revelation, chapter 20, you will then see the judgment of the wicked dead taking place at the close of the Millennium.

Perhaps Revelation 20:15 is the most tragic verse in the Bible.

It is preceded by verse 14 which states in the New American Standard Bible:

> *And death and Hades were thrown into the lake of fire. This is the second death, the lake of fire.*

Here we find that Satan is finally cast into the Lake of Fire with Antichrist and the False Prophet where he will forever remain.

> *But then in verse 15 we read that anyone whose name is not found recorded in the Book of Life is also thrown into this same Lake of Fire.*

To the unbeliever—to the person who does not accept Christ as his personal Saviour and Lord—to the person who (in terminology of Christians) is called "unsaved" or who has not been born again—his final destiny in this world is the Lake of Fire.

This is not speculation. This is not the opinion of theologians or world leaders.

The Word of God tells us that if you have not accepted Christ as your personal Saviour then your name will not be recorded in the Book of Life.

Therefore, if your name is not recorded in the Book of Life, regardless of what good deeds you accomplished on earth, regardless of what good works you did on earth, regardless of how kind or considerate you were, regardless of how generous you were on earth...because of your sins, and because you did not believe in Christ as your personal Saviour that your sins might have been forgiven, Christ having paid their penalty—you will be thrown into the Lake of Fire along with all other unbelievers and along with Satan, Antichrist and the False Prophet.

This leaves you with a decision to make, doesn't it?

You must accept Christ as your personal Saviour and Lord.

Or you must reject the Bible and follow your own beliefs or the beliefs set down by man or tradition.

If you decide to follow the latter, I would suggest you read Revelation 20:15 over and over and over again and keep this verse in a plaque above your door for through your unbelief you are determining your own destruction.

For Revelation 20:15—repeated again—tells us that:

> *And if anyone's name was not found written in the book of life, he was thrown into the lake of fire.*

You have just read about the bloodiest war in history—the war between the nations of the world and God—the Battle of Armageddon.

But you as an individual will also have to fight a great war —that is the war between the forces of good which are of God against the forces of evil which are of Satan.

This will be the great war in your life.

What will be your decision?

Will you take your stand with the forces of good and become a believer, joining the armies of Christ?

Or will you through indifference and neglect automatically side with the forces of evil and by so doing, commit your life to an eternity in the Lake of Fire?

My sincere prayer is that you will find Christ as your personal Saviour and Lord.

(For an interesting study on what life in the Millennium is like, we suggest you read **1000** by Salem Kirban. $4.95. **1000** is a novel and a sequel to the book **666**.)

13
God's Prophecy and Why It Is True

God's Prophetic Promise to Abraham • Jesus of Nazareth—
Predictions Fulfilled • Prophecies by Jesus Fulfilled

The fulfilled prophecies in God's Word are one of the best
evidences that the Bible is the Word of God!

In Isaiah 46:9, 10 we read:

> Remember the former things long past, For I am
> God, and there is no other; I am God, and there
> is no one like Me. (9)

> Declaring the end from the beginning And from
> ancient times things which have not been done,
> Saying, 'My purpose will be established, And I will
> accomplish all My good pleasure'; (10)

Let's look at some fulfilled prophecies:

In the eighth century B.C. Nahum, the prophet, said this
about Nineveh, the wicked capital of Assyria:

> Whatever you devise against the Lord, He will
> make a complete end of it. Distress will not rise
> up twice. (9)

> The Lord has issued a command concerning you:
> Your name will no longer be perpetuated. I will
> cut off idol and image From the house of your
> gods. I will prepare your grave, For you are con-
> temptible. (14) (Nahum 1:9, 14)

> Behold, I am against you, declares the Lord of
> hosts. I will burn up her chariots in smoke, a
> sword will devour your young lions, I will cut off
> your prey from the land, and no longer will the
> voice of your messengers be heard. (Nahum 2:13)

Nearly a century later Zephaniah echoed this prophecy about Nineveh:

> *And He will stretch out His hand against the north*
> *And destroy Assyria, And He will make Nineveh a*
> *desolation, Parched like the wilderness.*
> *(Zephaniah 2:13).*

At the time these prophecies were made, Nineveh was the queen city of the world. It was the capital of the greatest nation in the world...with a population of hundreds of thousands. It had walls 100 feet high—broad enough to accommodate three chariots abreast. It supported 1500 towers 200 feet high.

What a prediction by God! It would be like saying today that 100 years from now NEW YORK CITY will be completely destroyed so that no trace will be found of it!

But what happened? One hundred years after Nahum's prophecy Nineveh DISAPPEARED! And for centuries even the location of the site of the city was completely unknown.

GOD'S PROPHETIC PROMISE TO ABRAHAM

About 2000 B.C. God made a prophetic promise to Abraham.

> *And I will make your descendants as the dust of*
> *the earth; so that if anyone can number the dust*
> *of the earth, then your descendants can also be*
> *numbered. (Genesis 13:16).*

Abraham had no child and he and his wife were old WHEN THIS PROMISE WAS MADE. But today there are estimated to be over 14,000,000 Jews, and both they and the Arab nations are considered Abraham's seed.

JESUS OF NAZARETH—PREDICTIONS FULFILLED

In Matthew's Gospel alone, 106 Old Testament prophecies are fulfilled in the life of Christ.

Here are some of the messianic prophecies from the Old Testament that were fulfilled in the New Testament:

> *Prophecy:* "But thou, Bethlehem Ephratah, though thou be little among the thousands of Judah, yet out of thee shall he come forth unto me that is to be ruler in Israel; whose goings forth have been from of old, from everlasting" (Micah 5:2,; 700 years before Christ).

Fulfillment: "Now when Jesus was born in Bethlehem of Judea in the days of Herod the king..." (Matthew 2:1). "Jesus said unto them, Verily, verily, I say unto you, Before Abraham was, I am" (John 8:58).

Prophecy: "Rejoice greatly, O daughter of Zion; shout, O daughter of Jerusalem: behold, thy King cometh unto thee: he is just, and having salvation; lowly, and riding upon an ass, and upon a colt the foal of an ass" (Zechariah 9:9; 450 years before Christ).

Fulfillment: "And the disciples went, and did as Jesus commanded them, And brought the ass, and the colt, and put on them their clothes, and they set him thereon...And the multitudes that went before, and that followed, cried, saying, Hosanna to the son of David: Blessed is he that cometh in the name of the Lord..." (Matthew 21: 6, 7, 8).

Prophecy: "I gave my back to the smiters, and my cheeks to them that plucked off the hair: I hid not my face from shame and spitting" (Isaiah 50:6; 700 years before Christ).

Fulfillment: "Then did they spit in his face, and buffeted him; and others smote him with the palms of their hands" (Matthew 26:67).

Prophecy: "...and he was numbered with the transgressors; and he bare the sin of many, and made intercession for the transgressors" (Isaiah 53:12; 700 years before Christ).

Fulfillment: "And with him they crucify two thieves; the one on his right hand, and the other on his left" (Mark 15:27); "Then said Jesus, Father, forgive them; for they know not what they do..." (Luke 23:34).

Prophecy: "They part my garments among them, and cast lots upon my vesture" (Psalm 22:18; 1000 years before Christ).

Fulfillment: "Then the soldiers, when they had crucified Jesus, took his garments, and made four parts...now the coat was without seam, woven from the top throughout. They said therefore among themselves, Let us not rend it, but cast lots for it, whose it shall be..." (John 19:23, 24).

Prophecy: "I may count all my bones. They look and stare at me." (Psalm 22:17; 1000 years before Christ).

Fulfillment: "But when they came to Jesus, and saw that he was dead already, they brake not his legs" (John 19:33).

Prophecy: "For thou will not leave my soul in hell; neither wilt thou suffer thine Holy One to see corruption (Psalm 16:10; 1000 years before Christ).

Fulfillment: "And the angel answered and said unto the women, Fear not ye: for I know that ye seek Jesus, which was crucified. He is not here: for he is risen, as he said..." (Matthew 28:5,6).

PROPHECIES MADE BY JESUS FULFILLED

What about the prophetic statements made by Jesus which have been fulfilled?

Three years before it occurred, He announced his own crucifixion (John 3:14).

He described exactly the treatment He would receive at the hands of His enemies (Mark 10:32-34).

He announced his resurrection three years in advance of the event (John 2:19, 21).

There have been hundreds of predicted prophecies in the Bible that *already* have been fulfilled *to the letter.* To the doubter isn't this reason enough to believe that unfulfilled prophecy dealing with events to come *ALSO WILL BE FULFILLED TO THE LETTER.* Tomorrow's news has been in the Bible for many centuries! How challenging it is to see these events of the Last Days occur before our very eyes as foretold by God's inspired writers thousands of years ago!

14
Passport To Freedom

Detours to Destruction • Christ to Rule the World • What Will You Do With Jesus? • Your Most Important Decision in Life

In this book, GUIDE TO SURVIVAL you have read about:

A. Current events that show a world engulfed in lawlessness and reckless pursuit of earthly pleasures.

B. A rapid advancement towards a One World Church.

C. A modern technological age whose growth brings with it air pollution and the fear of a population explosion.

D. Man's growing ability towards mass destruction, coupled with famines, rampant disease and an uncontrollable arms race.

E. A trend in the United States to place more and more power into the hands of one man and in the Federal Government.

In light of these current events we also discussed the following:

A. The soon coming day when tens of thousands and perhaps even millions will suddenly vanish from the earth "in the twinkling of an eye." This is the day when the believers will be caught up to meet Christ in the air at the Rapture.

B. The coming into power of the Antichrist; his being hailed as a man of peace while the major European nations probably including the United States, appoint him as their head and give him unlimited powers; and his subsequent take over of world power.

C. The emerging of the False Prophet who will work many miracles and because of these many miracles, cause people to worship the Antichrist as their Messiah.

D. The first 3½ years of the Tribulation Period which, amid difficulties, will give a hope of security to the nations of the world—but will turn out to be a false security that will lead to terror and tragedy.

E. The day Russia invades Israel and is finally defeated.

F. The last 3½ years of the Tribulation Period which will be a time of reckoning wherein the sinister intents of Antichrist and the False Prophet will be made known— a time when everyone will be forced to accept the mark of the Beast (Antichrist) and bow down and worship him or face starvation and death.

G. The Great War called the Battle of Armageddon in which armies from all of the nations of the earth war against God and God pours His judgment upon them. Millions are killed and Antichrist and the False Prophet are thrown into the Lake of Fire while Satan is thrown into the bottomless pit for a thousand years.

H. The Millennium and the judgment of the unsaved dead which follows it. This is then followed by God's creation of New Heavens and Earth wherein the redeemed will dwell with God in joy forever in a sinless world.

Here then is a picture of the Last Days and the coming events as they will occur. In this scientific day and age, people are always looking for cold hard facts. Very few people will purposely exercise faith although they do so unconsciously every day when they fly in an airplane, cross a bridge, listen to a radio or watch a television program. In these above cases, they may not be able to understand electricity or the inventions that man has discovered—but they blindly accept them.

In writing this book GUIDE TO SURVIVAL, I accept the entire Bible—all 66 books from Genesis to Revelation—as the inspired Word of God.

My references regarding the events that will occur in the Last Days and during the Tribulation Period are found directly in God's Word.

Where the Bible speaks, I have tried to speak...and where the Bible remains silent...I have endeavored to remain silent. While some will differ from me on the details of the coming prophesied events certainly the main thrust of these things has been represented. All of the details will not be revealed until the actual events occur.

DETOURS TO DESTRUCTION

If you accept the Bible as the Word of God then you will have no trouble understanding much of God's blueprint for things to come.

God has told us in His Word:

> But we speak God's wisdom in a mystery, the hidden wisdom, which God predestined before the ages to our glory. (7)

> The wisdom which none of the rulers of this age has understood; for if they had understood it, they would not have crucified the Lord of glory. (8)

> But just as it is written, things which eye has not seen and ear has not heard, and which have not entered the heart of man, all that God has prepared for those who love Him. (9)

> For to us God revealed them through the Spirit; for the Spirit searches all things, even the depths of God. (10)

> For who among men knows the thoughts of a man except the spirit of the man, which is in him? Even so the thoughts of God no one knows except the Spirit of God. (11)

> Now we have received, not the spirit of the world, but the Spirit who is from God, that we might know the things freely given to us by God. (12)

> Which things we also speak, not in words taught by human wisdom, but in those taught by the Spirit, combining spiritual thoughts with spiritual words. (13)

> But a natural man does not accept the things of the Spirit of God; for they are foolishness to him,

and he cannot understand them, because they are spiritually appraised. (14) (I Corinthians 2:7-14)

If you do not believe the Bible as the verbally inspired Word of God or if you only believe parts of the Bible, or if you believe that only men in certain religious offices of a certain church can interpret the Bible, then you will find this book a great stumbling block to you.

You in your own personal life must make the decision whether you will accept the Bible as the verbally inspired Word of God, and believe that it means what it says—and by so believing in its Christ...gain entrance into Heaven.

Or by your disbelief in Christ—you are automatically condemning yourself to an eternity in Hell.

The Bible does not give any specific date when the Rapture will occur or when the Tribulation Period will begin.

Some Bible scholars differ on when the Seven Seal Judgments, the Seven Trumpet Judgments and the Seven Vial Judgments will occur; and on which events will occur during the first 3 1/2 years of the Tribulation, and on which events will occur during the second 3 1/2 years of the Tribulation or throughout the entire 7 years of the Tribulation Period.

Some Bible scholars believe that some of the judgments will occur slightly before the Tribulation and before the Rapture occurs.

However, this is the important thing to remember!

God has not chosen to reveal everything regarding His program through His Word. As we approach each step nearer to the Last Days and the Tribulation Period these prophecies will become clear to those people at that time.

These things, however, are very definite!

1. The Bible does state that there will be a Rapture of the saints.

   For the Lord Himself will descend from heaven with a shout, with the voice of the archangel, and with the trumpet of God; and the dead in Christ shall rise first. (16)

   Then we who are alive and remain shall be caught up together with them in the clouds to meet the Lord in the air, and thus we shall always be with the Lord. (17) (I Thessalonians 4:16,17).

2. The Bible does show that there will be a Tribulation Period of seven years—(Daniel 9:27 compared with Revelation 11:2; 11:3; 12:6; 12:14 and 13:5 referring to the various halves of the Period).

3. The Bible does show that Russia and her allies will march into Israel and attempt to conquer that country. God will open the heavens and cause earthquake and rain and hail and the Russian army will be destroyed finally quenching the power of Russian Communism in the world—(Ezekiel 38; 39:1-16).

4. The Bible does state that there will be Seven Seal Judgments—(Revelation chapters 6, 8).

5. The Bible does state that there will be Seven Trumpet Judgments—(Revelation chapters 8, 11).

6. The Bible does state that there will be Seven Vial (Bowl) Judgments—(Revelation chapters 15, 16).

7. The Bible does state that at the end of these judgments will come the Battle of Armageddon—(Joel 3; Isaiah 63; Revelation 14:14-20; 16:12-16; 19:11-21).

8. The Bible does state that at that time the False Prophet and the Antichrist will be thrown into the Lake of Fire—(Revelation 19:20; 20:10).

9. The Bible does state that Satan will be cast into the bottomless pit—(Revelation 20:1-3).

10. The Bible also states that at that time Christ will return to earth with his saints (believers) to reign for a thousand years—(Revelation 10:14, 20:4-6).

11. The Bible also states that at the end of these thousand years Christ will loose Satan from the bottomless pit and allow him once more to work his wicked ways—(Revelation 20:7-10).

12. The Bible also states that multitudes who have been born and raised in the Millennial Kingdom will, nevertheless, reject Christ to follow Satan—(Revelation 20:7-9).

13. The Bible also states that at the end of this period, God will finally cast all unbelievers into the Lake of Fire where they will remain with Satan, Antichrist and the False Prophet and be tormented forever and ever—(Revelation 20:10).

CHRIST TO RULE THE WORLD

Half of the predicted prophecies of the Bible concerning Christ, are yet unfulfilled.

The same prophets who told us prophetically of Christ's First Coming and whose prophecies have been literally fulfilled, tell us about His Second Coming and what will take place when He comes. Since they were right about what they said about His First Coming we should believe the same of His Second Coming.

One of the most important doctrines in the Bible next to those relating to salvation (accepting Christ as your personal Saviour) is the doctrine of the Second Coming of Christ.

No future subject is so frequently predicted in the pages of God's Word as those events surrounding Christ's return.

In these days of tremendous stress and strain, it is of great importance that we should fix our eyes upon Christ.

Perhaps, this is the very meaning of His own words when He told us:

> But when these things begin to take place,
> straighten up and lift up your heads, because
> your redemption is drawing near. (Luke 21:28).

Therefore don't allow differences over prophetical details to detour you from God's plan of salvation. It is of no importance to your accepting Christ as your personal Saviour whether the sounding of the Second Trumpet Judgment occurs in the first half of the Tribulation Period or the second half of the Tribulation Period.

It is of no importance to accepting Christ as your personal Saviour whether it will be Russia, Germany and the Arab countries coming down upon Israel or Russia, Japan and the Arab countries coming down upon Israel.

These facts are of little consequence on your making the decision of a lifetime—the decision that will determine whether you will spend an eternity in Heaven or be destined to an eternity of constant torment in Hell.

The important question that you must answer before you die is the question:

WHAT WILL I DO WITH JESUS?

Will you accept Jesus Christ as your personal Saviour and Lord or will you reject Him?

This you must decide yourself. No one else can decide that for you. The basis of your decision should be made on God's Word—the Bible.

God tells us the following:

> *All that the Father gives Me shall come to Me; and the one who comes to Me I will certainly not cast out. (37).*
>
> *Truly, truly, I say to you, he who believes has eternal life. (47) (John 6:37,47).*

He also is a righteous God and a God of indignation to those who reject Him....

> *He who believes in Him is not judged; he who does not believe has been judged already, because he has not believed in the name of the only begotten Son of God. (John 3:18).*
>
> *And if anyone's name was not found written in the book of life, he was thrown into the lake of fire. (Revelation 20:15).*

YOUR MOST IMPORTANT DECISION IN LIFE

Because sin entered the world in the days of Adam and Eve and because God hates sin, God sent His Son Jesus Christ to die on the cross to pay the price for your sins and mine.

If you place your trust in Him, God will freely forgive you of your sins.

> *For by grace you have been saved through faith; and that not of yourselves, it is the gift of God. (8)*
>
> *Not as a result of works, that no one should boast. (9) (Ephesians 2:8,9)*
>
> *Truly, truly, I say to you, he who hears My word, and believes Him who sent Me, has eternal life, and does not come into judgment, but has passed out of death into life. (John 5:24)*

What about you? Have you accepted Christ as your personal Saviour?

Do you realize that right now you can know the reality of this new life in Christ Jesus. Right now you can dispel the doubt that is in your mind concerning your future and that of your loved ones. Right now, you can ask Christ to come into your heart. And right now you can be assured of eternal life in heaven.

All of your riches here on earth—all of your financial security—all of your material wealth, your houses, your land will crumble into nothingness in a few years.

And as God has told us:

> *And inasmuch as it is appointed for men to die once, and after this comes judgment. (27)*
>
> *So Christ also, having been offered once to bear the sins of many, shall appear a second time, not to bear sin, to those who eagerly await Him, for salvation. (28) (Hebrews 9:27,28)*

Are you willing to sacrifice an eternity with Christ in Heaven for a few years of questionable material gain that will lead to death and destruction?

Or would you right now, as you are reading these very words of this book, like to know without a shadow of a doubt that you are on the road to Heaven—that death is not the end of life but actually the climactic beginning of the most wonderful existence that will ever be—a life with the Lord Jesus Christ and with your friends, your relatives, and your loved ones who have accepted Christ as their Saviour.

It's not a difficult thing to do. So many religions and so many people have tried to make the simple Gospel message of Christ complex. You can not work your way into heaven —*heaven is the gift of God to those who believe in Jesus Christ.*

No matter how great your works—no matter how kind you are—no matter how philanthropic you are—it means nothing in the sight of God, because in the sight of God, your own righteousness (merits) are as filthy rags.

> *For all of us have become like one who is unclean, and all our righteous deeds are like a filthy garment; and all of us wither like a leaf, and our iniquities, like the wind, take us away. (Isaiah 64:6)*

Christ expects you to come as you are, a sinner, recognizing your need of a Saviour, the Lord Jesus Christ.

Understanding this, why not bow your head right now and give this simple prayer of faith to the Lord.

Say it in your own words. It does not have to be a beautiful oratorical prayer—simply a prayer of humble contrition.

My Personal Decision for CHRIST

"Lord Jesus, I know that I'm a sinner and that I cannot save myself by good works. I believe that you died for me and that you shed your blood for my sins. I believe that you rose again from the dead. And now I am receiving you as my personal Saviour, my Lord, my only hope of salvation. I know that I'm a sinner and deserve to go to Hell. I know that I cannot save myself. Lord, be merciful to me, a sinner, and save me according to the promise of Your Word. I want Christ to come into my heart now to be my Saviour, Lord and Master."

Signed. . . . .

Date . . . .

If you have signed the above, having just taken Christ as your personal Saviour and Lord...I would like to rejoice with you in your new-found faith.

Write to   ...SALEM KIRBAN, Kent Road, Huntingdon Valley, Penna. 19006...and I'll send you a little booklet to help you start living your new life in Christ.

If you prayed this in humble sincerity and really meant it—you are saved, and are a saint of God. This is sometimes referred to as being "born again."

The Bible says:

> For whoever will call upon the name of the Lord
> will be saved. (Romans 10:13)

The life of a Christian is not an easy one. Accepting Christ as your personal Saviour does not mean that from now on everything will be a bed of roses.

Because now as a Christian (a believer—one who has been born again or saved) Satan, who may have been leaving you alone up to this point, will now more than ever before try to make you doubt that there is a God and that the step you have just taken is of any consequence.

In fact, your own feelings may change from day to day regarding God's Word.

However, it is important to remember this. God's Word never changes and He does promise:

> *All that the Father gives Me shall come to Me; and the one who comes to Me I will certainly not cast out. (John 6:37)*

My one central purpose in writing this book was not to display all of the consequences that will be yours in the Tribulation Period should you not accept Christ. Rather my sole purpose in writing this book was that you, seeing God's prophetic Word for the coming days, might *now* turn to Him and accept Him as your personal Saviour and Lord.

If you have accepted Him as your personal Saviour and have signed the simple prayer of faith that was given on the previous page—why not go back and read over some of the chapters in this book. They will now give you an even greater insight on the Word of God in these Last Days.

This then is my prayer: that God will use the book, **GUIDE TO SURVIVAL,** as a further testimony to His Holy Word— the Bible—and turn you to His Word, and in so doing, make possible your PASSPORT TO FREEDOM.

God's promise is:

> *"...Surely, I come quickly..." (Revelation 22:20).*

My prayer is that you will be among the number who joyfully say.

> *"...Even, so come, Lord Jesus." (Revelation 22:20).*

And until Christ does come, let us remember that this dark earth's night is still the opportunity of grace, and let us not forget the offer of His mercy:

> *And the Spirit and the bride say, "Come." And let the one who hears say, "Come." And let the one who is thirsty come; let the one who wishes take the water of life without cost. (Revelation 22:17).*

SALEM KIRBAN BOOKS
First in Books with a Message!

**S HERE! Special Prophecy Edition of the Bible!
cludes REVELATION VISUALIZED!**

lem Kirban's

EFERENCE BIBLE KING JAMES VERSION

w! You can be among the select few to possess the rare First
tion of the Salem Kirban REFERENCE BIBLE. It is the complete
g James Version of the entire Bible. Plus! Bound in the back of
Bible, right after the book of Jude, is the complete 480-page
VELATION VISUALIZED with over 200 Full Color Illustrations and
e Charts!

$39.95*

ok at These Special Features

**Complete King James Version of the
entire Bible.** Large, easy-to-read type

36 Exclusive Charts on Prophecy.
Includes all 21 Tribulation judgments
illustrated ● Three Decisive Wars ●
Judgment Days ● The Resurrections ●
The Three Heavens and much more!

32 Full Color Photographs. Holy Land
pictures personally taken by Salem Kirban

Rare Old World Bible Engravings.
Unusual etchings of Bible scenes
designed by craftsmen over 100 years ago!

Prophecy Time Symbols. All Bible verses
that relate to future events identified with
Time Symbol illustrations.

Special Feature. Every Bible Text Page,
from Genesis to Jude, has COMMENTARY
NOTES at the Bottom of the Page. These
1500 Commentary notes are written by
Salem Kirban (sparkling commentary),
Gary G. Cohen (difficult verses explained)
and **Charles Haddon Spurgeon**
(Promises to Live By devotionals).

lem Kirban's REFERENCE BIBLE durably
und in sturdy text binding. Page size: 6″ × 9″

PLUS REVELATION VISUALIZED

Co-authored by Salem Kirban and Dr. Gary
Cohen. REVELATION VISUALIZED is bound in
the back of the REFERENCE BIBLE, right after the
book of Jude. 480 pages in FULL COLOR!

Look at These Exclusive Features:

1 Promise Verses in BLUE. Judgment Verses
in RED.

2 Commentary on same page as related verse.

3 Illustration on each right hand page. Over
200 Charts and Photos in FULL COLOR!

4 Background Commentary by Salem Kirban.

5 TIME CHART on every Page Unit. Red Arrow
points to TIME PERIOD verses relate to
(Rapture, Tribulation, etc.)!

JIDE TO SURVIVAL (Over 300 pages/over 75 photos and charts) $4.95

antity Prices: 3 copies: $12 (You save $2.85) 10 copies: $34 (You save $15.50)
                25 copies: $74 (You save $49.50) 100 copies: $247 (You save $248)

e pay all shipping charges.

SECRET ORGANIZATIONS ACTIVE TODAY
invading even the Church
and Sunday School are part of

SATAN'S ANGELS
EXPOSED!

by Salem Kirban

$3.95
ILLUSTRATED

AT LAST! SATAN'S STRATEGY REVEALED!

Most people are unaware that Satan's subtle deception has now infiltrated the Christian church. Many imagine Satan as a grotesque individual with horns. But Satan, who before his fall was an angel of light, now cleverly deceives even those who are born again by his "imitation holiness."

SATAN'S ANGELS EXPOSED reveals how Satan is using an army of Judas Iscariots to undermine believers through "Christian" music, through false healers, through powerful religious groups that reach millions with a polluted, watered-down doctrine.

This "Angel of Light" as the Great Imitator is the "prince of this world" and his successes in the Church and in high political places are exposed ... clearly, concisely. Protect your children and those you love. You need to know the facts!

From Baal worship

To Witchcraft

To Satan worship

And Now Even Infiltrating The Unsuspecting Church!

Satan's Symbols Explained

How to recognize
doctrines of demons!

SPECIAL SECTION Reveals

How secret organizations, whose threads of terror reach back centuries ago, are carefully weaving their power plot to control the world for Satan. Illustrated chapters reveal the behind-the-scenes manipulation of:
The Illuminati, The Golden Dawn, and **Druid Witchcraft.**

Plus! Exposing the strange rise of political and economic power of:
The Bilderbergers, The Trilateral Commission, and the **Bancor Plan**
for a universal money system!

SATAN'S ANGELS EXPOSED!   (Publication Date, Feb. 1979) **$3.95**

Salem Kirban Family Catalog Order For

Salem Kirban, Inc.
Kent Road, Huntingdon Valley, Penna. 19006

Please Print

Mr./Mrs./Miss _____

Address _____

City _____ State _____ Zip _____

Name of Item	Qty.	Price Each	Total Price
Total			
Less Discount			
Sub Total			
Add PACKING charge			$1.00
TOTAL PAYMENT enclosed			

SHARE YOUR HAPPINESS WITH A FRIEND

Do you have friends or relatives who are interested in **Prophecy Books** that uplift and bring joy? Let us send them a 1-year subscription to our FAMILY CATALOG **free!** Just print their names and addresses below.

Mr.
Miss
Mrs. _____

Mr.
Miss
Mrs. _____

Address _____

Address _____

City _____ State _____ ZIP

City _____ State _____ Z

Salem Kirban Family Catalog Order Form

Salem Kirban, Inc.
Kent Road, Huntingdon Valley, Penna. 19006

Please Print

Mr./Mrs./Miss _____

Address _____

City _____ State _____ Zip _____

Name of Item	Qty.	Price Each	Total Price
Total			
Less Discount			
Sub Total			
Add PACKING charge			$1.00
TOTAL PAYMENT enclosed			

SHARE YOUR HAPPINESS WITH A FRIEND

Do you have friends or relatives who are interested in **Prophecy Books** that uplift and bring joy? Let us send them a 1-year subscription to our FAMILY CATALOG **free!** Just print their names and addresses below.

Mr.
Miss
Mrs. _____

Mr.
Miss
Mrs. _____

Address _____

Address _____

City _____ State ____ ZIP

City _____ State ____ ZI